THE INDOCHINA STORY

THE INDOCHINA STORY

A Fully Documented Account

BY
THE COMMITTEE OF CONCERNED
ASIAN SCHOLARS

PANTHEON BOOKS
A Division of Random House, New York

Library of Congress Catalog Card Number: 75-141620

ISBN: 0-394-47015-X

Manufactured in the United States of America

9 8 7 6 5 4 3 2

To the peoples of Indochina

On this land
where each blade of grass is human hair
each foot of soil is human flesh
where it rains blood
hails bones
life must flower

NGO VINH LONG

Contributors[*]

Frank Ackerman
R. David Arkush
Dennis Bathroy
Sidney Beech
Richard Bernstein
Michael Bierman
Herbert Bix
Karen Burke
Noam Chomsky
John Collins
John Dower
Thomas Engelhardt
Thomas Ferguson
Cynthia Fredrick
William Haseltine
Charles Hayford
Carl Jacobson
Leigh Kagan

Richard C. Kagan
Madeleine Levine
Steven Levine
Perry Link
Ngo Vinh Long
Edwin Moise
Victor Nee
James Sanford
Cheryl Payer
James Peck
Daniel Pool
Earl C. Ravenal
Larry Rottman
Jon Sherwood
Douglas Spelman
James C. Thomson, Jr.
John Wheeler
James A. Whitson

Ernest Young

[*] Individual contributors do not necessarily agree with all of the views expressed in this book.

Preface

In the spring of 1968, a small group of Asian scholars met in Philadelphia to form the Committee of Concerned Asian Scholars (CCAS). Their interests were narrow enough. They meant, in their own fashion, to protest American aggression in Vietnam, the blanket of misinformation about the war, and the complicity or silence of so many of those in Asian studies with respect to American policy. Since then, much has changed. The CCAS has grown into a loosely organized nationwide committee with numerous university based chapters. What was in 1968 simply a protest against aggression in Vietnam has become a protest against American imperialism in Asia, and an attempt to develop a sympathetic understanding of Asian revolutionary movements as they confront poverty, oppression, and imperialism.

This CCAS book was written in the wake of the invasion of Cambodia. The people who took part in putting it together have sought to contribute to ending the bloodletting of this war—by presenting in a comprehensive and comprehensible form to the American people what they have often seen only through the fragmenting and distorting eyes of their television sets and local newspapers; by bringing together all the essential information about the war now scattered among the myriad books; and by providing a readily usable handbook containing the arguments for total and immediate American withdrawal from Indochina. There was another, equally compelling reason, for writing this book. It was to show the faces of our "faceless enemies," to suggest the hope and alternatives the revolutionary movements in Indochina offer their own people, and to indicate why American policy has sought for so long to contain or destroy them. Ending this war may be just a part of a broader struggle to end American imperialism in Asia. But it is an essential beginning from which to build.

COMMITTEE OF CONCERNED
ASIAN SCHOLARS

Contents

Introduction

Troops of the Americal Division were burning down suspected Vietcong villages near Songmy, the scene of an alleged massacre of South Vietnamese civilians last year by American soldiers, as recently as last month.

"Within a matter of a week at the end of October, we destroyed 13 villages," said Second Lieut. Norman E. Cuttrell, aged 22, of Terre Haute, Ind. . . . According to Lieut. Col. Russ Whitla of Ganado, Ariz., the burning by "Zippo squads," so named for their cigarette lighters, is intended to "deny the villages to the Vietcong." It is part of the pacification program in Quangnai Province . . . The inhabitants are . . . placed in newly constructed "resettlement villages," which are often enclosed by barbed wire . . .

"If it's all a free-fire zone, you can sit on the hills and see the dinks [Vietnamese] running around, so they call in big air strikes," he said.

Lieutenant Cuttrell added: "What we try to do is to get all of the people out of the ville [village] before we start burning. Because of the psychological effect, of course, they don't want to go—that's their home and everything."

"So what we do," he said, "is to get them all out of the ville and out of sight before we burn it so they won't have to stand and watch their houses burn."[1]

This Reuters dispatch conveys the essential features of the American war against the peasants of Indochina: its primary tactics—massive bombardment, destruction, and population removal to concentration camps; the disdain of the American soldiers for the dinks whose villes they are forced to burn, or whom they destroy when seen where the Americans have decided they have no right to be;

and the unquestioned acceptance by most soldiers, and by the majority of the American reading public, that this is perfectly all right. There will be no court-martials to deal with the war crimes described here and elsewhere in this book, or thousands of other atrocities of the same sort that have been bombarding the sensibilities of the American people for the past ten years.

The American war against the peasants of Indochina is, beyond doubt, one of the most barbaric and vicious of modern history. It is perhaps remarkable that the American people continue to believe, by and large, that they are expending their lives and treasure to help the poor people of South Vietnam, just as it is remarkable that government propaganda has succeeded in convincing most of the population that the war is against "Hanoi," or "Communist aggression," despite overwhelming evidence to the contrary. [See especially part III.] If the United States government has succeeded in nothing else, it has surely proven itself masterful in the techniques of brainwashing which it is so fond of attributing to others— though it would be only fair to add that it has received assistance from the American intellectual community in this enterprise of deceit. For example, even many of those who now belatedly oppose the war have pretended that the United States is defending "South Vietnam" against "aggression from the North," when the plain fact is that it has been protecting a Saigon elite from its own population. As detailed in the text which follows [see part III], the largely peasant forces of South Vietnam received meaningful support from North Vietnam only when the American assault intensified beyond the point where they could resist by their own means. The direct involvement of North Vietnam followed the onset of the bombing of the North which destroyed virtually everything outside of the major cities. Much the same has been true in Laos, and will no doubt be true in Cambodia as well, if not beyond.

Senators who follow the war closely have not been fooled. Senator Symington recently stated:

It has been my impression, after visits to Vietnam,
that one of the problems is that a majority of the people in Vietnam support the guerrillas in the countryside
but do not support the Thieu government. There
would be people who would disagree with that, but
that is my considered opinion after talking to people
below the top.[2]

Over the years, others have supported this assessment.
Robert Scigliano wrote that "Communist adherents are
much more numerous than those of all the nationalist
opposition groups put together"; in 1961, "it appears that
80 percent of the [South] Vietnamese countryside had
come under Communist influence"; ". . . using the estimate of American officials in Saigon at the end of 1962,
about one-half of the South Vietnamese support the National Liberation Front . . ."[3] Douglas Pike, the American Foreign Service officer who is the main spokesman
for the American government on affairs having to do with
the Viet Cong, reports that in 1963, "perhaps half the
population of South Vietnam at least tacitly supported the
NLF."[4] Elsewhere, he explains that it was impossible for
the Saigon government to consider a coalition regime with
the NLF in late 1964 because it would have simply been
swallowed up by the more powerful force (it would hardly be reasonable, as he put it, to expect the minnow to
enter into a coalition with the whale). Detailed studies
of particular provinces show that in case after case the
Saigon regime had been defeated by local forces recruited
and trained within that province, despite the enormous
American support for the Saigon regime and the direct
American military involvement by the early sixties. All
authorities agree that the United States had essentially lost
the war by late 1964.

Similar judgments persist, even among those who, like
the sources just cited, are extremely hostile to the NLF.
The Council of Vietnamese Studies of SEADAG, in its
meetings of May 3, 1969, struggles with the fact that
the NLF is the "best organized political group," the
"strongest political group in South Vietnam." Peter Kumpa

of the *Baltimore Sun,* who has long experience in South-east Asian affairs, wrote that "a broad spectrum of South Vietnamese politicians" believes the Thieu–Ky regime utterly incapable of competing for power with the NLF: "Interviews with the most important political parties, fronts and religious blocs did not turn up a single individual who believed that the present Thieu government could win in any reasonably fair and open political competition with the Communists . . ."[5] The Thieu–Ky government of course agrees. Pressed by the Americans, Thieu made some gestures toward creating a political force that would support him, but these attempts have been abandoned. Daniel Southerland writes from Saigon:

> . . . the government has yet to come up with anything even approaching a political force in the villages which can compete in terms of discipline, dedication, and organizational skill with the political cadre of the NLF . . . "We have a huge army and administration on our side," a government Cabinet minister said recently. "But without a political organization, we cannot win a clearcut victory." "The Viet Cong have a political organization and a cause to serve," he continued. "But on our side the cement is lacking to pull the people together. They are just like so many grains of sand."
>
> Not everyone would agree with this official's views. But there is a widespread awareness here that the country's non-Communist forces simply are not organized for a political fight with the Viet Cong."[6]

For this reason, Prime Minister Khiem made it clear that Communists would "never" be allowed to run for office. President Thieu agrees.[7] These comments are characteristic. The Saigon regimes installed by the United States have always insisted that they cannot compete politically with the NLF, and have therefore demanded that the United States destroy the peasant-based opposition by force. The American government has been only too happy to oblige.

Many American apologists argue that the NLF is only a minority, so therefore the United States has a right, even a duty, to defend the non-Communist majority from the better-organized opposition. A British apologist in 1776 might have argued along similar lines, observing that Washington's subversive forces could hardly claim the support of a third of the population.[8] But the true cynicism behind this argument lies elsewhere. Because of the immense popular support for the NLF the United States was forced to undertake a sadistic policy of massacre and destruction. The result is social demoralization on such a scale that it is meaningless to speak of "the extent of political support" manifested—and as to support that is latent, no American has the slightest idea what is happening in the teeming slums of Saigon or the villages of Vietnam.

Bernard Fall—no alarmist, and fundamentally a military man who wanted the United States to win in Vietnam —wrote in one of his last essays that "Vietnam as a cultural and historic entity . . . is threatened with extinction," as "the countryside literally dies under the blows of the largest military machine ever unleashed on an area of this size."[9] Undersecretary of the Air Force Townsend Hoopes writes that the rebels are "inviting the West, which possesses unanswerable military power, to carry its strategic logic to the final conclusion, which is genocide."[10] No matter what the future may hold, the culture and society of Vietnam and its neighbors have already been dealt a blow from which they may never recover. Only the most malicious of hypocrites can justify continued American involvement on grounds that the United States is "defending the majority of the population" from this or that threat. As the information presented in the body of this book testifies, the tragedy of Vietnam lies in the fact that a society which finally freed itself from colonial oppression—and was in the process of establishing peace within its borders, addressing its own problems, and bettering the lives of the majority of its people—was plunged instead into an orgy of bloodletting by the intervention of the Western powers, first France and then the United States. Now the conflict has expanded even further. And the greatest threat to the peoples of Southeast Asia is unmistakably the United States.

In fact, America's "strategic logic" in Indochina has been dictated precisely by the fact that the resistance is so deeply embedded in the villages of Vietnam and Laos and increasingly Cambodia. Americans are not destroying these lands and their people because they enjoy the role of barbarians and sadists, but because there is no other way to defeat a deeply rooted people's war. Such a war as that conducted by the United States is possible because the victims obviously lack the capacity to strike back at the source of aggression. Therefore Washington can, with impunity, experiment with any technique of repression and destruction that tacticians can devise. The time has surely come for the American people to face this simple fact: that, as documented in part II of this book, the American response to rural-based people's war in Asia has been a war against the people, a war whose objective has been to depopulate the countryside by all techniques available short of nuclear weapons—the most massive aerial bombardment in history; the most diabolic arsenal of anti-personnel weapons ever designed to kill indiscriminately; the unprecedented heavy reliance upon chemicals to destroy the very ecology of a land and visit the war upon generations unborn; the forced removal of millions of peasants from their traditional homes and fields and their relocation in centers which can only be described as concentration camps.

By the end of 1964, the NLF had won the civil war in the South despite extensive American intervention and the enormous effort over the preceding decade to establish an effective pro-American government to control the country. But although the NLF was able to win in South Vietnam, it could not win in Thailand, or in the China Sea, or the Philippines, or Okinawa, or Hawaii, or the continental United States. Nor could it conquer the U.S. military bases in Danang or Camranh Bay. In the Tet offensive, "Communist" forces, overwhelmingly NLF, were able, with ease, to take over most of the cities of

South Vietnam, but they could not prevent these cities from being destroyed by American air power. It may be that the NLF can conquer South Vietnam, but they know that if they do, they may be wiped out in the process. There is no doubt that the United States has the material strength to destroy Indochina, and in this sense, a victory for the Vietnamese revolution can be prevented. Administration spokesmen like to say that the "Communists" are hoping to win in the United States, and in a sense they are correct, for if the people of the United States are willing to see Bernard Fall's prophecy fulfilled, if they are willing to see their government carry its strategic logic to the final conclusion, then the United States can surely win a victory of the graveyard in Vietnam. Furthermore, although the Vietnamese resistance to American aggression has been amazing in its heroism and dedication, it still remains possible that the vast American reserves of terror and violence will succeed in bringing about such extensive demoralization in Vietnamese society that the Quisling regime established by the United States will be able to maintain control of a subject population. Other conquerors in other lands have succeeded with far slighter means.

Does the United States really intend to withdraw from Vietnam? At the time of the Nixon inaugural, *U.S. News & World Report*—in general, a reliable guide to Nixon administration policies—reported that "those most deeply involved in overall strategy" foresee a slow reduction of U.S. forces in Vietnam to 200,000 men by the end of 1971, as "the basis for a long-haul, low-cost effort in Vietnam that could continue indefinitely" (Jan. 27, 1969). The terminology is that of Sir Robert Thompson, who has long argued that the United States relies too heavily on massive armies and short-range tactics, and that it might be possible for the United States to win in Vietnam at a lesser tempo with a "long-haul, low-cost strategy"— though "it will certainly take at least ten to fifteen years."[11] Nixon has since identified Sir Robert as his favorite strategist, and it seems that he intends to follow at least some of his recommendations. American troop levels are being slowly reduced, and most analysts believe that the goal is an army of about a quarter of a million—an immense army of occupation—operating from the impregnable bases that the United States has built throughout Vietnam and that it presumably intends to hold permanently. Meanwhile, the war will become more "capital-intensive," in the apt phrase of Herman and Du Boff.[12] By March 1969, for example, Melvin Laird announced that consumption of air ordnance would remain at the highest level reached during the war, almost 130,000 tons a month.[13]

Testifying before Congress in October 1969, the secretary of the army, Stanley Resor, refused to predict how long the war would last, though he reported that time is "running on our side":

> Therefore if we can just buy some time in the U.S. by these periodic progressive withdrawals and the American people can just shore up their patience and determination, I think we can bring this to a successful conclusion.

Chief of Staff William C. Westmoreland added: "I have never made the prediction that this would be other than a long war."[14]

The goal of American policy in Vietnam remains military victory. Based upon his long career among Washington's decision makers, Townsend Hoopes explains that military victory "appears to be a necessary precondition for the realization of a U.S. political objective which defines 'free choice' for the people of South Viet Nam as a process necessarily excluding the NLF/VC from participation in either elections or government."[15] The American government has been pursuing this policy in one or another variant for twenty years, first through support of the French in their attempt to reconquer their former colony, and then by direct intervention, when the French proved unequal to the task. In the process, tactics have been altered repeatedly but the goal of creating a pro-American, anti-Communist group of states in Southeast

Asia has remained constant. Here is another point to consider: that to accept the view of many present critics that the war in Indochina is a tragic departure from a generally benevolent policy which the U.S. has traditionally pursued toward Asia is to obscure the historic roots of American intervention and the complex web of ideological, political, economic, and military considerations which has fixed the United States to this accelerating course of destruction. [See parts I and III.] Such a view may be personally consoling, but it contributes little to an understanding of the causes of this war and the threat of continued and expanding American wars in Asia.

At the outset of U.S. involvement in Vietnam, Dean Acheson's State Department explained that we were supporting the French to save Vietnam from Russian imperialism. The absurdity of this claim has not prevented others—the Rostow brothers for example—from repeating it, with minor changes of phraseology, in later years. Acheson's verbal overkill was part of the policy of "scaring hell out of the American people," in Senator Vandenberg's words, in an effort to whip them into line in support of American global initiatives. The strategy worked only too well. The United States is barely beginning to emerge from the psychosis induced by Acheson and his successors.

As Hoopes relates, the policy makers of the Kennedy administration operated on "the implicit assumption that henceforth Washington would be predisposed to view an effort to overthrow the existing order *anywhere* as a national-liberation war fomented by and for the benefit of Russia or China," and Johnson's principal foreign policy advisers, Kennedy men, "all carried in their veins the implicitly unlimited commitment to global struggle against Revolutionary Communism . . ." He quotes Philip Geyelin's remarks on "the backstage Johnson," who "was quite capable of telling one of the Senate's more serious students of foreign affairs that 'if we don't stop the Reds in South Vietnam, tomorrow they will be in Hawaii, and next week they will be in San Francisco'!" The "prevailing assumption" among Kennedy's close advisers was "that the 'Communist Bloc' remained an essentially cohesive international conspiracy manifesting itself primarily in military and paramilitary assaults against that other comprehensible entity, the 'Free World.' "[16]

Virtually nothing in the historic record supports this stereotyped and apocalyptic view, and in light of the evidence available, one can only marvel at the extent to which American intervention in Southeast Asia has been based upon myths and theories abstracted from any close examination of either the concrete situation in Asia or real trends and relationships within the so-called Communist world. The postwar history of Southeast Asia, described in chapter 1, reveals beyond a shadow of a doubt that the great disruptive and destructive alien presence in this area since 1945 has been, not outside Communist agitators, but the military machines of the French and Americans. The myth of global communism disintegrates upon examination of the independent and frequently fractious activities of the Soviet Union, China, North Vietnam, and the National Liberation Front. [See part III.] Assertions of Chinese aggressiveness fail almost without exception to withstand close scrutiny. And on the other side of the coin, the various popular movements of the world which have been simply painted over with the label of "communism" have, in the orthodox American view, been denied their dimensions of humaneness and reform in such a manner as to make their successes inexplicable indeed unless one conjures up a devil thesis. Such perspectives are offered in greater detail in the body of this work, but it remains a sad and striking commentary upon American society and the American intelligence that they will seem heresy when introduced before the paranoid vision of world politics held by most Americans, victims of twenty years of relentless indoctrination.

Today there are many influential people in the United States who think their country should terminate its effort to conquer South Vietnam if only because the costs are too painful to bear. "Its penalties upon us all are much too great," McGeorge Bundy put it in October 1968 when he switched from hawk to dove, joining those he had dismissed not long before as "wild men in the wings." The costs and penalties are surely severe. But the anti-Communist crusade cannot be turned on and off at will. Only broad popular pressure and a political leader of great courage and imagination would be able to reverse the American policy of twenty years in the face of the tempest that would be sure to break out.

It is an axiom of politics that no army ever loses a war. Rather, it is the treacherous, lily-livered civilians who snatch defeat from the jaws of victory. If the United States were, in fact, to return Indochina to its own people, it is of course the "Communists" who would benefit, since they constitute the only organized mass-based political forces existing in Indochina. Hence to the cries of "stab in the back" would be added the accusation of "betrayal to the international Communist conspiracy." What is more, there are those 3 billion people in the world, as President Johnson warned, who outnumber us 15 to 1 and might "sweep over the United States and take what we have."[17] Those who have spent a quarter of a century scaring hell out of the American people now have to face a population that is, in fact, badly frightened of "Communists," of "have-nots" and "yellow hordes," not to speak of the domestic dangers: Panthers, the unemployed in the ghetto, hippies, students. A recent survey of public attitudes reports a conversation between a construction worker and his wife in San Diego. They mentioned that their daughter was dating an organizer of the Vietnam moratorium:

> "She came into our room the other night yelling about peace and love," said the wife. "Too many groups are coming in with this militant talk," added the husband."[18]

Unfortunately, such reactions are nothing to laugh about. That kind of "militant talk" will indeed frighten those who take seriously the propaganda of the past twenty-five years, and who recognize the severity of the social and economic crisis that is barely kept at bay as the U.S. devotes its resources to waste and destruction.

In short, even if there were some intention of terminating the American intervention in the internal affairs of Indochina, such a policy would require the kind of courage and imagination that one can hardly find among the current political elite. And there are no discernible signs of any such intention. Rather, there is every prospect that the people of Indochina—and very possibly of other lands whose people seek true self-expression—will continue to be subjected to the military assault of the great superpower of the Western world.

It would be a mistake to suggest that the American crusade against communism is nothing but a reaction of frightened men who could not comprehend the realities of international politics. For one thing, Russian imperialism is no invention of American ideologists, as the Hungarians and Czechs know well enough. But Russian imperialism does not suffice to explain the pretense by American ideologists that the Russians were provoking the guerrillas in Greece, Mossadegh in Iran, Arbenz in Guatemala, the Viet Minh or the Viet Cong, the Boschists in Santo Domingo. Rather, just as the Russians exploit the threat of the West to whip up popular support for the Czech intervention, so the anti-Communist crusade has proved an excellent device to mobilize the American population in support of the far vaster designs of American imperialism. The cold war has functioned as a device for enhancing the power of hard-liners on both sides of the iron curtain. It has served both nobly as an ideology for empire. Hence its persistence, in the face of numerous chances, over the years, to bring it to a close. For the ruling elites of the great world empires, the optimal situation is one of cold-war tension, neither war nor peace, so that within each system the population will be silent and obedient while order is preserved in the colonies by force.

The function of the cold war—on the American side, the anti-Communist crusade—in reinforcing the status quo is quite apparent in the writings of American ideologists. For example Eugene Rostow, in a book that was widely praised by liberal intellectuals and political figures, explained why the United States must be "largely responsible for peace-keeping in Asia," exactly as it was in Greece and Berlin, in the face of "Soviet or Chinese experiments in limited aggression," which now take the form of such "new styles of aggression" as "wars of national liberation" supported by Soviet or Chinese power. Rostow agrees that "in many countries, the demonstrators seek liberty and social advance," but

> hostile forces seek to exploit these feelings, and to turn their manifestation into revolutionary channels— that is, into channels seeking a truly revolutionary transfer of power or a situation of suicidal chaos, and not simply the acceleration of social change within the pattern of the existing order. And, of course, in the face of such threats governments have to intervene finally to restore and preserve public order.

He then adds wistfully that "the result could be incalculable" if only "those in Western countries who protest in the name of peace conclude that certain Communist countries are in fact responsible for the absence of peace," and he warns of the "demons of force . . . slipping their chains" as the "precarious minimum of order that has been ours since 1945" begins to slip away.[19] Characteristic of American propaganda is the assumption that a revolutionary transfer of power must be resisted and the pattern of the existing order preserved. And this overriding principle is juxtaposed to the claim that it is the Communist countries that are solely responsible for the absence of peace. This amalgam serves to justify counterrevolutionary repression as defense of "order" from Communist aggression.

There are other factors that reinforce the system of

cold-war paranoia. Consider, for example, the economic dimension and the problems—generally taboo in American publications—of capitalism. The United States escaped the depression only with the government spending of World War II. The New Deal softened many of the rough edges, but by no means succeeded in overcoming unemployment or restoring the economy. It was commonly assumed that foreign markets would be needed in the postwar period to absorb the output of American industry, and that government spending would be necessary both to guarantee foreign markets (through "aid") and to maintain domestic production. In fact, the primary economic lesson of the war was that extensive government-induced production could restore the faltering economy to full vigor. But to preserve foreign markets, it is necessary to insure that other societies remain "open," that they do not set up barriers to trade or attempt, "irrationally," to use their resources for their own development rather than for the benefit of the great centers of world capitalism. And as to government spending, it is not very easy to invent forms of government-induced production that meet the several conditions that are necessary under corporate capitalism: that this spending enhance, rather than injure, the interests of the corporations that control the economy; that it be tolerable to the population, which must pay the bill; that it be extremely wasteful, so that more is always needed; that it not produce capital goods and thus contribute to the crisis of "overproduction." An arms race seems the optimal solution to this problem; it is only necessary to convince the population that disaster threatens if we relax our guard. Again, the cold war and the yellow hordes provide the answer.

An arms race requires strategic stockpiles, reserves of materials—nonferrous metals, for example—that are available only in the "third world." It requires that our access to these resources be free and unhampered. This too contributes to the demand that the societies of the world remain open to American economic penetration. All of these factors, and others as well, combine to reinforce the cold-war system of anti-Communist paranoia that would now block the effort to extricate ourselves from Vietnam, even if the will to abandon this venture were there.

This system of domestic and foreign repression is very stable and, as the final chapter of the book reveals, no present policy—no "Nixon Doctrine"—even remotely begins to address the dilemma at its roots. The system will not be easily modified. It constitutes an American crisis, a severe crisis of modern state capitalism. The people of Indochina have been the victims of this crisis, and there is every reason to suppose that they will continue to suffer because of the failures and internal problems of American society. Furthermore, the threat of a major war is not small. It is quite possible that the American position in Indochina, tenuous at best, will suddenly begin to erode. It is possible that continuing American provocation may finally cause China to abandon its policy of passive support and actively engage itself in the conflict on its southern borders. The Soviet Union, which has suffered a severe blow to its prestige and influence as a result of the latest American escapade in Cambodia, may decide to try to recoup its losses elsewhere, perhaps in the Middle East, where the situation is highly inflammatory. There are those in the American government—President Nixon among them—who have spoken in the past of the necessity for using nuclear weapons if the United States becomes engaged in an Asian war. Bernard Fall, among others, warned of those who hope that "the Vietnam affair could be transformed into a 'golden opportunity' to 'solve' the Red Chinese problem as well . . ."[20] and there are surely military men who are convinced that it is foolhardy to permit China—the repository of all evil, in the dominant American vision of international affairs—to continue to develop its economic and military potential in peace. It is not unlikely, then, that the American people too may be drawn directly into the war, not as observers from afar who bear only its indirect costs, but as victims who suffer the fate of those whom they now attack with relative impunity.

No serious person will treat these possibilities lightly. Now is the time to launch a major campaign against the possible use of nuclear weapons in Indochina, and against any further participation in this miserable war. There are many avenues of protest and resistance that are open, and it is the duty of the citizen to pursue these opportunities. Within the narrow domain of electoral politics, there is, for the first time in many years, a possibility of influencing national policy. Congress has lost whatever role it may have had in the design of foreign policy except in one respect: it holds the purse strings. Effort by senators such as McGovern and Hatfield to withhold appropriations for a continuing or expanding war have established a sharp criterion by which it can be determined whether a senator or representative is for peace or war, and efforts to support those who are for peace in this sense should be pursued. Beyond this, citizens have the right, the responsibility in fact, to refuse complicity in the criminal acts of the government—by refusal to pay war taxes, support for those who refuse to serve in the armed forces, encouragement of freedom of speech (which will lead to resistance) in the military, and by many other means of principled resistance to continued American aggression. Furthermore, the task of dismantling the "military-industrial complex"—that is, the present form of militarized state capitalism in the United States—will be long and arduous. It must engage the resources of many people for many years in educational and political efforts. It is necessary to overcome the prevailing repressive ideologies, demystify existing institutions, investigate and explain the structure and dynamics of American society, and build popular forces that can undertake a humane and truly revolutionary transformation of American society. The United States, more than any other country, has the technological and material resources to carry out a truly democratic revolution that will place all social and economic institutions under popular control. Within the American tradition, there are strong libertarian elements that can provide the basis for a revolutionary transformation to truly democratic forms of social organization. The future need not be bleak, despite problems and dangers that no serious person will disregard.

PART I

Who Is the United States Fighting in Indochina?

CHAPTER 1

Vietnam: The Open War

The Legacy of French Colonialism

In May 1954, the Great Powers convened a conference at Geneva, Switzerland, to discuss a resolution of the Indochina war. There, the Western powers had a harsh fact to face. France had been badly defeated. For almost seventy years, France had dominated Vietnamese life, undermined her society, disfigured her cities, taxed her peasants, and extracted her wealth. Now, after a decade of savage warfare, she had lost. The Viet Minh held three-quarters of Indochina. In the spring of 1954, they had decisively humiliated the "finest" of French armies. Thousands of France's best-trained troops had been taken prisoner.

This was not a new phenomenon in Asia. In the wake of the defeat of the Dutch in Indonesia, the American-backed Chiang Kai-shek in China, and the collapse of the British colonial system, it was becoming almost a familiar process. In fact, for almost two decades the West's position of dominance in Asia had been crumbling. Only the United States, after World War II, had seemed capable of continuing in that well-worn role. Already, with her money and her armaments, she was replacing France in Indochina. Yet what was a new role for the United

States was an old story to the Vietnamese. "We have fought a thousand years," was the proud claim of Vietnamese nationalists. "And we will fight another thousand if need be."[1] It was no exaggeration. They had defended their independence against the Chinese, the Mongols, sometimes the Thais, and only recently, the Europeans, the Japanese, and the Americans. Despite their continuing divisions and intermittent wars, the French, arriving in the nineteenth century, were impressed by the unified sense of resistance that the Vietnamese maintained.[2]

Before the arrival of the French, Vietnamese life was regulated according to custom within the confines of the village, the basic unit of Vietnamese society. As the Vietnamese moved south from their traditional homeland in the Red River Delta, spreading their villages and culture to those areas suitable for rice cultivation and relatively free of malarial mosquitoes, each new village was "incorporated" into the national community by the emperor. The point of contact between the Vietnamese imperial system and rural Vietnam was the village unit, not the individual peasant. That village was required to pay taxes, provide labor for public works and men for the army. Beyond these tasks, village affairs were self-directed and the village autonomous. "The king's law bows before village custom" was the saying. Within the village, a strong cooperative tradition existed. While there was a village elite which exploited the peasantry, extremes of poverty and wealth were avoided, education was widespread, and ownership of the land was dispersed among the vast majority of the populace. In addition, the villages maintained communal lands. A part of these lands was set aside for the support of the old and the poor, who could also rely on the rice granaries in times of need. Yet, this tradition of local "democracy" never was meant to challenge the supreme and overriding authority of the emperor's government.[3]

Such a decentralized society hardly suited French needs. They proceeded to remodel it to their specifications—often by force. The first skirmishers of the emerging French colonial empire, Catholic missionaries, with their naval allies, took advantage of Vietnamese dynastic rivalries to establish a foothold in the country. By 1862, they held in hand Cochin China (the present-day Mekong Delta region of South Vietnam). By 1885, they had added Annam (central Vietnam) and Tonkin to the north. Claims to large parts of Laos and Cambodia were rigorously enforced. Yet it was not until the 1890s that all of Indochina was "secure." Even then resistance lingered on, flaring fiercely from time to time. In fact, for every French general who commanded troops on the Indochinese peninsula, there was a leader of Vietnamese resistance. What the French had taken by force, they had to hold by the overwhelming power of their arms.

The French soon moved to ensure that no further unified resistance to their rule could arise. They used a policy of "divide and rule" to break down the Vietnamese sense of national tradition. They cut the country into three administrative areas (plus Laos and Cambodia), ruling through a variety of petty bureaucrats. They even outlawed the expression "Vietnam" used by the Emperor Gialong when he briefly unified the country early in the nineteenth century. They exacerbated regional differences in interest and character and set one group of Vietnamese against another. At the same time, they gathered all real power, economic and political, into their own hands. These two processes, the purposeful fragmentation of the society and the consolidation of power, served the same end: the enhancement of the ability of the French to extract from the country as much wealth as they could with as little opposition as possible.[4]

In sum, they disfigured the shape of Vietnamese society to suit their own needs. The result was disastrous for the Vietnamese peasant. The pattern of land distribution changed, enlarging the gap between rich and poor. In order better to extract rubber and rice for export in Cochin China, the French created a large plantation system on which the peasant could work as a penniless tenant. In the twentieth century, in the Mekong Delta, out of a population of 4 million, only 255,000 still owned land. And in one Mekong province, 9.6 percent of these landowners held 65.5 percent of the province's cultivable land. In the north (Tonkin), the situation was not so severe in numerical terms. Of a population of 6 million, 965,000 were landholders.[5] Yet the size of the holdings of individual peasants decreased significantly, while large estates arose. Sixty-two percent of the Tonkinese peasantry came to own less than nine-tenths of an acre each.[6]

Better to insure their profits, the French administrators created monopolies for consumer goods (salt and wine), so that the peasant would have to buy what he wanted (or in the case of French wine, what he did not want) from the produce of land he no longer owned at prices he could not afford. The French administration had a particular interest in spreading the use of alcohol and, to a lesser extent, opium. It profited directly from their sale. At first administrators simply prevented the distillation of the traditional Vietnamese rice wine (used mainly for ceremonial purposes), enforcing its replacement with a much stronger, more expensive French-made alcohol. There was a decline in consumption. Resourcefully, the French then assigned each village a quota which it was required to consume. As one French prefect, setting exorbitant quotas, commented, "The villages which have consumed much will be recompensed, and the villages which have consumed little will be punished." The smoking of opium, a criminal offense in France, served similarly as a financial prop for the French colonial regime. So, too, did the salt tax. By allowing the price of salt to jump 500 percent in twenty years, by wiping out local salt producers, the salt monopoly did grave damage to the health of the Vietnamese people, destroying an indispensable part of their daily diet.[7]

The French colonial regime exercised its power largely for profits. Indeed its own budget statistics are damning. In the annual statistical report on Indochina (1943), for instance, the governor-general reported these figures:[8]

For schools	748,000 piasters
For hospitals	71,000 piasters
For libraries	30,000 piasters
For purchase of opium by state monopoly	4,473,000 piasters

While the French engaged in large-scale public works programs (roads, canals, rail lines, irrigation projects), these proved of little value to the Vietnamese peasantry. Between 1880 and 1937, for instance, the French constructed drainage and irrigation canals which freed 4.5 million new acres for cultivation.[9] This meant considerable increases in rice production; yet export of this rice to China and Japan offered such enormous profits to the French that per capita intake of rice, for the peasant, actually declined.[10]

French factory goods were forced into the rural areas where they competed favorably with traditional handicrafts. The individual was, in addition, heavily taxed. Hundreds of thousands of landless peasants lived in poverty. Even the large estates of absentee landlords (built, through usury, on the poverty of their countrymen) in turn fell into the hands of the powerful (French) Bank of Indochina.

In these ways, the French administration controlled the wealth of Vietnam. Though the Indochinese colony was a financial drain for the French people as a whole, it proved a rich and open mine for small groups of French businessmen in Indochina and their allies in French officialdom. For the Vietnamese, however, increasing misery was the lot of all but the few who collaborated with the French. The real standard of living fell during this period. The rate of literacy among the population decreased considerably. Higher education ceased altogether.[11]

> Forty years after the conquest, there was elementary education of a crude kind available for 2 percent of the population and secondary education available for one-half of 1 percent. Three libraries and one so-called "university" were established in the country.[12]

Education exposes in microcosm both the French methods of controlling the country and the seeds of conflict hidden within those methods. Essentially, the French attempted to retrain a part of the educated elite of Vietnam. They did this primarily through their education system—a system which, they liked to boast, brought a "civilizing mission" to colonized peoples. To a significant degree this education was designed to rob the educated native few of any sense of their own nationality. They were to know more of Joan of Arc and Napoleon than of their own patriotic tradition. Schoolchildren, prohibited from celebrating their national holidays, observed French ones.

Yet among this tiny educated class they were fostering, there was a danger—not least in the French revolutionary tradition itself, a tradition encompassed in the words "liberty, equality, fraternity," all notably absent in French Indochina. Even without such an education, a Vietnamese intellectual needed no more than his eyes to see gross injustices in his surroundings, to feel the humiliating highhandedness of his French "compatriots."

> The rare Annamite able to go through the polytechnical school and graduate as a modestly equipped engineer could earn 400 piasters a month. The French concierge of the University of Hanoi—a slightly glorified sort of janitor—earned 1,404 piasters per month.[13]

Instead of the gratitude the French expected for the gift of their culture, numerous Vietnamese intellectuals throughout the period of French rule opposed foreign domination. "It was indeed a fact," noted one visiting American journalist in the late 1940s, "that almost every Annamite graduate of a French lycee or university took his post-graduate degree in French colonial culture at any of a score of prisons, at Sonla or Banmethuot, or on the island penal colony of Poulo-Condor."[14] As one governor-general bitterly exclaimed, "We want no intellectuals in Indochina. They are a misfortune for the country."[15]

For the Indochinese elite, there were only a couple of paths into opposition. One possibility was to go into opposition in the cities themselves. This was the European revolutionary model. Yet to do this meant fighting the battles on the enemy's home ground, for the cities of Vietnam had become as much French as they were Vietnamese. This was natural enough. Coming from an urban industrial society, the French logically chose to dominate Indochina through its cities. They changed the very physical layout of the cities to suit their own tastes. "With its buff-colored homes with their red-slate roofs bordering quiet tree-lined streets, Saigon might have been almost any drowsy, southern French provincial town."[16] In their sculpted cities, French *fonctionnaires* lived a life of relative ease while their Vietnamese opposites tried to make ends meet. One budget of the 1930s, for instance, provided 15 million piasters for about 30,000 Vietnamese employees and functionaries of the government, and 40 million piasters for 5,000 French functionaries.[17]

More important, the French changed the relationship of urban to rural areas. Traditionally, the rural mandarin elite, while exploiting the peasantry, had served as a buffer between them and the imperial government in the capital. With the French, the rural elite no longer served even this mediating role. Instead cities were made the direct control mechanism for the whole country. They were made centers of investment and, from these command posts, the local French administration sallied out to exploit the wealth of the countryside. In sum, the French fortified the cities as the counting and sorting houses for the wealth of Vietnam and suitable abodes for invading Europeans.

By turning the eyes of the urban-educated to the West and overburdening the peasant, the French hoped to prevent any effective opposition to their rule from arising. A measure of their success was that while they built only thirty-one new hospitals, they were forced to construct eighty-one new prisons (not including concentration camps).[18] Resistance in the cities was either of a token kind, existed underground, or was crushed. It also meant resistance largely apart from the populace of Vietnam, 85 percent of whom lived in the rural areas. There was, though, an alternative—to go into the countryside and make an alliance with the Vietnamese peasantry.

World War II and the First Betrayal of the Viet Minh Resistance

During the early periods of resistance to the French (1858–96), many of the leaders of the opposition had been the old mandarin elite. But by the turn of the century, their time of armed rebellion was over. Resistance, when it was resumed, was led by new men, inspired by new ideas, impelled by new forces, organizing along new lines. All these nationalist groups had long been convinced that independence could only be won by force. Yet among these growing opposition forces of the early 1920s, none had a coherent formula for nationwide resistance. Most intellectuals, while sympathizing with the plight of the peasant masses, never articulated a program of social reform applicable to them. The rights they demanded were of concern mainly to the tiny educated middle class immersed in city politics. None were likely to rally the entire Vietnamese people behind the independence movement.

Only in the late 1920s was a group formed which focused on the long history of isolated peasant uprisings and protests bloodily put down by the French. This group, the Communists, concluded that the peasants and urban workers of Vietnam would enter the struggle only when independence was related to their desperate needs. Independence, they explained, would be but one result of a continuous battle on concrete issues of immediate interest to them. They spoke of the need for lowering taxes, of the distribution of land among the landless, of higher wages and medical care for plantation workers, of the right of workers in the cities to organize unions. Only within this context, they felt, could "nationalism" serve to generate peasant support and participation in the movement to overthrow French rule.[19]

Not until the Second World War did the resistance forces gain real strength. Before then, the French exploited the advantages of overwhelming power (and the history of the colony is filled with its use, right up to 1940) against fragmented opposition groups. Long before the days of Hitler, as one observer commented, the French "employed the method of wiping out whole villages and towns in reprisal for the acts of individuals."[20] The colony supported a top-heavy and heavy-handed bureaucracy. Its garrisons, composed of Foreign Legion units, African Senegalese, and other colonial levies, often engaged in punitive expeditions against the dissident and the rebellious. In the rebellion of 1930, the French killed an estimated 10,000 and deported 50,000. "People," concluded one scholar, "were killed not in the heat of battle—there were no battles—but rather they were chased, hunted down, and murdered by a soldiery drunk on blood."[21]

It was the Japanese who first swept the European colonialists out of Southeast Asia, shattering forever the myth of white invincibility. In 1941 they occupied Indochina, incorporating it into their "Greater East Asian Coprosperity Sphere." Yet, they left the Vichy (collaborationist) French government to run the country. Indeed, the harsh rule Japan imposed through these French bureaucrats belied her pan-Asian rhetoric. In response, various parts of the Vietnamese nationalist movement came together in May 1941 to form a united front organization, the League for the Independence of Vietnam (Viet Minh, for short). At its head was Ho Chi Minh, ex-merchant seaman, assistant chef (London), photographic retoucher (Paris). For many years he had struggled for Vietnamese independence and had been imprisoned at various times by the French, British, and Chinese. He was an eclectic thinker, at home in French culture, persuaded by its revolutionary tradition, yet deeply immersed in Vietnamese history. In the 1920s, he turned to Marxism-Leninism not as an abstract philosophy, but as a potent tool for analyzing the world situation and, in particular, the plight of colonial peoples. By the late 1930s, Ho (now head of the Indochinese Communist party) was the most widely known of the nationalist leaders; and his party, although prevented from effectively organizing in the countryside, managed to ally with a wide range of groups: traditional-style secret societies, mountain tribes, labor organizations, student groups.

During the war, his new united front, the Viet Minh, established a small territorial base in the mountain highlands of present-day North Vietnam. They made wide contacts internationally, did intelligence work for the Allies, and received substantial aid from the American OSS (Office of Strategic Services, the wartime predecessor of the CIA). Toward the end of the war, the Japanese, mistrusting the colony's French administrators, removed the puppet French government. In its place they proclaimed Bao Dai, the last twig on the Vietnamese imperial tree, emperor of an "independent" Vietnam.

This Japanese coup gave the Viet Minh (whose forces at that time numbered only a few thousand) an unprecedented opportunity. The Japanese, preoccupied elsewhere in the Pacific, made no attempt to replace the French in their mountain defense positions. Nor did they have the time to set up a police apparatus in the colony as efficient as the French one had been. The Viet Minh quickly moved in, disarming many of the French occupation troops in their rural outposts. Soon the whole traditional system of French control over rural Vietnam began to disintegrate, and the Japanese found themselves confronted with a rapidly spreading revolutionary movement. Securing arms from American airdrops or abandoned French supply depots, the Viet Minh attacked local Japanese fortifications. Between March and August 1945 they cleared large areas of five of the northern provinces and engaged the full attention of the Japanese Twenty-first Division.[22]

Suddenly the war ended. After a few brief clashes, the Viet Minh troops marched triumphantly into Hanoi and set up a government. Days later, in Saigon, the Viet Minh's People's Committee, declaring itself a representative of the provisional government in Hanoi, took power.

While the Japanese armies awaited their fate and thousands of French looked helplessly on, the Democratic Republic of Vietnam was created. And the new regime, through its energetic actions, took swift hold among the Vietnamese people. They distributed French lands and the landholdings of "collaborators" among the landless peasants. By requisitioning all untilled land for those who would work it, they wiped out the then widespread famine within six months. Quickly, they reversed the French-encouraged trend of illiteracy, set up new schools, made the eight-hour working day law in the cities, lowered taxes, nationalized all public utilities (previously controlled by foreigners), helped the workers set up their own unions, and opened the jails to release the many thousands of political prisoners incarcerated by the French regime.[23]

But this period was brief indeed. It had been arranged that the Japanese surrender would be taken by the British in the southern part of the country and by the Chinese Nationalists in the North. Their task was supposedly the "round-up and disarming of the Japanese, and the recovery of Allied Prisoners of War and Internees."[24] While the Chinese warlord given the job in the North was interested primarily in booty, the British systematically sought to enable the French to return to power. They went to some lengths. They rearmed the French troops interned in the Saigon area. On September 23, the French launched a coup d'etat. The British commander looked the other way. Saigon fell and the Viet Minh troops retreated into the countryside. There, a combined force of British-Indian and Japanese soldiers fought on until the French could find and muster reinforcements.[25] As General MacArthur paternalistically summed it all up, "If there is anything that makes my blood boil, it is to see our Allies in Indochina and Java deploying Japanese troops to reconquer the little people [sic] we promised to liberate. It is the most ignoble kind of betrayal."[26]

Yet the Viet Minh held back. Twice Ho signed agreements which gave the French more than he felt they were entitled to. Finally, when asked virtually to surrender, he is reported to have said that "in the French Union [the commonwealth proposed at that time] there is no place for cowards; if I accept these conditions I would be one."[27] In late November 1946, ships of the French fleet bombarded the Vietnamese sections of the port city of Haiphong. The commander of the French naval forces in the Far East estimated that 6,000 Vietnamese civilians had died in the unexpected onslaught.[28] It set a precedent for the many atrocities to follow. On December 20, the Viet Minh struck back inside Hanoi; but, poorly armed, they were unable to sweep the French from the city. That afternoon, with some difficulty, the Viet Minh leadership and their ill-armed soldiers slipped away into the countryside.

The First Indochina War, 1946—54

With the French back in the urban saddle, increasingly arrogant and intransigent, and the Vietnamese firm but not well armed, the war for independence was on in earnest. The pattern of the war emerged quickly. "Today it is a case of the grasshopper pitted against the elephant," stated Ho Chi Minh succinctly, "but tomorrow the elephant will have its guts ripped out."[29] On balance, the French had the advantage of superior armaments; the Viet Minh, peasant support. The French held the cities; the Viet Minh, the countryside. The French could go practically anywhere they wished, as long as they had the military forces to clear the way. The Viet Minh, hard pressed at first, kept the number of their fighting units low. They patterned their strategy to their situation, emphasizing extreme mobility of combat groups and relying on the support of the Vietnamese villagers. A symbiotic relationship developed. Where the Viet Minh went, they began to promote agrarian and educational reforms, new health measures, new political organizations. With the villagers, the Viet Minh began to find food and hiding places, information on French positions, sons and daughters to fill their ranks.

The very focus of power in Vietnam began to change. The cities, which had been the hub of Indochinese politics during the period of French rule, gained a peripheral (almost ephemeral) existence—decaying frontier outposts of a dying empire. Power had returned to the villages, traditional centers of Vietnamese culture, and living place of the great majority of Vietnam's people. In those villages the Viet Minh, increasingly strong as the war progressed, continually developed that form of revolutionary struggle now known as "people's war."

For many Americans, people's war has become synonymous with the swift ambush of the lingering patrol, the sudden attack on an unwary garrison. Yet these are its military tactics and little more. At the heart of people's war are "people," not military tactics. In fact, the real task for the Viet Minh was not primarily to outfight, but to outadminister the French on the village level. What became important was not the reported battles, nor the pronunciamentos from the capital, but the unnoticed happenings in local villages. It was there that the Viet Minh was able to break the old links between urban and rural areas, displacing French bureaucrats and their Vietnamese headmen, tax collectors, and police inspectors, with revolutionary cadres drawn from among the peasants. It was a crude yet constructive undertaking, this attempt, in the most primitive of conditions, under the extreme hardships of a war situation, to build a new society.

The Viet Minh war, even its harshest Western critics have admitted, was clearly nationalistic, anticolonial, and popular among all strata of Vietnamese.[30] But, like guerrilla tactics, nationalism alone does not make a people's war. It is important to remember that within this framework of nationalism and resistance to the French, the Viet Minh concentrated upon the immediate needs of the peasants—on increasing food supplies, encouraging the growth of local industries, building roads, improving production, setting up basic health facilities. There, in the northern forests, they set up crude factories. An American visiting the area in 1952 reported "a glimpse of this process in a visit to the M.K. factory, an arsenal making small arms, bazookas and hand grenades. It was quite unlike anything we would think of as an industrial plant." The machines rested in sandbagged huts, the power lines were strung from palm trees.

> Everything had to be learned the hard way. Old Japanese bombs were dug up and taken apart for chemicals. Melanite had to be stolen. Nitrates were smuggled from Hanoi. Design-makers had to be trained. There were explosions and accidents. Old rails were reforged into gun barrels. The wrecks of French half-tracks, old boats and armored cars were dragged into the jungle. Lathes, pulleys and boilers were rigged up. The workers lived on soup and corn and had to plant their own crops as well as work, and sometimes fight. By 1949, the plant was producing recoil-less bazookas, said the factory director.[31]

Other factories worked on ferrous and nonferrous metals, made sulfuric acid, paper, textiles for local use, soap, and medical supplies (including penicillin).[32]

"Study to Resist" was the slogan the Viet Minh cadres brought to the villages. So that the peasant might gain new tools for learning how to improve his world, the Vietnamese alphabet was simplified, new schools established in liberated areas, and mass literacy campaigns carried out. But at the base of village reforms lay the land policies. It was this that peasants from the Mekong Delta village of Tan Phu recalled most vividly in an interview with a French journalist:

> In 1945, we learned at Tan Phu that the Japanese were leaving, beaten. It's at that time that the Viet Minh settle into our village and administered it: the cadres gain in importance; the people linked to the French are superseded. In speeches people begin to refer more than ever to independence, social revolution, agrarian reforms: They propose to limit rents to 25%, to divide up the great plantations, to regulate

leases on farm lands; and they begin to plan for the distribution of confiscated lands to the peasants.[33]

The reforms of 1945, 1949, and the Land Law of December 19, 1953, had the effect of winning large-scale peasant support for the guerrilla troops. The peasants had gained a clear-cut stake in the developing struggle. For the first time, they began to feel themselves to be participants in the planning of their own lives.

This interaction between leaders and those being led is basic to people's war. From it, a new spirit arose in the areas under Viet Minh control, a spirit even the hawkish American journalist Joseph Alsop could not overlook. In the winter of 1954, traveling through the Viet Minh areas of the Mekong Delta, he commented:

> I would like to be able to report—I had hoped to be able to report—that on that long, slow canal trip to Vinh Binh, I saw all the signs of misery and oppression that have made my visits to East Germany like nightmare journeys to 1984. But it was not so . . . At first it was difficult to conceive a Communist government's genuinely 'serving the people.' I could hardly imagine a Communist government that was also a popular government and almost a democratic government. But this is just the sort of government the palm-hut state actually was while the struggle with the French continued. The Vietminh could not possibly have carried on the resistance for one year, let alone nine years, without the people's strong, united support.[34]

From the beginning, the French reacted conventionally—as if they were engaged in no more than a colonial war of reconquest. They relied mainly on the military tactic called *tache d'huile* (oil slick). In French North Africa, where this tactic had been developed, the taking of an oasis sometimes led to the surrender of whole tribes. From this key center, the occupying forces could spread into sparsely populated surrounding areas, using *"quadrillage,* the splitting-up into small squares, or 'gridding,' of the countryside, with each grid being carefully 'raked over' (the *'ratissage'*) by troops thoroughly familiar with the area, or guided by experts who know the area well."[35] This "pacification" tactic, so useful in the Moroccan desert fighting of the 1920s, was particularly inapplicable in Indochina. There, in areas either densely populated or forbiddingly mountainous and forested, the French did not even have adequate forces to secure all the major population areas against Viet Minh resistance. Yet the French commanders clung tenaciously to oil slick operations almost to the end.[36]

By the fall of 1950, immobilized French garrisons were being overrun throughout northern Vietnam. The Viet Minh troops under General Vo Nguyen Giap inflicted a series of stunning defeats on their retreating forces.

> When the smoke cleared, the French had suffered their greatest colonial defeat since Montcalm had died at Quebec. They had lost 6,000 troops, 13 artillery pieces and 125 mortars, 450 trucks and three armored platoons, 940 machineguns and more than 8,000 rifles. Their abandoned stocks alone sufficed for the equipment of a whole additional Viet-Minh division.[37]

By the end of October, all of northern North Vietnam was an impenetrable Viet Minh fortress. Despite setbacks to the Vietnamese forces early in 1951, the French position continued its speedy disintegration.

The Viet Minh were no longer the poorly armed guerrillas who had proclaimed the Democratic Republic of Vietnam in August 1946. By the spring of 1954, they controlled three-quarters of Vietnam in its name. Their troops, well armed with American weapons (many left on the mainland by Chiang Kai-shek's defeated armies and shipped across the border by the Chinese Communists) passed easily throughout most of the country. Their support among the Vietnamese was overwhelming. The French, while still having a numerical superiority in troops, were desperate. Navarre, the French commander, ignoring (as a later French government investigatory committee put it) the fact that "there are no blocking positions in country lacking European-type roads," had set up a "land-air" base in the valley of Dienbienphu. It was supposed to lock the "back door" to the kingdom of Laos. Now twelve French divisions within the fortress were besieged by the Viet Minh. Viet Minh artillery was raking the valley floor.[38]

In April 1954, the French appealed to the United States for direct intervention. United States officials, behind closed doors, proposed a joint British-French-U.S. offensive against the Viet Minh.[39] It was to include air strikes around Dienbienphu from U.S. carriers cruising in the South China Sea on "training missions."[40] To French Foreign Minister Georges Bidault, Secretary of State John Foster Dulles suggested the possible "use of . . . one or more nuclear weapons near the Chinese border against supply lines," and "two" to be used against the Viet Minh at Dienbienphu itself.[41] On April 7, then Vice-President Nixon stated "off the record":

> The United States as a leader of the Free World cannot afford further retreat in Asia . . . if this government cannot avoid it, the Administration must face up to the situation and dispatch forces.[42]

But the plans aborted. British Prime Minister Winston Churchill flatly opposed British involvement. His foreign minister, Anthony Eden, warned that such military acts would destroy the possibility of a negotiated settlement. Within the U.S., opposition to a possible intervention proved particularly strong in the Congress—from men like Russell, Stennis, Kennedy, and Johnson who feared domestic and international complications. Most important, the French people were sick of *la sale guerre* (the dirty war) and wished to end it. On May 7, the Viet Minh overran Dienbienphu. Close to 10,000 men from among the French forces were made prisoner. Another 2,000 lay dead in the valley. Only seventy-three managed to escape.[43] "When the battle ended, the 82,926 parachutes expended [by the French] in supplying the fortress covered the battlefield like freshly fallen snow. Or like a burial shroud."[44]

Geneva, the United States, and the Second Betrayal of the Resistance Movement

Yet Dienbienphu proved the occasion, not the cause, for a decision in Paris to terminate the war. A conference had already been convened at Geneva, Switzerland, attended by China, Russia, France, Britain, the United States, and the Democratic Republic of Vietnam. While only one indigenous group, the Viet Minh, had major political power throughout Indochina, in the conference's final settlement, "the Viet Minh, the winners, lost, or were sold out. Ho Chi Minh was somehow persuaded—apparently by a joint Sino-Soviet effort—to settle for half the country."[45] The agreement signed between the French and the Viet Minh provided for a regroupment of military forces pending the arrangement of national elections. The seventeenth parallel, dividing the country in half, was chosen as a demarcation line. Civil administration of the respective territories was to be in the hands of the Viet Minh in the North and the French (not Bao Dai's government) in the south. It was written into the provisions that the Viet Minh were to participate fully in the political activities of the South prior to the elections. No reprisals were to be taken against individuals or organizations in either zone for activities during the war. Civilians were to be allowed to cross the borders freely during the ten-month period provided for military regroupment. In an attempt to neutralize the country, both zones were forbidden to make military alliances with other nations or to receive troop reinforcements and military supplies from outside. An International Control Commission (ICC) composed of India, Canada, and Poland was formed to supervise the execution of the agreement.

In retrospect, the most important aspect of these accords, signed in July 1954, was what they did not say. Specifically, they *in no way* partitioned Vietnam into two separate and independent nations. They were no more than a "cease-fire" accord between the two sides, and the seventeenth parallel only a "provisional military demarcation line" that "should not in any way be interpreted as constituting a political or territorial boundary" (articles 1 and 8; article 6, Final Declaration). This was only a means, in a war without clear-cut front lines, of separating the two sides. In a Final Declaration, endorsed by all the nations at the conference (except the United States) the temporary nature of the demarcation line was emphasized and it was specified that elections should be held in July 1956, under the supervision of the ICC representatives.[46]

Even today, what pressures were put on the Viet Minh by the Russians and the Chinese is not clear, nor is it clear why they compromised, giving up so much that they had won. The promise of elections within two years probably helped to convince them. While their ultimate victory over the French was assured, the campaigns needed to oust the French (particularly if the U.S. were to become further involved) would have been costly indeed— especially when it was generally assumed that Ho Chi Minh would win the election in a reunified Vietnam hands down. Yet the agreement was, despite compromises, a ratification of the Viet Minh's victory over the French and of a future unified Vietnam governed from Hanoi.

For American officials, it was a bitter pill to swallow. At the conference table, Secretary of State Dulles refused even to shake hands with Chou En-lai, negotiating for the Chinese. As Assistant Secretary for Far Eastern Affairs Walter S. Robertson commented in August, "It would be an understatement to say that we do not like the terms of the cease-fire agreement just concluded."[47] It would be equally a mistatement to say that the United States had any intention of abiding by them. The U.S. issued a frosty declaration of its own (stating that it would refrain from the use, or threat, of force to disturb the agreements, and that it would view the renewal of "aggression" in violation of the agreements with grave concern) and went right on with its pre-Dienbienphu planning. Before the ink was dry at Geneva, according to General James Gavin,

> Admiral Radford was emphatically in favor of landing a force in the Haiphong-Hanoi area even if it meant risking war with Red China. In this he was fully supported by the Chief of Staff of the Air Force and the Chief of Naval Operations.[48]

Secretary of State Dulles and the Central Intelligence Agency generally agreed. It was assumed that the "expeditionary force" would be "eight combat divisions, supported by thirty-five engineer battalions, and all the artillery and logistical support such a mammoth undertaking requires."[49] It was further assumed that to land in the Red River Delta area of North Vietnam would necessitate taking Hainan Island from the Chinese.

That American officials were considering such far-reaching plans just before and just after the "settlement" at Geneva belies the popular American conviction that the U.S. assumed a whole new role in Indochina after 1954. In actuality, America's role in Indochina began as early as the late 1940s when the colonial expedition directed from Paris turned into a Franco-American anti-Communist crusade. The growth of the American commitment, first to French Indochina, then to Diem's Vietnam, is a study in the American way of empire.

During the Second World War, President Roosevelt had mentioned the possibility of making French overseas territories into trusteeships of the United Nations. But when he died, this vague possibility passed away with him. Truman and his advisers, primarily concerned with European problems, focused their attentions on shoring up their weakened French ally. For them, Indochina was of little importance, a mere appendage of France. For France's glory and pride, they were quite willing to sacrifice and humiliate the people of Vietnam. They gave in quickly to the French government's desire to reestablish its colonial prerogatives throughout Indochina. Indeed, though the French returned to Indochina first in a few symbolic

French transports, these were followed by a long succession of American ships, flying the American flag, manned by American crews. The French army, disembarking from these ships in American-made uniforms, launched their first assaults with American lend-lease weapons, tanks, trucks, and jeeps.

Yet even in those early years, U.S. officials realized the futility of fighting Ho under the French imperial flag. Seeing Ho as a nationalist, they urged the French to create some alternate nationalist movement which might compete with his appeal to Vietnamese patriotism. By 1949, however, with the intensification of the cold war in Europe and the unification of mainland China under the Communists, they began to look at the struggle somewhat differently. Washington began to downplay the nationalist (and colonial) face of the Indochina war, while playing up its "international" aspects. In January 1950, Ho Chi Minh's government was recognized by the Russians and Chinese. Shortly thereafter, Secretary of State Dean Acheson replied that such recognition "should remove any illusions as to the 'Nationalist' nature of Ho Chi Minh's aims and reveals Ho in his true colors as the mortal enemy of native independence in Indochina."[50] On February 7, both Britain and the United States recognized the government of Bao Dai as the legitimate representative of the Vietnamese people. Washington's recognition was followed by massive financial support. In June 1950, the Korean War began. All Asian wars, like all Asians, apparently looked alike from Washington's vantage point. Korea and Indochina came to be seen as twin battles in the same international Communist drive to take over Asia. The dollar flow supporting the French military campaign rapidly increased. From $150 million in 1950, it soared to $1 billion four years later. By 1954, the United States was underwriting 80 percent of the cost of the war. On April 6, 1954, in the middle of the battle of Dienbienphu, the U.S. announced that in the next fiscal year it would increase its aid to $1.33 billion.[51]

Geneva brought almost no halt to this process. While

the extreme military measures suggested by Admiral Radford and others were finally rejected by President Eisenhower himself, a "compromise" was reached. It was decided, as General Gavin has reported, that "we would not attack North Vietnam, but we would support a *South Vietnamese government* that we hoped would provide a stable, independent government that was representative of the people."[52] This flagrant violation of the Geneva accords marks the essence of American policy since 1954. It was pursued both internationally and on the level of Vietnamese politics.

Undermining Geneva: SEATO, Diem, and "South" Vietnam

Just a month after Geneva, Dulles convened a conference at Manila more to his liking. At this conference, SEATO (Southeast Asia Treaty Organization) was formed. The signatories of this mutual defense pact, in addition to Great Britain, Australia, New Zealand, France, and the United States, included just three Asian countries (Pakistan, Thailand, and the Philippines). In a protocol, SEATO protection was unilaterally extended to Cambodia, Laos, and the "free territory under the jurisdiction of the State of Vietnam" (that is, the regroupment area below the seventeenth parallel).

In this way, SEATO proved to be Dulles's answer to the Geneva agreement's ban on military alliances for either of the two zones. It also reflected the American commitment, in total violation of the accords at Geneva, to underwrite a separate state in the southern half of Vietnam. Yet SEATO in no way "committed" the signatories to intervene in Indochina (all they had to do was consult with each other). In fact, as an alliance, it was always weak and powerless. Yet, in Dulles's eyes, it served a much more significant end: "SEATO's *principal* purpose," he said, "was to provide our president *legal* authority to intervene in Indochina."[53]

In Saigon, General J. Lawton Collins, special American envoy, promptly announced that the U.S. intended to supply $2 billion in equipment and advisers to the South's armed forces.

> This American mission will soon take charge of instructing the Vietnam Army in accordance with special American methods which have proved effective in Korea, Greece and Turkey, and other parts of the world. . . . The aim will be, however, to build a completely autonomous Vietnam Army.[54]

Shortly after, President Eisenhower sent a letter to Prime Minister Ngo Dinh Diem promising his government aid "in developing and maintaining a strong, viable state, capable of resisting attempted subversion or aggression through military means."[55] Already, it seems, the cards were on the table.

The decision to prevent the prescribed reunification elections, however, concretely demonstrated the U.S. commitment to a permanent division of the country.[56] Washington has always tried to blame the "Communists" for this failure to call the 1956 elections. As *A Threat to Peace,* the State Department's December 1961 white paper, stated: "It was the Communists' calculation that nationwide elections scheduled in the Accords for 1956 would turn all of South Vietnam over to them . . . The authorities in South Vietnam refused to fall into this well laid trap."[57] This clever Communist "plot" to win the elections through popularity was carefully avoided by Diem. With American backing, he refused all overtures from the North. He refused to attend any preliminary conferences on the holding of elections (stipulated at Geneva). He refused even to state the electoral and supervisory conditions under which he would permit free elections to be held. Time and again, the North Vietnamese requested conferences to discuss the elections. Diem gave an adamant "no." Hanoi's subsequent requests for postal, cultural, or economic exchanges between the two areas were met with stony silence.[58]

To explain his actions, Diem put forward an argument repeated ad nauseam in later years by American officials. Truly free elections, he claimed, were unfeasible because the Communists in control of the North were unwilling to "allow each Viet-Namese citizen to exercise democratic liberties and the fundamental rights of man."[59] In that region, he added, brainwashing and the fear of reprisals made free elections impossible. In these rationalizations, both Diem and his American backers consciously ignored the fact that only Ho was willing to discuss internationally supervised elections to be held under the auspices of the ICC. They ignored as well the Geneva agreements: Viet Minh "control" of the North was an essential feature of the *preliminary* arrangements which were to be *followed* by elections; on the other hand, until the elections, France was expected to retain administrative control of the South, not Diem or the Americans. "We are not entirely masters of the situation," admitted the French Minister of foreign affairs in February 1956.

> The Geneva Accords on the one hand and the pressure of our allies [i.e., the Americans] on the other creates a very complex juridical situation. . . . The position in principle is clear: France is the guarantor of the Geneva Accords . . . But we do not have the means alone of making them respected.[60]

Nor do arguments about coercion and reprisals in the North hold water. Everyone knew that Ho was a popular figure. As President Eisenhower stated in his memoirs, *Mandate for Change*: "I have never talked or corresponded with a person knowledgeable in Indochinese affairs who did not agree that had elections been held as of the time of the fighting, possibly 80 percent of the population would have voted for the Communist Ho Chi Minh as their leader rather than chief of state Bao Dai."[61] Diem proved in practice that it was he, not Ho, who feared elections. In his race against the discredited Bao Dai for presidency of the South in 1955, he rejected the suggestion of American advisers that he settle for 60 percent of the vote. Instead, he made sure he got 98.2 percent, including 605,025 votes from among the not very selective 450,000 registered voters of Saigon.[62]

The truth was that American officials had never taken seriously the agreement at Geneva to hold elections within two years. They saw the election clause as a two-year breathing space in which to organize a base in the South. As Dulles put the matter, somewhat euphemistically, "American public opinion would never tolerate 'guaranteeing of the subjection of millions of Vietnamese to Communist rule.' "[63] The only question was how to organize it and through whom. In Ngo Dinh Diem they had found their answer.

By Mandarin background, personal inclination, and training Diem was a member of Vietnam's feudal aristocracy. He firmly believed in the Vietnamese monarchy; but was, as well, a Catholic. Under the French, he rose to the rank of governor of Phan Thiet province. His reputation as a governor was better than most. He judged fairly, and was not known to take bribes. From the beginning, he was a militant anti-Communist. As early as 1933, he gave the French a hand against the Communist-led insurgents, just then emerging as leaders of the Vietnamese anticolonial struggle. In May 1933, he became Emperor Bao Dai's minister of interior; but proud of Vietnamese traditions, he fell out with his sovereign over the French unwillingness to implement in any way his proposed "reform" programs. Publicly accusing the emperor of being "nothing but an instrument in the hands of the French authorities," he resigned and went into retirement.[64]

Unlike so many other Vietnamese, though, he never actively opposed the French. Rather he chose exile. He preferred to trust in fate and await some new opportunity to step back to the center of Vietnamese politics. In 1950, one quick leap ahead of history, he went to the United States. He spent most of the next three years in that country, living long stretches of time in Maryknoll seminaries in New Jersey and New York. Through his brother, Bishop Can (of the Vietnamese Catholic Church), he

gained a close relationship with Cardinal Francis Spell-
man, and a useful reputation as a militant *anti-Communist*
reformer. Launched on a career as a political lobbyist, he
came to meet and be admired by a diverse group of
senators, congressmen, intellectuals, and CIA agents. De-
spairing for an alternative to waning French power in
Indochina, they mistook his position of standing aside
from the struggle in his homeland for their long-desired
"middle course." "Ngo Dinh Diem," eulogized Supreme
Court Justice William O. Douglas, "is revered by the
Vietnamese because he is honest and independent and
stood firm against the French influence." Others came to
echo his words.[65]

In June 1954, the French, at American urging, accepted Diem as premier of the Bao Dai regime. While
Diem floated into power on a wave of American publicity
as a "reformer," "nationalist," and "anti-Communist," his
potential bases of power were quite limited. His reforms
were directed mainly toward the consolidation of those
bases. It was, in fact, a great irony of Diem's nationalist
career that the first and most important of them lay outside his country. His enemies, the Viet Minh, already
wore the halo of victory against the French colonists. To
defeat them, Diem had no alternative but to become almost
totally dependent on another foreign power, the United
States.

Even before Geneva, the United States had been involved in planting the seeds of a future "Free Vietnam."
Often American officials had attempted to supply their
aid directly to local Vietnamese forces, establishing independent ties with them while enraging French bureaucrats. After Geneva, America poured $250 million per
year into the country—in support of Diem.[66] Wheeling and
dealing, withholding funds from the army at a key moment,
American officials helped Diem undercut his more powerful opponents. With the money came American military advisers for the army, new American military equipment,
CIA agents to train his police force, professors from
Michigan State to provide a respectable front for these

activities, and publicity men to help his image in the United States.

Diem desperately needed this help. In Vietnam itself, his authority in 1954 was reported to extend to no more than a dozen square blocks of downtown Saigon. It was from this urban center that he sought to expand his control, gain supporters, and destroy the Viet Minh organization in the countryside. There were just two groups he could turn to. The first of these was the large landowners of the Mekong Delta region. This tiny, highly influential group was a creation of the French plantation system. Naturally enough, they identified with the French because of class interests and supported Diem for the same reason. Under the Viet Minh, much of the land they owned had been redistributed and many of them had fled to the cities to await events. With Diem they could only stand to gain. But for their support Diem had a price to pay. His lauded "land reform" program, designed and supported by American advisers, is only understandable within this context. The program was carried out primarily in those areas where Viet Minh land reforms had been most sweeping and successful. The return of Diem's soldiers to these areas meant that many peasants who had been cultivating the land for a decade as de facto owners were suddenly forced to pay rent—or they were "permitted" to purchase land they had long regarded as their own. The government's reforms, in the end, reduced rents which the Viet Minh had abolished, sold land which the Viet Minh had given away, and reestablished estates which the Viet Minh had broken up. The results of such an agrarian program were hardly popular in the countryside.[67]

The second group Diem looked toward was the Catholics. A minority of the population in primarily Buddhist Vietnam, they held a privileged position under the French. French policy, which had encouraged Catholicism, tried as well to tie Vietnamese Catholics to the colonial regime. They were exempted from military service and offered tax relief. In return they loyally staffed much of the colonial bureaucracy. During the first Indochina war (1946–54), nearly all sided with the French. In many northern Catholic communities, militia were specifically raised to fight the Viet Minh. The most important American propaganda victory of the Diem period, the dramatic story of the flight of 880,000 refugees to the South in 1954–55, must be seen against this backdrop.[68] This exodus has been cited repeatedly by American officials as a warning that the North is a place of horror and a bloodbath would follow any withdrawal from the South. An examination of the circumstances reveals something quite different.

First of all, these refugees consisted of only two groups. The first was the more than 100,000 Vietnamese troops of the colonial army and their dependents.[69] These men, who had fought many years against the Viet Minh, were certainly fearful of staying in the North. The second group was about 660,000 Vietnamese Catholics. Their fears and their flight could hardly be called spontaneous. For one thing, Diem, with foreign teams to aid him, flew to Hanoi on June 30, 1954, to set up a "Committee for the Defense of the North." Through it he hoped to galvanize the Catholics into flight.[70] With the help of the Catholic hierarchy in Vietnam and local parish priests in the tightly knit Catholic communities, his agents began to pass rumors among the Catholic peasants: the Communists would prohibit all religious service or religious symbols, "the Virgin Mary has departed from the North," "Christ has gone to the South," if they stayed the Americans would drop nuclear bombs on their villages, their priests would be put on trial. The Catholic peasants were terrified. Led by confused parish priests, manipulated by Catholic leaders and their bureaucratic allies in the cities, they began their flight south. There, they were told, was a Catholic president waiting to provide for them. As the French scholar Bernard Fall concluded,

> the mass flight was admittedly the result of an extremely intensive, well-conducted, and, in terms of its ob-

jective, very successful American psychological warfare operation.[71]

Units of the U.S. Seventh Fleet played a major role in moving the refugees south, and the U.S. government provided $93 million for their resettlement.

It was not so much that Diem feared for the safety of the Catholics in the North, but that he so desperately needed them in the South. These northern Catholics were Diem's real political base. With their arrival in the South they more than tripled that region's Catholic population, bringing it to slightly over 1 million. This was only 7 percent of the South's total population.[72] In coming south, they became socially rootless exiles. They were totally dependent on the good graces of Diem. They could be relied on to be uncompromising with the Viet Minh, and their fervent anticommunism recommended them to the Americans. The Catholic peasants were settled in their own communities mainly around Saigon and just south of the seventeenth parallel (two areas Diem was particularly interested in securing). Many of their leaders were appointed to top bureaucratic posts in his administration. New provincial and local offices were also filled out with them. In short, these northern Catholics "provided Diem with his most reliable and effective element in his power base."[73]

Repression and Resistance Under Diem

From the beginning, Diem attempted to weave together these potential sources of support—the Catholics, the large landholders, and the Americans—in the most personal way possible, through his own family. His brother, Archbishop Ngo Dinh Thuc, as dean of the Catholic episcopacy of Vietnam, provided a much needed religious sanction for Diem's policies at home. Through his links to prominent Catholics within the United States there was an equally effective channel for propaganda abroad. Ngo Dinh Can, another of Diem's brothers, became the "viceroy" of central Vietnam. By far the most famous of Diem's family advisers, however, were his brother Ngo Dinh Nhu and his wife. With the help of the CIA and various American advisers, Nhu developed South Vietnam's vast internal security system, including its secret police. At the international level, another brother, Ngo Dinh Luyen, served as ambassador to England, while Madame Nhu's father served as the ambassador to Washington. An early American supporter of Diem concluded:

> Abuse of power, nepotism, corruption, contempt for inferiors, and cruel disregard of the needs of the people were the example set by the "Family" for the ministers, legislators, generals, province chiefs, and village commissioners whom they used as pawns.[74]

Behind the family stood the United States. Below it stood very little at all. It threw its shadow over all Vietnamese society; yet its roots penetrated shallowly indeed into Vietnamese soil. This predetermined the methods by which Diem could extend his control over the country. His main problem was to break down already organized centers of resistance. While he first attacked religious-political groups, his real target was the far stronger Viet Minh, its cadres and supporters among the peasantry. Yet he had nothing to offer the peasantry that the Viet Minh had not already offered them better. In fact he could afford to offer them nothing at all without losing the support of the large landholders who stood by his side. Only one way was open: repression and further consolidation of power in the hands of his brothers and their followers.

In June and August 1956, Diem abolished the elected councils which ruled the villages of South Vietnam. He replaced these councils with officials appointed directly by his provincial governors (after approval from Nhu's Ministry of Interior in Saigon). With this single decree, Diem abolished the autonomy enjoyed by the South's 2,560 villages. For local autonomy, he substituted a city-directed administration which could hardly be expected to be in touch with local village problems.[75] Of course, Diem was basically interested not in local problems but in breaking the control that the Viet Minh and other groups held at the grass roots.

Centralized appointments were, however, only a part of his ambitious program. In 1959, he introduced a new, fairly sophisticated system of "relocation centers" for the peasants. These centers, under the administrative control of brother Nhu, were called "agrovilles"—a pre-1954 French term. (They, failing, were superseded in 1961 by the euphemistically entitled "strategic hamlets," and in 1964 by the "new life hamlets.") Under the agroville program, new rural villages, built by "forced labor," were surrounded by barbed-wire fences and spiked moats to make them militarily and politically impregnable. They bore, as American officials came to concede, a strange similarity to "concentration camps."[76] By 1963, 8 million villagers were living in the descendants of the original agrovilles.

Diem's policies toward the hostile peasantry were matched by his policies toward various minority and religious groups. The Montagnards (condescendingly called "Moi" or "savages" by Vietnamese), who lived a nomadic life in the central and southern highlands, were continually persecuted by the Diem regime. Unlike Hanoi, which allowed the northern Montagnards a significant degree of administrative and cultural autonomy, Diem denied them any measure of independence, even revoking some of the rights they had held under the French. The Hoa Hao and Cao Dai, powerful religious sects possessing both armies and territory, were also targets of persecution. Despite 12 million CIA dollars, Diem managed to antagonize as many of their leaders as he succeded in bribing. Dissident branches of these two sects accounted for most of the armed resistance to Saigon during the initial years of Diem's rule. Later, they were to constitute the largest part of the membership of the National Liberation Front in the first years of its existence.[77]

Yet none of these policies solved Diem's problems. He had no choice but to launch, along with them, a gigantic system of police terrorism and repression against rural Vietnam. As early as 1955 Diem launched wholesale acts of retaliation. These were not aimed just at Communist or non-Communist members of the Viet Minh. "Nearly all Vietnamese who had actively opposed French rule were now declared enemies of Diem's state of Vietnam."[78] Full-scale manhunts against dissidents were organized in the rural areas in 1956, and increased in later years as the situation deteriorated. The pattern of these manhunts is clear:

> . . . denunciation, encirclement of villages, searches and raids, arrests of suspects, plundering, interrogations enlivened sometimes by torture (even of innocent people), deportation, and regrouping of populations suspected of intelligence with the rebels, etc.[79]

Seventy-five thousand or more people were killed in this campaign.[80] As many or more were incarcerated under Presidential Ordinance No. 6, signed in January 1956. "Individuals considered dangerous to national defense and common security," it said, could be confined by executive order in a "concentration camp."[81] Conditions in Diem's "reeducation centers," brought to light only after his overthrow in 1963, were sordid indeed. Deliberate starvation, deliberate blinding, deliberate maiming. The list is long.

North Vietnam protested the slaughter and repression in the South to the ICC with increasing bitterness, but Ho's government did not directly interfere. In an unexpectedly partitioned country, the North found itself in a precarious economic position. While industrially more developed, it was dependent on the South for many of its food staples. This caused great hardships. Yet, exhausted from over a decade of constant warfare, northern leaders desired to avoid the cost of another prolonged conflict. They opted instead for developing self-sufficiency in their own area. Ho was confident that, even with massive American assistance, the attempt to build a separate state in the South would fail by itself. He seemed to believe that, in time, there would arise a new government in Saigon willing to negotiate renewed economic ties with the North and ultimately a peaceful reunification.[82]

But in the South, for the ex-Viet Minh cadres, the situation seemed far more serious. Slaughtered for their past political convictions, they were driven underground. In the end, they felt betrayed by the Geneva conference and abandoned by their northern comrades. Many, desperate, fled to the forests. Once again, in the late 1950s, small groups took up the guerrilla struggle. In March 1960, some of these ex-resistance fighters gathered in Zone D (eastern Cochin China) and issued a "general call" for the creation of a front to deal with the "intolerable" repression in the South.[83] From "somewhere in Nam Bo [Cochin China]" in December 1960, close to a hundred persons announced the creation of the "National Liberation Front of South Vietnam." They called for a nationwide uprising against the Saigon regime. Despite a certain reluctance, Hanoi had little choice but to sanction this southern initiative or lose whatever moral influence it had south of the Demilitarized Zone.[84]

The National Liberation Front

From the beginning, the Front had a certain heritage to fall back on. The Viet Minh organization in the South had retained its political influence even without its troops —both in the villages which had been in liberated zones during the war and in villages from which the French withdrew after 1954. Joseph Alsop wrote at the time that, according to American information in Saigon, "outside the feudal domains of the military religious sects, anywhere from 50 to 70 percent of the southern Indo-China villages are subject to Viet Minh influence or control. French experts give still higher percentages, between 60 and 90."[85] Yet neither the Viet Minh strength nor its programs had been as fully implemented there as in their northern stronghold. Faced with Diem's onslaught of repression, and unarmed, the Viet Minh cadres had been pushed into a temporary retreat.

This chronology of events puts in a different light the image many Americans have been given of the guerrilla: he is an "outside agitator" entering the village, upsetting the order of things or the forces of progressive change, using terror to manipulate and control a passive populace for ends of little interest to them. Walt Rostow, assistant to President Johnson, said typically that the guerrilla's "task is merely to destroy, while the government must build and protect what it is building."[86] Or, as Dean Rusk used to like to state, the NLF "has no significant popular following . . . It relies heavily on terror."[87] In Vietnam, however, it was Diem, not the Viet Minh or NLF, who fitted this image. What Diem and his American supporters described as an effort to establish an orderly system of government linked to Saigon and to "pacify" the countryside was to the peasants the destruction of reforms already won through the Viet Minh. For these villagers, it was Diem's agents and soldiers who were the intruders, manipulating them against their own interests.

Of course, from Saigon, the response to this intrusion seemed truly malevolent. Diem's appointed village chiefs were murdered, his police informers driven out, landlords fled to the safety of the large cities, government officials either joined the NLF, served with their tacit approval, or lost their lives. The NLF employed terror tactics, specifically against those whom the peasants feared. Orders from Saigon were ignored, feedback ceased to exist in whole areas of the countryside—the government came to see that it ruled in a void. All, claimed the government, due to simple "terrorism." Yet the peasants saw things quite differently. As a South Vietnamese peasant told Jacques Doyon, an independent French reporter who traveled in NLF territory in 1968,

> [The NLF soldiers] are very nice to us, very polite. They don't take anything in our homes or anywhere else in the village. . . . If they want something, they

ask for it, and if they can, they pay for it. Even the
rice! . . . not like the government's soldiers who help
themselves, taking the animals and the fruits, pillaging
when they're on an operation in the village.[88]

Discussing relations between the NLF cadres and the village peasants, Doyon observed that "the local cadres of
the NLF have captured their confidence, because, like
them, they are close to the soil; and it is this soil, of the
villages, of the province, and of the country, about which
the Viet Cong cadres talk to them." The peasant, added
Doyon, "fears them a bit . . . [but] he appreciates their
politeness, their language, their total poverty, and their
life so similar to his own."[89] The contrast with government appointees from the cities or landlords in their fine
homes was striking.

For Diem's government, by late 1961, the situation
had deteriorated drastically. One American administrative
adviser estimated that the NLF had already extended its
control in varying degrees to 80 percent of the countryside.[90] They could move almost anywhere in the country
with impunity. "The sun was just setting . . ." reported pro-
NLF Australian reporter Wilfred Burchett. "We rested
on a rice field terrace, drank some bottles of Saigon beer
and watched bombers roaring down the runway of Saigon's main airport."[91] He wrote this in late 1963 while
touring *NLF* hamlets at the very edge of the national
capital. It only reflected the fact that while the Saigon
regime retained its bureaucracy, a ubiquitous police, and
a powerful army, it controlled little more than the cities of
Vietnam.

In the countryside, the NLF was carrying out sweeping programs of economic and social reform. Land reform,
particularly in the Mekong Delta, was the initial and key
phase in the effort to redefine village life. The program
was pushed hard. As USIA official Douglas Pike comments, "the land distribution system was pressed until,
by the end of 1964, the DRV could claim that 'the
peasants in the areas under NLF . . . control have become masters of more than 1.3 million hectares (3.2 mil-

lion acres) of South Vietnam's total 3.5 million hectares (8.6 million acres) of cultivated land.' "[92] Doyan, observing these areas four years later, suggests an even higher figure.[93] This program of land redistribution (and rent reduction) had many effects in the villages. It tied the interests of the peasants clearly to the Front's guerrilla struggle. It helped identify the enemy in the Vietnamese countryside (i.e., those who would take the land back from the peasants). It taught self-sufficiency and self-reliance, key attitudes in a guerrilla struggle. It was also meant to increase crop production and to assure that food was not siphoned from the peasantry and the guerrilla army into the hands of absentee landlords and city bureaucrats.

Another aspect of the NLF's programs was the encouragement, among the peasantry of cooperative efforts and individual participation in the resolution of local problems. The NLF's educational and literacy campaigns were directed toward these ends. To cite but one example, an NLF document relates how villagers in a "government-controlled" area petitioned the government district office for a school. When the request was denied, a movement was initiated (with NLF help) at the local level to build and manage a school. The result was that the Saigon government's

> failure then appeared to the villagers as a striking contrast to their own ability to meet the need, inspiring confidence in their own capabilities. Furthermore, activities of managing the school, such as hiring teachers, deciding on curricula, and observing and evaluating its progress were an ongoing community concern. By carrying the political struggle efforts against GVN to their logical conclusion, villagers find encouraging examples of the strengths and potential of human effort in the liberation movement and simultaneously provide services to the community, which increase the involvement of the community members in new self-sustaining integrative interaction.[94]

From this sort of popular participation in decisions that affected their lives, there developed a "rudimentary society" of a new sort in many areas of the South. As Pike concludes, "the group norm in the liberated area was characterized by a greater sense of equalitarianism, greater social mobility, with individual merit counting for more and family for less."[95]

The NLF drew strong support from Vietnam's women. As an NLF document explains, under the French "not only did [women] share the state of slavery of all the people but as a class had to endure special oppression at the hands of society as well as within the family. They were despised, ill treated, without rights, regarded as private property." Vietnamese women, as the saying went, led the "life of a water buffalo."[96] To combat this, in March 1961, a Women's Liberation Association was formed in the liberated zones. As Pike comments,

> Even at the risk of treading on masculine sensibilities, the NLF took a strong prowoman stand and maintained it consistently: 'Women represent half the population and at least half of the revolutionary effort. If women do not participate in the Revolution, it will fail.'[97]

And, in fact, women have emerged as a strong force in all parts of the society forming in the liberated zones, including taking on a fighting role in the army.

As for health care, the NLF has established complex underground surgical hospitals and large medical training programs. In most villages, infirmaries have been installed and treatment is free. However, facilities almost everywhere are crude at best. A Japanese newsman has described a "clinic" he visited in a Mekong Delta village:

> It was a nipa palm hut, but larger—about 12 ft. x 12 ft. wide—than ordinary huts. . . . This was a field hospital of the NLF.
> The chief of the hospital was a 16-year-old boy orderly. . . . There were some beds made of nipa palm leaves enough for several patients, and some ordinary medicines and injection equipment. There were some American-made medicines and first aid kits, but no

large-scale equipment for surgery. We were told that
sometimes a doctor, like the 28-year-old we had seen
at the skirmishing area, would come to perform an
operation.

. . . For six months [the boy] had been receiving
training in a medical unit [about 170 miles away]. . . .
The boy told us that he was going to be a physician
after more study and experience under the guidance of
senior army surgeons of the NLF.[98]

Yet this level of medical care is so far above what was
previously available to most Vietnamese that people from
Saigon-controlled hamlets and Saigon itself sometimes trav-
el to the NLF areas for treatment.[99]

Reforms like these lent the peasants a strong sense of
change for the better. Even among those exhausted by
twenty years of war and hardship, there was no mistaking
this emphasis. Doyon interviewed a deserter from the
Delta area who had been the head of a small NLF guerrilla unit. He had fought for twenty-two years before
"breaking" under American bombardment and immense
physical hardship. Here, in part, is his testimony:

In 1946 [he told Doyon] I became a member of the
Viet Minh. I fought nine years against the French . . .
When peace was restored, in 1954, Diem sent troops
to fight and arrest the former Viet Minh partisans.
They arrived one day, in my village, and arrested fifteen of them whom they executed publicly. I learned
of this afterwards for I was not in the village that day.
I decided, with eight other former partisans, to go
underground once again . . .

—and the organization of the [National Liberation]
Front in Long Duc [asked Doyon]?

Five cadres took charge of the hamlet . . . [The
Front] is strict and the discipline is strong, but we have
local autonomy. The hamlet chief is elected, as in the
case of the village, and he chooses his own assistants.
The big decisions are discussed between the village
chief, the Front cadres, and the peasants . . .

The Front organized the land reform: certain peasants left the ricefields to go over to the government's
side. The land was divided and distributed among the

old Resistance [Viet Minh] fighters, the supporters of
the Front, the poor peasants and the community at
large.

In 1964 they opened a school, then a maternity
ward. Local nurses took care of the population; due
to the insecurity, the wounded were sent to hospitals
on the Camau peninsula. The medicines came from
China, the USSR and Czechoslovakia . . .[100]

For all its crudeness and difficulties—the lack of
trained cadres, the bluntness and sometimes harsh treatment of the peasantry, the constant threat of government
reprisals—the NLF offered hope to the peasant. And because of this, the NLF found a sanctuary not in China,
not in Russia, not in North Vietnam, but among the peasantry itself.

The Fall of Diem and After: America Against the Peasants

As Diem's power base shrunk, the president grew more
paranoid, and his regime even more repressive. Particularly
harsh was the Ngo family's repression of the Buddhists.
Religious tensions reached a climax in May 1963 when
government troops in the old imperial capital of Hue shot
into a crowd of unarmed Buddhists celebrating the Bud-
dha's birthday. Nine were killed. In response, the Buddhists launched large-scale protests against Diem's auto-
cratic rule. As the violence of these demonstrations
increased, several monks burned themselves to death before a shocked international audience. ("All the Buddhists have done for this country is to barbecue a monk,"
commented the Catholic Madame Nhu to an American
TV newsman.)[101] The protests, in the ensuing uproar,
turned into riots. At the highest levels American officials
began, none too quietly, to reconsider whether Diem was
the best man to run the country. As American ambivalence
became common knowledge around the capital, a military
clique led by three of Diem's discontented generals began

to plot a coup d'etat. They were reportedly in constant contact with the American embassy, and had the tacit approval of Ambassador Lodge. On November 1, as their tanks rumbled into position in Saigon, Diem's nine-year rule came to a bloody end.[102]

While the bodies of Diem and Nhu were photographed by newsmen, the overthrow was hailed in Saigon as the beginning of a new revolutionary era. What followed, though, was a seemingly endless series of military coups, countercoups, and counter-countercoups. Generals Minh, Don, and Dinh were followed by General Kanh, the civilian premiers Nguyen Xuan Oanh and Tran Van Huong, then by Dr. Phan Huy Quat. Charges of "neutralism" and corruption were exchanged among competing factions, but behind this game of musical chairs lay a two-fold problem. The U.S. refused to support any group which seemed inclined to seek an end to the war—particularly the militant Buddhists; yet none of the factions they would support was capable of providing a viable alternative to its predecessors. These various splinter factions included remnants of the pre-World War II "nationalist" parties (like the Dai Viet and VNQDD), adherents of the Cao Dai and the Hoa Hao delta sects, various moderate Buddhist factions, the Catholics, "independent" intellectuals, and professional organizations. Motivated mainly by their narrow personal interests, they could not even agree on a workable coalition among themselves. Consequently, the military, considered by the Americans as the one "viable" political force in the country, retained a tenuous control.

What these events showed, as Pike comments, is that "aside from the NLF there has never been a truly mass-based political party in South Vietnam."[103] Their strong support among the peasantry and the growing willingness of disillusioned elements from the protesting city groups to make accommodations with them allowed the NLF to center their struggle against the various governments of Saigon mainly at the political level, rather than at the level of massed military might. In fact, the confusion created by the disputes in the capital resulted in further deterioration of the government's position in the country-side. By 1965, Saigon stood on the verge of total defeat. At this point, to save the government in Saigon, the Americans made their well-known massive commitment of armed power. They sent in large numbers of troops and be-gan the regular bombardment of North Vietnam. Shortly thereafter, in June 1965, the military government of the flamboyant northern air force vice-marshal Nguyen Cao Ky was installed. In 1967, his former right-hand man, General Thieu, gained control of the government. Ky had to take a back seat as vice-president. The Americans thought their problems were solved. According to their computers (in their Hamlet Evaluation System), by Octo-ber 1967 more than 60 percent of South Vietnam's hamlets were "secure"; commanding General Westmoreland pro-claimed the NLF incapable of launching major assaults; "the light at the end of the tunnel," claimed American officials, was in sight.

All this was shattered in February 1968, during the Tet (New Year's) festival. Fifty to sixty thousand NLF soldiers launched a major offensive across the whole of South Vietnam. In most areas of rural Vietnam, the "paci-fication" program simply disappeared. With the large-scale aid of city dwellers, the guerrilla soldiers managed to take over most of Vietnam's urban areas. The Americans' re-sponse was simply to destroy an estimated 50 percent of each major city from the air to "retake" it. Hue was almost totally demolished by American aerial bombardments and artillery strikes. Unable to tear the NLF from its peasant supporters (or even from their allies in the cities), the Americans had little recourse but to redouble their efforts to force the peasants from their lands by endless bomb-ings, defoliation, and the destruction of crops and arable land with air-dropped chemicals. For such a war against a political foe deeply immersed in the infrastructure of Vietnamese rural society meant, in reality, a war against the peasants themselves.

CHAPTER 2

Laos: The Secret War

For this country finally to make some progress, everything would have to be leveled. The inhabitants would
have to be reduced to zero and rid of their traditional
culture, which is blocking everything.[1]

There is nothing metaphorical about this statement,
made by an American diplomat in Vientiane, Laos. For
several years now, two-thirds of the territory of Laos, with
a population of close to half of the country's 3 million
people, has been subjected by the American military to
the most intensive aerial bombardment in history. Countless Laotian villages have been destroyed. An estimated
600,000 refugees have been created. As the French journalist Jacques Decornoy reported after a trip through this
area in 1968:

The inhabitants ask themselves the reasons for this de-
luge of fire and steel. 'I don't even know where
America is,' says a peasant woman whose daughter has
just been killed and who has lost all her belongings.
[Another] peasant remarked: 'Before, I understood
nothing about what was said against American aid,
against the United States. After the raids on my village,
I know what they mean.' Everything American, far and
wide, is hated by the people.[2]

Yet the people of the area, which is governed by the revolutionary Pathet Lao, have refused to give in. Abandoning the sunlight, they live in caves or hide in the forests, farming at dusk—in their own words, "Owls by day, foxes by night." In their caves they have set up primitive industrial shops, weaving plants, hospitals, and schools, tenaciously awaiting that day when they may be able to attempt to build a more normal life.

There is another Laos as well, more familiar to Americans and almost the complete antithesis of the Pathet Lao areas. This is the society of the cities, particularly of Vientiane, the administrative center of the American-supported Royal Laotian Government (RLG). As Decornoy comments:

> Presently in Vientiane, a city which is becoming 'Saigonized' and which is rotting morally and culturally, it is possible to observe an irrational and futureless mixture of traditional Laotian life and a search for Western 'values': rudiments of French and English, a fascination with money, Japanese motorcycles and cars. The nightclubs are filled with Thai prostitutes and talentless Filipino orchestras. . . . The people survive in this dream world without faith, knowing 'this cannot last.'[3]

Since 1962, American military aid to the urban-based RLG has totaled more than $200 million annually—with the exception of Vietnam, the highest per capita military assistance program in the world. The entire Laotian economy is in fact supported by the U.S., with immense personal profits being derived by some 200 to 300 prominent Lao families.[4] Both the military and governmental bureaucracies are sustained directly by Washington, while parallel rule at all levels of the government has been established by the CIA. The society of the cities, in short, survives largely via the proceeds of American aid.

The corrupted cities and the devastated countryside, and America's role in the creation of both: these are some of the striking parameters of the complex Laotian tragedy. Where did it begin?

Laos and the Outbreak of the Indochina War

The war did not really spread to Laos; in a very important sense it has always been there. Shortly after World
War II, a small group of Lao nationalist leaders, in exile
in Thailand, created the Lao Issara ("Free Lao") to work
for independence from the French. To the French, looking
at all of Indochina, Laos seemed of secondary importance.
In 1950, therefore, they offered these exiles a degree of
Laotian "independence" within the French Union. For the
French, this was an admirable solution. It seemed to eliminate the possibility of a second front in Indochina. It
left the French free to concentrate their entire effort on
the struggle in Vietnam. In fact, it converted Laos from a
battlefield into a staging area for the French army and
a recruiting ground for the incorporation of large numbers
of Laotian tribesmen into the French colonial army.[5]

This arrangement was accepted by the Lao Issara exiles,
who with one notable exception returned to Vientiane to
take up positions in a new government. That exception
was Prince Souphanouvong, a dissident member of the
royal Laotian family. He has written little about himself
and it is hard to know what his aspirations were. An
engineer, trained in Paris, he had spent some years in the
Public Works Department of the French colonial administration, traveling across the Laotian countryside. Certainly, like the French themselves, he looked at events in Laos
in a broader Indochinese perspective. In contact with the
Viet Minh, both in Paris and Vietnam during the war,
he was impressed with their revolutionary ideology and
program of resistance to the French. When his two royal
brothers (Phetsarath and Souvanna Phouma) left Bangkok
for Vientiane, Souphanouvong went into the hill country
of northeastern Laos. There, with Viet Minh assistance,
he helped to organize the Pathet Lao, a revolutionary
movement dedicated to throwing the French out of Laos

and to creating a socially viable Lao nation. "Peace in Indochina," it declared, "is indivisible." By 1954, it controlled more than half of rural Laos and, at Geneva, its troops were given two northeastern provinces as regroupment zones.[6]

The Pattern of Laotian Politics

By 1954, then, a situation had grown in Laos similar to that in its neighbor, Vietnam. In large areas of the countryside, the Pathet Lao predominated; in Vientiane and Luang Prabang, the two major cities of Laos, the French had managed to establish a small elite of ruling aristocrats, with few ties to the rural areas and a high standard of living based on foreign luxuries and supported by foreign aid. These men were linked to a nascent middle class, set in budding commercial operations and government positions, fearful of losing the benefits of wealth and power which had only recently come into their hands. Interested largely in maintaining or improving the status quo, they were the natural allies of the United States, which stepped into Laos, as into Vietnam, before the French could even exit gracefully.[7]

A good example of this urban ruling group was the rightist general Phoumi Nosavan, leader of two American-encouraged coups. Phoumi's preeminence in Laotian politics, achieved at the joint expense of the American taxpayer and the Laotian peasant, gained him "a monopoly of imports of gold, wines, and spirits as well as ownership of the biggest opium parlor in Vientiane."[8] With men like these, the United States was able, from early on, to prevent the incorporation of the Pathet Lao into a "neutralist" government in Vientiane. American support of the Laotian right wing initiated the collapse of the 1957 agreement among various factions in the capital and the Pathet Lao for a "neutral" Government of National Union. In 1958, a calculated suspension of American aid forced the neutralist prime minister out of office. American-instigated coups of 1959, 1960, and 1964 had approximately the same effect. Several times Laos was on the verge of a neutral coalition; each time the delicate balance was destroyed by a right-wing grab for power. Despite the common American propaganda image of "Communist subversion" of Laotian neutrality, extralegal politics has been the preserve of that faction of the Lao ruling class supported and emboldened by American power.

Even during the Kennedy administration, when the attempt to turn Laos into a pro-Western bastion seemed for a time abandoned, American support for the right wing continued. The new administration negotiated in 1962 a new Geneva agreement on Laos, prohibiting foreign intervention of any kind and guaranteeing its neutrality. The Pathet Lao was included in the new government in Vientiane. Again however, the Laotian right, with the largest army in the country (built up by the Americans) began to move. In April 1963, two left-wing members of the coalition government were assassinated. In April 1964, in a rightist coup the remaining leftists were expelled from the cabinet, the "neutralist" leader was placed under house arrest, and rightist control over the army was consolidated.[9] The Pathet Lao, its very survival threatened, its cabinet posts empty, took up arms again in the northeast. This act is now referred to by American officials as the starting point of renewed "Communist aggression" in Laos.

With no base of support in the countryside and almost no industrial sector in the cities, these politicians all (except the Pathet Lao) were dependent on American support for their very existence. Through its aid program, the Americans have assured this, pumping wealth into Laos far in excess of the absorptive capacity of its economy. While peasants in the hills practice ancient forms of slash-and-burn agriculture, the commercial elite of Vientiane live in French-style villas and drive Mercedes Benz cards, all purchased with the proceeds of American aid.[10] Over the last twenty years, on the average, imports have exceeded exports by 1,400 percent and the

U.S. has picked up the tab. In fact, the Royal Laotian Government, which has given up even its minor tax-collecting forays into the countryside, is quite simply a creature of the American aid program.[11]

All along, the United States has supplied, supported, and paid for the upkeep of the Royal Lao armed forces. In addition, the CIA, using AID as a front, provided a similar service for its own "clandestine army" (*armée clandestine*) of Meo hill tribesmen in northeastern Laos.[12] A large secret headquarters for this army of 15,000 was built at Long Cheng, staffed by scores of American pilots, technicians, communications experts, and Special Forces personnel. Air America and Air Continental, two private airlines under charter to the CIA, keep together the far-flung American military establishment, flying supplies to remote bases in Laos, while keeping open the lines of communication with the huge American installations in Thailand and Vietnam.[13] This was the background for America's "secret war" in Laos.

And in 1964, before the Tonkin Gulf incident, that secret war took a quantum leap forward. American planes began bombing the Ho Chi Minh Trail. Soon the bombing was extended to Pathet Lao areas far removed from the trail. These flights, referred to as "unarmed reconnaissance flights" by American officials, rose to 12,500 sorties a month. After the bombing halt over the North, they grew to anywhere from 17,000 to 27,000 per month.[14] By 1970, more bombs had been dropped in Laos than in both Vietnams. It seems clear that the United States, turning large areas of Pathet Lao territory into "free-fire zones," was attempting by air to dismantle and destroy any organized resistance in them. For peasants in these areas, a typical morning begins this way:

> . . . at 7 o'clock, an AD-6 plane prowls overhead. It circles for about ten minutes, then leaves. At 7:30 the plane returns, makes a pass and drops three loads several kilometres from the [cave]. At 8 o'clock, there is a flight of jets. At 8:30, new jets and bombs. The same operation at 9 o'clock.[15]

With this bombing goes a policy of emptying the country-side. The Plain of Jars, for instance, has been virtually depopulated in a coordinated program of "evacuation." It is estimated that already the American attacks have driven almost a fourth of the population into what are little more than concentration camps in government areas. Such a policy, as a reporter from the *New York Times* wrote, was an attempt to make it "increasingly difficult [for the Pathet Lao] to fight a 'people's war' with fewer and fewer people."[16]

The Pathet Lao

Despite the intention behind this attempt, by late 1969 "it was becoming increasingly obvious that Prince Sou-phanouvong and his allies held the country in their hands, and that if they did not take either Vientiane or Luang Prabang it was a political decision and not a strategic incapacity."[17] As a symbol of resistance, among a population jolted into political consciousness by American bombs, the Pathet Lao's popularity has increased.

This is not to say that the Pathet Lao is the Laotian equivalent of the Vietnamese revolutionary movement. In Laos, there has never been a comparable tradition of peasant rebellion and popular resistance. Nor has Laos ever enjoyed the sense of national and cultural identity characteristic of the Vietnamese. Historically, regional power was divided up among some forty-two different tribal groups, many speaking different languages, each jealous of its local autonomy.[18] Most Laotian peasants, in fact, did not even know that they were "Laotian." To build national unity out of such division and con-flict presented the Pathet Lao a formidable task indeed. Lacking much firsthand information, we can only speculate on how far it has progressed in the task.

But we do know one thing. Whatever the difficulties posed by the nature of Laotian society, the Pathet Lao, as the only articulate and effective political force in the country, has already taken the first steps toward forging a sense of Laotian nationhood. Within its program of anticolonialism, one of the first steps taken in the early fifties was to scrap the French educational curriculum. Out went the courses in French language, history, and geography with which the French administrators had trained the small Lao ruling class. In came courses emphasizing the Lao language, the *national* culture, and practical farming which was of use to the peasant. Advancement in school, formerly based on bribery and social position, was now dictated by merit.[19] In addition, the Pathet Lao took measures to overcome the inequality and exploitation whose roots lay deep in Laotian history. Racial equality among all Laotians was strongly emphasized in their program. Not surprisingly, their earliest successes were among the non-Lao hill tribes of the northeast, peoples traditionally considered inferior by the dominant lowland Laos.[20] For contrast, they pointed to the corruption and decadence of foreign-dominated life in the cities, often transporting village leaders to Vientiane so they could see for themselves the meaning of American control.[21]

The results have been impressive. In the only fair election ever held in Laos, in 1958, the Pathet Lao won thirteen of the twenty-one seats contested.[22] In the countryside, the job of expanding a political organization, teaching improved agricultural techniques, and building parallel administrations has continued despite the ever-increasing American attacks. By 1965, the Pathet Lao had organized at least eleven of its own provincial administrations (out of a total of sixteen provinces)—all of which had come to overshadow the "legal" but hapless Royal Lao administration.[23] At present, they seem to control at least two-thirds of Laotian territory outright. As for the attempt to build in the peasants a sense of "national" culture, under the most primitive and dangerous conditions, Decornoy reports:

> The laboratory for this experience—the caves, of course—is found at the training school for instructors and teachers . . . Students can be seen scattered about,

busy learning their lessons. They have made everything: the tables, the benches, the houses, the picture, the access ways to the rocky classrooms. Classes are difficult for study: young people seated near the opening of the cave are lucky enough to write by daylight, but the majority must be content with tiny oil lamps. The instruction aims at being comprehensive: everyone cultivates his own vegetables and his rice; everyone raises his own livestock. The goal to be reached is support oneself by oneself. Until this is achieved, rice is still received from the central administration.[24]

Certainly, the Pathet Lao has been forced to press hard on the limited resources of the peasants. In the primitive Pathet Lao areas, life remains precarious, poverty widespread, conditions harsh, resources few, and cadres ill-trained. Facing the massive and increasing American commitment to destroy it, the Pathet Lao has had to turn to North Vietnam for aid and, in recent years, troops. Yet in these same areas Laotian national identity, far from being reduced to zero, is for the first time in history beginning to emerge.

CHAPTER 3

Cambodia: The Balancing Act*

The Internal Situation Under Sihanouk

On March 18, 1970, Prince Norodom Sihanouk, at a Moscow airport, fresh from a "health cure" in Paris, was informed that he had been deposed as ruler of Cambodia. A coup d'etat in Pnompenh, the capital of his country, had displaced him. Already, as he flew on to Peking to denounce the new rulers of Cambodia, the land he had ruled for almost thirty years was on the threshold of a new era. For what had taken place

> . . . was far more than the overthrow of a head of state, a divine king, or a prince. With him vanished the Cambodia of the tourists marvelling at the riches of Angkor, the Cambodia of pretty little towns with parks and flowered walks, of the thousands of little villages dozing quietly near their pagodas, and of the staging posts where travelers were welcomed with smiling hospitality.[1]

With the American invasion forty-three days later, what had started as a shift of power from one faction of the Cambodian ruling class to another threatened to

*This chapter draws heavily on the work of Cynthia Fredrick.

53

change the whole fabric of Cambodian politics. A type of struggle long seen in Vietnam and Laos, but little known in Cambodia, was emerging. As Richard Dudman, correspondent for the *St. Louis Post-Dispatch,* observed, after spending six weeks as a captive of Cambodian guerrilla forces:

> The fleeing peasants had with them all the household goods they could carry. Several women whom we picked up with babies in their arms, [were] as well lugging bundles and chickens.
>
> In this great migration [from areas of American aerial bombardment] we felt that we were watching the terrorization of the peasants in Cambodia. We felt that we were observing the welding together of the local population with the guerrillas. The peasants were turning to the fighters as their best friends.[2]

This is what Cambodia, alone among her neighbors, had managed for years to avoid—thanks to Prince Sihanouk. In fact, its avoidance had been a prerequisite for his rule. Sihanouk's Cambodia, like that of his royal predecessors, required "peace." For him, however, peace meant mainly protection from Cambodia's traditional enemies, Thailand and Vietnam, and a passive, if not contented, peasantry. French rule had provided this "protection." True, during the Indochina war, numbers of young Cambodians, forming a Khmer National Union Front, tried to challenge the existing monarchical and colonial order. Yet these efforts faltered, due to personal rivalries, an inability to adopt a broad program capable of winning peasant support, and the deft maneuvers of Sihanouk himself. At Geneva, the Khmer rebels, far weaker than their Lao and Vietnamese compatriots, received no regroupment area for their military forces. And when independence came, in 1954, it came peacefully, without abrupt changes or serious challenge to the status quo. Cambodia's stagnant rural society remained undisturbed. French teachers stayed on in the *lycées,* French technicians in the ministries, French managers on the rubber plantations, French officers and professors in the military academies and universities. Their authority went almost unquestioned.

After independence, though, Sihanouk's political style underwent a change. As a descendant of the ancient Khmer kings, his political power rested on the prestige of the monarchy, and his personal charisma. In 1955, he abdicated. Organizing a political party, the Sangkum Reastr Niyum (Popular Socialist Community), as a tool for ruling the country, he descended into the arena of elite politics. At the same time, aware of the need to maintain his popularity with the peasants, he arranged public meetings, popular audiences in the capital, and extensive travels in the provinces. This was most effective. To the peasants, Sihanouk as protector of the state religion, Theravada Buddhism, and symbol of the monarchy virtually personified "Cambodia."[3]

Yet if Sihanouk, as a symbol, could bridge the immense gap between the rural and urban areas, his regime, nonetheless, had "widened the gulf between the peasantry and the other classes of Cambodian society."[4] While an urban elite lived exceedingly well on foreign aid, the peasant's life showed very little if any improvement. The prince's particular brand of economic planning, "Khmer socialism," resulted in a woebegone economy and a budget deficit (by 1969) of $20 million. In this situation, the peasant was helpless. Though he produced the food and wealth of the country, he remained totally divorced from political power. Even Sihanouk could not have greatly affected this. His appeal to the peasants was direct, but his rule over them was indirect, deflected through a small urban ruling elite. Headed by the prince and royal circles, this elite consisted primarily of commoners who managed to gain prominant positions in the Buddhist clergy, the government bureaucracy, or the armed forces. In more recent years, there had grown up as well a small urban middle class, mainly made up of white-collar government officials. In the end, seventeen years after independence, Cambodia remained "a good example of colonialist structures maintained under an outer wrapping of nationalism embodied in one man."[5]

Sihanouk's International Role

To neutralize opponents at home, and protect his country's independence, the prince engaged in an impressive international juggling act. In the first decade of independence, he rejected SEATO "protection" and criticized American intervention in Southeast Asia; yet he yielded to the demands of his opponents on the right by welcoming American aid. It amounted to more than $350 million between 1955 and 1962, and accounted for the high style in which the Pnompenh elite maintained itself. At the same time, by establishing good relations with the People's Republic of China, he reassured elements on his left. Peking's goodwill had the added benefit of protecting his country from its greedy neighbors, the Thais and Vietnamese. As Sihanouk remarked in 1961:

> Westerners are always astonished that we Cambodians are not disturbed by our future in which China will play such a powerful role. But one should try to put himself in our place: in this jungle which is the real world, should we, simple deer, interest ourselves in a dinosaur like China when we are more directly menaced, and have been for centuries, by the wolf and the tiger, who are Vietnam and Thailand.[6]

In this tangled web of national and international politics lay a dilemma. In a nutshell it was this: If Sihanouk allied his country with the West, insurgency groups backed by hostile Communist neighbors might spring to life in the countryside. If he aligned too closely with the Socialist countries, significant elements of the Cambodian elite (particularly the army) would surely balk. Like a nervous high-wire artist, he tried, with "neutralism" as his balancing pole, to stay on his feet.

After 1960, growing American involvement in Laos, support for Thailand, and rapid troop buildups in South

Vietnam made this increasingly difficult. As a U.S.-fostered Saigon-Bangkok anti-Communist axis emerged, Sihanouk found his nation dangerously wedged between two pro-Western, but hardly pro-Cambodian, states. The possibilities of playing upon traditional hostilities between Vietnamese and Thai waned. Indeed relations with Thailand were broken off in 1961, and with Saigon in 1963. To survive, Sihanouk moved toward accommodation with the North Vietnamese and the National Liberation Front. Sure of their ultimate victory, he was anxious to secure their guarantees of Cambodia's sovereignty.

By 1965, a series of informal agreements had been concluded with the North Vietnamese and the NLF allowing their forces to pass along the Cambodian border en route to South Vietnam. Permission was also granted for Soviet and Chinese ships to unload supplies at Sihanoukville. Transport of these supplies inland and high prices paid by the Vietnamese for rice and other Cambodian goods proved a boost to the stagnant Cambodian economy. The government simply closed its eyes. In the sparsely populated frontier regions where the NLF and North Vietnamese forces set up shop, the peasants also received certain benefits. They stated, for instance, that they were allowed access to local NLF hospitals and medical stations. In fact, the major disruptive element in these border areas was the savage attacks by American and South Vietnamese forces. According to official Cambodian statistics, before May 1969 there were some 1,864 such border violations, 165 sea violations, and 5,149 air violations.[7]

On an official level, Cambodia granted de facto recognition to the Democratic Republic of Vietnam (Hanoi) and to the NLF. In 1969, Pnompenh officially established relations with the newly formed Provisional Revolutionary Government of South Vietnam. In return, both the North Vietnamese and the NLF recognized the Khmer border claims. Despite American propaganda (and that of the new Lon Nol regime), it seemed hardly credible to suggest that the Vietnamese presence in the Cambodian border regions was considered by Sihanouk's government at the time to be an "invasion."

On the other hand, it was true that, long before the present coup, Sihanouk had been faced with a persistent American effort to undermine his policies—and his regime. After 1954, in direct violation of the Geneva accords, the United States sought to incorporate Cambodia into SEATO. "When I told the U.S. ambassador that we will not enter SEATO," said Sihanouk in 1956, "he replied, 'never mind, SEATO will protect you just the same.' But we reject SEATO 'protection.' We have never asked for it. We don't want it. We want absolutely nothing to do with SEATO or any other military pact . . ."[8] But the U.S. hardly limited its interference to Cambodia's neutralist foreign policy. In 1959, officials in Pnompenh bitterly accused the CIA of being the motivating force behind a plot to overthrow Sihanouk. Their prime piece of evidence was a letter allegedly from President Eisenhower, found in the villa of a conspiring general, "pledging full support to a projected coup and to a reversal of Cambodian neutrality."[9] Later, in the early 1960s, the CIA organized its own private army, from a rightist group called the Khmer Serai ("Free Khmer"), to oppose Sihanouk. (Its troops today defend Lon Nol's Pnompenh.) Sihanouk replied to all this first by rejecting American aid in November 1963, then by breaking off all relations in May 1965. Among merchants, university intellectuals, businessmen, and administrators, this move resulted in rising antipathy. "The urban elite—accustomed to a high standard of living sustained by American aid . . . is now finding it difficult to adjust to economic austerity," reported Michael Leifer in the spring of 1967.[10] But the army, deliberately held by Sihanouk at subsistence pay, proved the "most obvious candidate for an alternative government; it has suffered the most from the rejection of American aid.[11]

The 1970 Coup and the Rising Resistance Movement

On March 18, 1970, a military-civilian clique headed by Lon Nol formed a government of "national salvation." They were, Sihanouk charged, representing only the interests of "dishonest big capitalists," a "few big landlords and plantation owners," and the Americans. Whether or not (as charged) the CIA instigated the coup makes little difference. What is significant is that, left on its own, the new Lon Nol government probably could not have lasted a month. Strong support for Sihanouk among the peasantry, and the armed aid of the clandestine Khmer Rouge ("Red Khmer"), a rebel group which had patiently been biding its time since a brief period of armed struggle in 1967, would certainly have toppled the government—had it not tipped over of its own accord. However, the tottering regime, its base of support barely even extending to the ruling elite, defended itself the best way it knew how. It denounced the North Vietnamese and NLF presence in the border areas as an "invasion"; it spoke of "defending the race against 'Vietnamese imperialism' '"; and it called on American, South Vietnamese, and later Thai troops for defense.

On April 30, as if the legendary COSVN headquarters were an Asian-style Pentagon, tall and massive amid leafy ferns, the Americans and their South Vietnamese allies launched a full-scale conventional attack into Cambodia. The absurdity of this is evident. Even before the invasion, there had been wide-scale peasant protests, and "in the Vietcong zones [along the border], the Khmer peasants are even now being trained and armed," wrote Le Monde correspondent Jean-Claude Pomonti early in April 1970.[12] A strange sight, the Vietnamese "invaders" distributing arms to their "victims." In the wake of the American "success"—the massive bombardment of large swaths of Cambodia; the destruction of scores if not hundreds of towns and villages; the defoliation of the rubber plantations, a major part of the Cambodian economy—the peasant population, bitter and angry, is in armed revolt. The vivid testimony of American reporters, held captive there, confirms this: "A boy with a bandage over his eye glared at me for several minutes," reported Michael Morrow of Dispatch News Service.

> He looked at least part Vietnamese so I tried to break the ice by talking to him. "You've been wounded, haven't you?" He spat out his reply: "Yes, fighting the American aggression." I was glad Anh Ba [their guard] was standing nearby, for the boy or any number of the people would just as soon have killed me as not.[13]

Richard Dudman commented that in the areas of American incursion, "the villagers appeared to offer willing cooperation and friendship to the guerrillas." Already they were settling in for a lengthy struggle.

> 'As long as there is one of us left, we will fight on.'
> The toughness and dedication of the guerrillas in Cambodia as we came to know them in 40 days of captivity there made that seem a statement of fact rather than a propaganda slogan.[14]

Against the hapless Cambodian army, the guerrillas of the newly formed National Union Front of Kampucheia ranged across the countryside almost at will. By the end of June 1970, Lon Nol's regime had officially written off the four northeastern provinces. In other parts of the country, it controlled little more than some of the larger towns and pieces of road physically occupied by their own or South Vietnamese troops. More important, the whole fabric of traditional Cambodian society was being ripped to shreds; and the peasants, armed like their counterparts in Laos and Vietnam, were rapidly pulling power out of the cities into the rural heart of Cambodia.

Meanwhile, the desperate Lon Nol government, continually denouncing "foreign invasion," has placed its Eastern provinces under the informal protectorate of the

Thieu–Ky regime in Saigon. In the West, Thailand, eyeing Battambang and Siembriap provinces from which it was forced over sixty years ago, sits poised to take its share of the booty. In Cambodia, the choice seems clear: either FUNK (Front Unifié National Khmer) backed by Sihanouk and the peasants, aided by the NLF and the DRV, or a land grab by Cambodia's traditional enemies. Certainly, if Sihanouk again returns to Pnompenh, it will be a very different Cambodia which he will have to face.

CHAPTER 4

Thailand: The Client State

In 1969, U.S. Ambassador to Thailand Leonard Unger explained America's attitude toward Thailand in these words:

> Another factor is our general interest in encouraging the development of a world order in which independent nations may not be deprived of their independence by an outside aggressor's force. This perhaps has particular meaning in the case of a nation like Thailand, which has for a long time been a stable society with a capacity to govern itself and conduct itself responsibly among the nations of the world.[1]

The situation in Thailand, and the nature of the Thai-U.S. relationship, however, are somewhat more ambivalent than this official version suggests. Under three different military dictatorships this "model" country has been turned into the linchpin of the American empire in Southeast Asia. It may well be the Saigon of the 1970s. Training its armed forces, furnishing and later repairing its military equipment, lavishly funding its communication and transportation network, "advising" and training its constabulary and civil bureaucracy, the United States has guaranteed itself a predominant voice in Thai foreign and domestic policy. It has thrown its weight behind the Thai ruling class in which the army is the dominant stratum.

The Ruling Elite

As in Laos, Cambodia, and Vietnam, this ruling class is urban based. In shape, it has been described as a "three-tiered pyramid":

> The top level includes perhaps ten to fifteen persons who do or could dominate the ruling class and the country as a whole by manipulation of the various political forces. This group includes senior military commanders, a few men of great reputation gained in the revolution of 1932 or in the interplay of politics since, and perhaps two or three men around the throne. At any given time there has never been more than six or eight such men in power. The second level of the pyramid is made up of perhaps a thousand persons including military officers of the rank of colonel or general, special-grade civil servants, prominent members of parliament, some princes, and perhaps some particularly powerful businessmen. Although the top group dominates, it is only through their manipulation and control of the second group that they gain, hold and use power. The base of the ruling-class structure is what may be called the political public. It is made up of educated and articulate citizens in Bangkok and the provincial towns who interest themselves in the details of political activity. For the most part high school and university graduates, they are largely in the bureaucracy but also include professional people, journalists and other writers, and Thai members of the commercial white-collar group. It may be estimated that the ruling class as described is between 1 and 2 percent of the total adult population of the country.[2]

"National" politics, whose conflicts have been resolved since 1932 by coup d'etats, takes place solely among this 1 to 2 percent of the Thai people. In this context, self-interest serves as the main guide to Thai political figures. "From the standpoint of government officials," commented a Swedish observer, "the whole economy is one vast spoils system."[3] The rest of the Thai population exist outside this system (mainly in the countryside), their needs unrepresented by it.

The U.S.–Thai Military Relationship

Systematic American intervention in Thai domestic affairs can be dated from 1947. On November 8, Field Marshal Luang Pibul Songgram, the pro-Axis dictator of the 1930s, returned to power in a coup d'etat. Less than three months later the U.S. recognized the Pibul regime, sent a scientific mission to conduct a survey of the country's resources, and invited a Thai military mission to the U.S.[4] In October 1950, as part of an interlocking system of military alliances that it was then constructing throughout Asia to "contain China," the U.S. signed a military assistance agreement with Thailand. Within two years the American presence in Bangkok included a large embassy staff, the MAAG mission, and a USIS office. Within eighteen years U.S. military aid was to increase forty times over from the original $7 million to nearly $300 million annually.[5] The Americans did not have to wait long for results. Under Pibul, Thailand became the first Asian nation to "volunteer" to send ground forces to fight in South Korea. Later it recognized the Bao Dai regime in Vietnam and the French-sponsored governments of Laos and Cambodia; in 1954, it became the only Southeast Asian nation besides the Philippines to join SEATO.

Field Marshal Sarit Thanarat, Thailand's second postwar dictator, overthrew Pibul in September 1958. Indicative of Sarit's foreign policy was his "Bangkok plan." Together he and South Vietnam's Ngo Dinh Diem agreed "to dismember Cambodia and instigate civil war."[6] Before his death in December 1963, Sarit consolidated the Thai-U.S. military relationship. In the March 1962 Rusk-Thanat Khoman joint communiqué, the U.S. and Thailand agreed in essence that "if the eight-nation Southeast Asia

Treaty Organization failed to act against any aggressor, the US could act to protect an Asian member without approval of the treaty organization."[7]

It remained, however, for Thailand's third postwar military dictator, General Thanom Kittikachorn, to carry the alliance relationship with the U.S. beyond the point of no return. Ruling under martial law, with total suppression of political liberties, Thanom (officially only the Thai defense minister) acceded to U.S. demands that Thailand be brought into the war against the Pathet Lao and the NLF—ostensibly to protect Thai independence against Communist China. Sometime in early 1965, the commander of American forces in Thailand, General Richard G. Stilwell, and Thanom drew up a secret five-year plan committing one Thai mercenary unit (about 2,000 troops) to fight in South Vietnam, all expenses paid by Washington. It also allowed the U.S. to construct and use bases on Thai soil from which to bomb North Vietnam and Laos. (In return the Defense Department committed American troops to the defense of Thailand in certain circumstances.)

Central to this unannounced declaration of war against its neighbors was a call for the preemptive invasion of Laos. American and Thai troops were to enter the country if the political situation there deteriorated seriously.[8] It should be remembered that Thailand ruled parts of Laos before the French conquest of Indochina, had long been committed to keeping a pro-Thai government in power in Vientiane, and had just the year before sent 300 of its troops into Laos under the direction of the American ambassador to Bangkok, Graham Martin. With this in mind, the significance of the Thai Contingency Plan (known as COMUSTAF Plan 1/64) becomes clear: it was an American invitation to the Thais to destroy the very existence of an independent Laotian state.

In late 1967, the Thais sent their "Black Panther" division to Vietnam, bringing their troop strength there to 12,000. Not surprisingly, for their generous gift, they demanded and received a two-year $30 million subsidy, a battery of HAWK missiles, F-5 fighters, UH-1 "Huey" helicopters, and increased logistic and training support for the then 100,000-man Thai army.[9] In the wake of the American invasion of Cambodia, the Thai government moved to restore relations with Pnompenh, broken since 1961. The moment had arrived for actualizing the spirit of Sarit Thanat's Bangkok plan of 1958; but this time with Thieu–Ky, rather than Diem, in Saigon. On June 1, 1970, Premier Thanom announced that Thailand would send "volunteers" to bolster the rightist regime in Cambodia.

Calculated from 1950 through 1969, the U.S. has supplied an estimated $2 billion in aid to the Thais. Large sums of this have gone to support Thai mercenaries in Vietnam, Laos, and (perhaps soon) Cambodia. Much of the rest has gone into the suppression of peasant opposition to the Thai ruling class.

Guerrilla Activity and "Pacification"

The guerrilla struggles in Thailand have paralleled the growth of the American presence (47,000 troops and airmen in 1969). Martial law has not prevented the spread of guerrilla activities to thirty-five of Thailand's seventy-one provinces,[10] nor has the application of the "pacification" lessons learned in Vietnam lessened peasant estrangement from the Bangkok government. Yet so little information is available on the Thai guerrillas that it is not possible to do much more than enumerate the geographical areas where the struggle is now taking place.

In the fifteen provinces of the Khorat Plateau in the northeast, anti-Bangkok opposition predates the American presence. There, the Thai Patriotic Front, organized in January 1965 by the Communist party of Thailand, furnishes the leadership for a northeast guerrilla army estimated at 1,500 men. Members of the Front seem to have achieved some success over the past five years in transcending geographic isolation and ethnic divisions of the region. To the west, in the mountains of northern

Thailand, they have made their presence felt, giving leadership to the insurrection of 45,000 Meo tribesmen, who are reported to have about a dozen training camps along the Thai-Laos border.[11]

In the five rubber-producing provinces of southern Thailand, 80 percent of the population, 800,000 people, are Muslims who speak Malay rather than Thai. Their support for the small National Liberation Army of the Malaysian Communist party, led by Chin Peng, has enabled this army to withstand the combined assaults of U.S. Special Forces and the Thai-Malaysian joint command.[12]

Even in the central plains region there are indications that guerrilla insurrection has kept pace with the growth of absentee landlordism, tenantry, and rural indebtedness. In May 1970, a Japanese scholar visiting Thailand reported that in some parts of the central plains guerrillas and bandits operated unopposed even within sixty miles of Bangkok.[13]

Since Bangkok is one of the major military, political, and economic centers for U.S. activity in Southeast Asia, any guerrilla movement confronts a vast array of American war-making institutions. These include the large U.S. Air Force Command and the smaller Army Command which provides logistical support for such major bases as those at Udorn, Don Muang, Ubon, U-Tapao, Korat, Takhli, Nakhon Phanom, and Sattahip. Sattahip, a sprawling, permanent port installation built in 1967, is connected by a network of American-constructed roads to the "danger" areas of the northeast. It seems programmed as America's major future naval-air-military anchor for mainland Southeast Asia.

In Thailand, where Pentagon and State Department activities merge, Ambassador Leonard Unger and his "Special Assistant for Counterinsurgency," George U. Tanham, coordinate the Thai-U.S. counterinsurgency effort through the consular establishment over which they preside. A U.S. consul is stationed in each major area of insurgency. "In his travels throughout his district," Unger explained to the Senate Foreign Relations Committee, "[the consul] visits military units (Thai and U.S.) in the field, discusses ongoing and planned activities with advisers and commanders and generally keeps himself informed of military affairs in his district."[14]

Helicopters, napalm, defoliants, infrared electronic devices, and much of the other advanced technology tested in Vietnam and Laos have been made available to the Thai government in its attempt to crush the incipient guerrilla movements among its own people.

The U.S. effort to maintain law and order in the Thai countryside also operates through institutions and programs which bypass the regular Thai military establishment. The training by Green Berets of a 1,000-man Thai Special Forces Group is but one example. Another is a program of police expansion which the U.S. has been pushing on the Thais. A thousand police stations are being constructed, mostly in the northeast.

> [These will] be manned by at least twenty members of the Thai National Police or paramilitary Border Patrol Police. Before assuming their new posts, these officers will receive six weeks of counterinsurgency and jungle warfare training provided by AID's "public safety advisers."[15]

Another aspect of this pacification effort has been the construction of a military communications network. Between 1954 and 1962, the Americans spent approximately $97 million to build over a thousand bridges and a number of superhighways in Thailand, like the four-lane, 450-mile-long "Friendship Highway" connecting Bangkok to Vientiane. Between 1965 and 1969, another $113.4 million was spent by the Pentagon for similar purposes.[16]

Agricultural development has also been on the U.S. agenda for Thailand. This "development" seeks basically to preserve the political status quo for the rulers of Thailand. The Accelerated Rural Development program and the Mobile Development Units, active in the northeast, are key parts of the pacification effort. These are supplemented by village organizations akin to 4-H clubs, funded by Ford, Rockefeller, Esso, and Shell. Based on them, there is a rural reconstruction movement, designed to create a strong anti-Communist base in the villages.[17]

With over 5,000 troops reliably reported to be fighting in Laos (many disguised in Royal Lao army uniforms), another 12,000 in Vietnam, and more promised for the Cambodia battlefield, the Thais can hardly help but be drawn further into the expanding "Indochina" war. Nor is there much doubt that the war will be drawn into Thailand.

PART II

How Is the United States Fighting in Indochina?

CHAPTER 5

The "Science" of
Counterinsurgency

One of the more dubious products of the decade of the fifties was the notion of a "science" of counterinsurgency.* The sources of this science have by no means been exclusively American. The works of French theorists of the Algerian War and the writings of Sir Robert Thompson on the British counterinsurgency in Malaya were textbooks for the development of the theory and practice of counterinsurgency in the United States. During the early sixties, as the Kennedy administration began to move away from the massive retaliation doctrine of the Eisenhower period, counterinsurgency became a dominant theme in the new military goal of a "flexible response."

During these years, as the fear of a nuclear confrontation with the Soviet Union diminished, a new arena of conflict was seen emerging in the countries of the third world where, presumably, Peking-style local wars were to become the main tool for Communist domination of the world. The "Communist" guerrilla came to overshadow the "Communist" bomb as the chief American concern in the international world. Guerrilla warfare was granted almost magical power to destroy conventional forces, overthrow

*This chapter draws upon a draft manuscript by Eqbal Ahmad to be published in Aya and Miller, eds., *Revolution Reconsidered* (New York: Free Press, 1970).

existing governments, and establish Communist regimes.
To Hubert Humphrey, for example, guerrilla techniques
were so startling as to "rank with the discovery of gun
powder." They constituted the "major challenge to our
security."[1]

Accordingly, Americans took over leadership from the
French and British in counterinsurgency theory and practice. By 1961, the secretary of defense had requested
a 150 percent increase in the size of antiguerrilla forces.
According to the *New York Times,* counterinsurgency had
become "a fetish with the President." Schools and training
grounds for the application of theory proliferated rapidly
throughout the American military establishment. Antiguerrilla forces were trained in Latin America where real
jungle conditions prevailed, elite corps like the Green
Berets emerged as antiguerrilla specialists, a new and
ultrasophisticated weapons technology was developed for
use in guerrilla operations. And like every other military
technique devised by man, counterinsurgency came to be
used in a real combat situation. Vietnam became a kind of
counterinsurgency test tube; a field for experimentation
with the new theories. As the war became the primary
focus of American political life, counterinsurgency, the
methodology of the war, assumed corresponding importance. To some of its most avid proponents, its success
or failure would determine the course of civilization itself.
"If we have the common will to hold together and get on
with the job," argued Walt Rostow, "the struggle in Vietnam might be the last great confrontation of the postwar era."[2]

The same cold-war perceptions about monolithic world
communism that produced the ABM and an $80 billion
defense budget thus also produced the "science" of
counterinsurgency. The principal assumption was that all
revolutionary wars would follow the Communist Chinese
model of the war of national liberation; the corollary of
that assumption was that the new science of counterinsurgency would crush revolutionary wars wherever they
arose. The British success in defeating the Malay in-

surgency in the 1950s seemed to prove that similar measures would defeat any insurgency anywhere.

Principles of Counterinsurgency

Two major conceptions of counterinsurgency were developed during the course of the war in Vietnam. The first saw the problem posed by guerrilla war exlusively in terms of military technique. In this conception, guerrillas were successful because they had developed a method of waging war that could compete with larger, conventional forces. The way to defeat the guerrilla was to meet him on his own ground, to perfect his own techniques of fighting, and to beat him at his own game. Superior firepower, greater mobility through the use of helicopters, the use of air power—these were the military techniques of counterinsurgency.

But they were clearly not enough. As the position of the Saigon government in Vietnam went from bad to worse, a second conception of counterinsurgency was developed. This more sophisticated approach saw that the success of the Vietnamese revolutionaries lay in the combination of a military with a political program. To defeat the insurgency, then, military force designed to break the power of the insurrection would be combined with a political program that would rob the insurgents of their popularity · among the masses. "The answer," writes General Edward G. Lansdale, a chief American practitioner of counterinsurgency, "is to oppose the Communist idea with a better idea."[3] The lessons of Malaya and the Philippines, he says, teach that "there must be a heart-felt cause to which the legitimate government is pledged, a cause which makes stronger appeal to the people than the Communist cause." In a nation such as Vietnam, the general feels, there is no dynamic political tradition which can compete successfully with the Communist ideas introduced from abroad. Hence, counterinsurgency involves teaching the Vietnamese a new politics around which a new social life can be built.

This means that counterinsurgency must have a social vision as well as a military program. Counterinsurgency, like insurgency itself, seeks a transformation of society. In the words of Sir Robert Thompson, both must exist in "exactly the same element and have exactly the same purpose in life." Killing the revolutionaries, though critically important, is not enough; the program of the revolutionaries must be preempted as well.

The Fatal Flaw

On the surface this may appear to be a workable solution. In reality, however, counterinsurgency is a social transformation on paper only; it has produced no revolutions in the third world. Quite the contrary, in fact. Advertised by its proponents as a "science" for progress, counterinsurgency is in reality a euphemism for war against the people—as the following discussion of how the United States is fighting in Indochina amply testifies. The rhetoric of social progress is belied by the terrible facts of an antirevolutionary war fought more often than not on behalf of a corrupt and parasitic oligarchy. Its accomplishments are at best negative. As in Malaya, it may prevent a revolutionary takeover, but, having done that, the desire for a social transformation disappears and reforms are dropped. The success of a counterinsurgency operation lies in achieving the goals of stability, pacification, and control over the population. Social change, like refugee camps and free-fire zones, is only a means employed for gaining control, it is not an end in itself. Though it speaks of transformation, an antiguerrilla operation always stops short of meaningful change. It is a "success" that one should not want to inflict on the peoples of the third world.

Given the desperate need of many third world countries for revolutionary change, the concept of counterinsurgency is in itself pernicious. Counterinsurgency's need to build on established governmental elites usually means the perpetuation of the very conditions that breed popular discontent. Too often counterinsurgency does no more than enable one petty dictator or another to suppress the progressive forces of his nation.

But, quite aside from its undesirability, counterinsurgency theory, in its own terms, has severe limitations. Implicit in the doctrine is a distortion of the meaning of revolution. Counterinsurgency theorists tend to see revolution as a matter of terror, manipulation, and exploitation; it is a device by which a band of conspirators, usually inspired from abroad, assumes political control of a given country. Counterinsurgency thus concentrates on establishing alternative means of control by shoring up and attempting to reinvigorate an already established government. Revolutions however are not created by small bands of conspirators. They arise instead from the profound, and often irreversible, alienation of a people from its government. The success of a revolutionary movement is directly proportionate to the incapacity of an established government to create a sense of its legitimacy among its own people. Counterinsurgency can aim at restoring stability; it can never restore the legitimacy of a government that has lost the faith of its own people. Counterinsurgency practitioners can destroy the bodies of the insurgents, they can concentrate the people of a country in controllable "strategic hamlets," but they cannot invest a ruling elite with the symbols of legitimate authority. They are, in the words of I. F. Stone,

> . . . like men watching a dance from outside through heavy plate glass windows. They see the motions but they can't hear the music. They put the mechanical gestures down on paper with pedantic fidelity. But what rarely comes through to them are the injured racial feelings, the misery, the rankling slights, the hatred, the devotion, the inspiration and the desperation. So they do not really understand what leads men to abandon wife, children, home, career, friends; to take to the bush and live gun in hand like a hunted animal; to challenge overwhelming military odds rather than acquiesce any longer in humiliation, injustice or poverty.[4]

Once the moral isolation of the established government is complete, no amount of outside assistance can save it; indeed, if a government has lost the allegiance of its people, it is difficult to find a reason for wanting to save it. The example of Algeria is striking in this regard. The insurrection there had been defeated militarily by the French; yet the final outcome saw the insurgents the victors. The French forces enjoyed a numerical troop advantage of 23 to 1; near the end of the war only five thousand guerrillas were actively fighting against the entire French force. Nevertheless, in the face of the passive hostility of the Algerian population, the French could never regain their aura of legitimacy. As one Arab intellectual put it, "When [moral isolation] becomes total the war has been won, for the population will then fight to the last man."

Clearly this has been the case in Vietnam as well. The government in Saigon is a prototype of the government that has become morally isolated. Even Vice-President Ky has admitted that the men who comprise the Saigon regime "are not the men that people want."[5] Saigon has lost its mandate; like Humpty Dumpty, it has fallen from the wall, and all the king's horses and all the king's men can't put Humpty Dumpty together again.

CHAPTER 6

Pacification: The Name Game

Pacification is a process under which a military force establishes control of a civilian population. It has been going on in South Vietnam at least since 1958, when the Diem government launched a campaign for control of the villages. As Philippe Devillers puts it:

> In 1958 the situation grew worse. Round-ups of "dissidents" became more frequent and more brutal. . . . The way in which many of the operations were carried out very soon set the villagers against the regime. A certain sequence of events became almost classical: denunciation, encirclement of villages, searches and raids, arrest of suspects, plundering, interrogation enlivened sometimes by torture (even of innocent people), deportation and "regrouping" of populations suspected of intelligence with the rebels, etc.

He adds:

> . . . the insurrection existed before the Communists decided to take part, and . . . they were simply forced to join in. And even among the Communists, the initiative did not originate in Hanoi, but from the grass roots, where the people were literally driven by Diem to take up arms in their own defense.[1]

In fact, much of the early guerrilla strength came from the religious sects, which had never supported the Viet Minh in the war of 1946–54.

Thus, at the beginning, pacification was not a response to rebellion. On the contrary, rebellion was a response to pacification.

Drying Up the Ocean

Pacification has been going on ever since. Its purpose is to isolate the guerrilla forces from the rural population whose help they need. On November 18, 1969, Secretary of State Rogers testified before the Senate Foreign Relations Committee that "the Vietcong require a base of population to recruit or impress from, to transport ammunition and supplies, to grow foods, to supply information, to circulate propaganda, and to hide among."[2] The relationship between guerrillas and people in a rural revolution has been likened by Mao Tse-tung to that of fish in the surrounding ocean. There is abundant evidence that the U.S. military and its Saigon collaborators understand this relationship and have, accordingly, undertaken to "dry up the ocean." For this purpose Diem, with the aid of American "experts," divided the population into two groups—"loyal" and "disloyal"—and these were relocated in separate areas known as *qui-ap* and *qui-khu*. By February 1959, according to a top U.S. expert, "relocation of families within communities had begun and . . . these relocations were often forced."[3] The relocations were carried on without regard for the peasants' long-standing ties to their own rice fields, houses, and ancestral tombs.[4]

In April 1959, more "sophisticated" relocation sites were planned, with barbed-wire fences and spiked moats around them. These were euphemistically called "agrovilles," and they had smaller satellites called "agrohamlets." Peasants brought into "agrovilles" were required to do corvée labor and commute long distances to their fields.

When commuting distances were impossibly long the peasants' homes and fields were burned down to deny them to the NLF. As might have been expected, the populations of the "agrovilles" quickly proved to be too large, and too resentful, to be controlled by the Saigon regime. In 1961 the program was discontinued and followed by the tighter, more forcible, "strategic hamlet" program.

Strategic Hamlets

A "strategic hamlet" contained about one hundred families. Each family was assigned to a group of five families called a *lien-gia* who, as a group, were responsible for controlling and reporting on each other. The peasants were forced to work in the "hamlets," digging moats and ditches, etc., while the crops in their own fields wasted away either from lack of care or from the first effects of the chemical crop destruction program, which began in 1961. The burning down of peasant homes outside the "hamlets" was continued and increased. Peasants were not reimbursed for their burned homes, nor were they compensated for their forced labor. For economic support, they became more and more dependent on "strategic hamlet" handouts, the funds for which were of American origin.[5] (There are documented cases, though, of less than 8 percent of allotted American redemption money ever reaching the hands of "pacification" victims because of graft along the way.) Many thousands suffered hunger and starvation.[6]

While conditions in the "pacification" centers worsened, the aims of "pacification" escalated beyond what they had been for the "agrovilles." The foremost aim of the "strategic hamlets," which peasants were not allowed to leave between 6:00 P.M. and 8:00 A.M., was to make any popular support of a people's war impossible. Secondly, the aim was to solve the problem of *defining* the enemy: anyone outside the strategic hamlets could be considered a Communist.[7] Borrowing Mao Tse-tung's metaphor,

Diem's brother Ngo Dinh Nhu summed up the strategic hamlet policy by predicting that it would put the NLF in the position of "fish out of water."[8]

But the program proved to have quite a different effect. The exigencies of strategic hamlet life, together with the concurrent destruction of the surrounding countryside, so embittered the peasants that when the Diem regime fell in 1963, the "strategic hamlet" program fell with it.

American Intensification of Forced Relocation

By January 1964, the "pacification" program, with the same goals and methods, was revived under the name "new life hamlets." While "pacification" had been conceived and financed by Americans from the start, direct U.S. involvement now increased markedly. In 1964, the U.S. military completely took over chemical crop destruction operations. In 1965, U.S. Marines occupied "secure villages." In 1966, a CIA training center in the resort town of Vung Tau began producing "new life hamlet" cadres.[9] Security and surveillance were made much tighter than ever before, and consequences were extremely severe for those finding themselves on the wrong side of the national police, the PRU (Provincial Reconnaissance Units, CIA-supported), or the CIDG (Civil Irregular Defense Group, Green Beret-supported).[10]

At the same time, America became more deeply involved in the actual population relocation process. An example of American-style relocation during 1967 is described in detail by Jonathan Schell for the case of a village called Ben Suc. The scenario was as follows: U.S. troops surrounded the village while, with no advance warning, more troops were dropped into the middle of the village. The people were herded onto trucks and transported out. Then the village was burned, razed by bulldozers, and abandoned. Finally, the rubble was bombed by B-52s to make certain that absolutely everything, including the deepest tunnels, was totally destroyed.[11]

Following such destruction of their homes, the people were then driven to "new life hamlets" or, if there were no room, simply released and called "refugees." The number of peasants killed by these operations may be small (as in the case of Ben Suc) or large (as in Mylai), depending in part upon whether trucks and other facilities are available to transport the villagers and also upon whether nearby relocation areas have vacancies. In recent years "new life hamlets" and other "safe" areas have been extremely overcrowded. To be admitted to a "new life hamlet" a peasant frequently must offer huge bribes —amounting to a lifetime's savings—to the authorities. The alternative is indefinite imprisonment—"detention for further investigation."[12]

WHAM, RevDev, and Atrocity

In time, popular resentment to "pacification" grew so strong that U.S. officials could no longer ignore it. Thus was born "the other" war—"winning hearts and minds" of the people (WHAM). "Pacification" as a term was discarded because of its unsavory associations, and the Vietnamese words for "rural reconstruction" were substituted. The Americans, though, preferred "revolutionary development" (RevDev) as the new English name because of its progressive-sounding ring. At the same time that RevDev came in, the Saigon regime decided to change the name of "new life hamlets" from *Ap Tan Sinh,* which had antinationalist connotations because the words were of Chinese origin, to *Ap Doi Moi,* which means exactly the same thing using words of Vietnamese origin. The Americans, who had spent years proliferating names for "pacification"—agrovilles, agrohamlets, strategic hamlets, new life hamlets, WHAM, RevDev, etc.—finally found themselves at a loss terminologically and, to translate *Ap Doi Moi,* came up feebly with *"new* new life hamlets," the latest in the series.

But to the Vietnamese peasant, terminological changes are irrelevant. What matters to him is that the nature of "pacification" has not changed. For more than ten years his countryside has been bombed and poisoned almost beyond recognition, while he has lived under increasingly crowded, unsanitary police state conditions. The "pacified" Vietnamese does not view himself as an accidental refugee of an unfortunate war. He correctly understands that removal of countless peasants from their native place is an American program and a deliberate policy. His resentment is directed against America and her Saigon collaborators. As one South Vietnamese official put it, "Instead of separating the population from the Viet Cong, we were making Viet Cong."[13] And as a recent *New York Times Index* puts it, under its subheading "Pacification Program in South Vietnamese Villages"—"see subhead 'Atrocity Charges.' "[14]

Precise figures on how many Vietnamese have been and are being "pacified" in American-sponsored "hamlets" are difficult to obtain. U.S. advisers prefer to release statistics only for the total Vietnamese population "under Saigon control" which, in addition to people in "pacified" camps, also includes city dwellers, people in villages over which Saigon has only nominal daytime control, and refugees. American figures for April 1970 count 88.9 percent of the South Vietnamese population as "pacified."[15] The percentage not securely "pacified" live, of course, under the constant threat that bombs, napalm, and poison will fall on them from the sky or that the next American to see them will shoot them on sight. Therefore in one sense the percentages are unimportant: the "pacification" program is an unrelenting menace to a South Vietnamese peasant whether or not he is actually "pacified."

In Laos, the Plain of Jars, once the home of approximately 150,000 persons, has been almost completely evac-

uated in the course of the little-publicized war there. In January 1970 about half of the 30,000 Laotians still remaining there were evacuated in a CIA-directed project. Peasants were given as little as an hour's warning to leave their homes and were made to march for hours, sometimes, to airfields where CIA charters (Air America and Continental Air Services) would fly them to refugee camps. As of February 1970, approximately 600,000 Laotians had been made refugees.[16] Within little more than a month following the invasion of Cambodia in the spring of 1970, administration officials indicated that they foresaw the necessity of a comparable "pacification" program to shore up the rightist regime of Lon Nol. According to newspaper accounts in early June, South Vietnam and Thailand had been encouraged to assist Pnompenh in setting up a control system which "would be a small-scale version of the pacification effort conducted by the United States in South Vietnam."[17]

"Pacification" in Indochina is not and never has been conceived by its American designers as an end in itself. It has always been simply another tool in the American arsenal of counterinsurgency. To win against a people's war a foreign power must either eliminate the people or eliminate their ability to support a war. One should not, therefore, be confused that America's overall tactics range in style from the Ben Suc (eliminate-the-village) paradigm to the Mylai (eliminate-the-people) paradigm, for the objective is the same throughout: to prevent people from supporting a people's war.

CHAPTER 7

Weapons and Tactics: Three

Generations of Technological

Death

The war in Vietnam is a war against an entire people and an entire country. Nowhere is this more apparent than in the tactics and weapons used by the United States.

To date Vietnam has seen three generations of American military technology and tactics. The first weapons and tactics used by the U.S. were similar to those used in Korea, with one important exception: the army relied much more on "air-mobile" or helicopter-borne troops. The second generation began in the early sixties and was marked by the introduction of new weapons systems designed specifically for counterguerrilla wars. Introduction of new electronic sensing and detection devices in 1968 marked the beginning of the third generation of weapons, which is still being tested and perfected in Vietnam. In general, the new weapons do not replace previous ones, but are merely added to the existing arsenal.

First Generation: War Without Battle Lines

Reliance on helicopter-borne troops and equipment represents a radical departure from combat in previous wars. In Vietnam there is no front line and there are no concrete enemy strongholds. Fighting flares wherever contact is made. The goal of ground forces is not to occupy territory; it is to deny it to the enemy. Units are no longer assigned a section of the front. Instead, they are made responsible for an area.[1] Their job is to find enemy units in their territory and destroy them. Units are lifted by helicopter from heavily fortified bases to the fighting and transported back to their base when the battle is over. This is the only tactic possible when an entire country is hostile and every inhabitant is a potential enemy. The change from fixed battle lines to air-mobile operations marked the initial change from a war against an army to a war against the people.

Second Generation: Antipersonnel Weapons

This change was made more explicit with the introduction of the second generation of weapons, the antipersonnel weapons specifically designed to kill or maim large numbers of defenseless people. These new weapons have several characteristics in common. They are primarily effective against decentralized agricultural populations; they devastate broad areas, killing people yet leaving property relatively unharmed; they are designed to be used against defenseless people; and they demand undisputed air superiority to be effective. Use of the weapons results in the indiscriminate slaughter of civilians and soldiers alike.

Typical of these weapons are the "cluster bomb units." These are large bomb casings filled with hundreds of smaller bomblets. They may contain a variety of different bomblets, ranging from fragmentation or incendiary bomblets to CS gas canisters. The guava bomb, for example, is a large shell resembling a 750-pound bomb filled with hundreds of spherical bomblets or "guavas" each of which releases 260–300 steel pellets. As the mother bomb falls it releases the "guavas" which spew the pellets in "an isotropic sunburst pattern for a distance of about 15 meters."[2]

These bombs and others like them are dropped over wide areas of the countryside, especially in areas such as War Zone C, designated as "free bombing zones." Each bomb can fill the air over half a mile with a hail of deadly missiles indiscriminately killing and maiming anyone above the ground.

In a sense all bombs and shells used in Vietnam are fragmentation bombs, for they are all made from material which fragments into double-edged machetelike slivers. The wounds caused by fragmentation bombs and antipersonnel weapons are irregular and hard to cure. According to *Aviation Week* these painful wounds build "a deterrence capability into conventional ordinance" and give them a "separate and distinguishable psychological impact . . . apart from the actual destruction which they caused."[3]

Another weapons system designed specifically for counterguerrilla warfare is "Puff the Magic Dragon." Puff is a C-47 airplane mounted with three miniguns each capable of shooting 18,000 rounds a minute. It is used to saturate suspected enemy positions with bullets, and in three seconds can cover an area the size of a football field with one bullet to every square foot. Puff is a large slow plane with limited maneuverability, so it is used primarily at night or against targets which are not heavily defended.

A Quaker working in Quang Ngai, South Vietnam, in 1969 describes Puff in action.

Several of us went to the roof about 3 a.m. The Americans unleashed the terrifying "Puff the Magic Dragon."
. . . As I watched it circle overhead last night, silhouetted against the low clouds in the light of the flares, flinging indiscriminate bolts of death earthward, I could vividly visualize the scene below. Men, women, children and animals, caught like rats in a flood. No place to hide, no way to plead their case of innocence to the machine in the sky, no time to prepare for death. The beating the civilians are taking in this war is beyond adequate description.[4]

The list of new antipersonnel weapons is long and gruesome. They range in sophistication from bombs guided by TV cameras on their noses to the medieval caltrops, multipointed spikes strewn over the ground, once used to maim knights' horses, but now designed to injure and maim anyone walking through an area where they've been dispersed.

When many people are killed, the survivors are terrorized, but where terror is the objective, severe injuries may be even more effective. *Weapons for Counter-Insurgency,* by the American Friends Service Committee NARMIC Project, reports that

. . . most of the victims of anti-personnel bombs are not killed, rather they are maimed. The pellets from anti-personnel bombs are designed to cause irregular and hard-to-cure wounds. This serves two functions. First, it means that instead of a single man dead and withdrawn from military production, six to ten people (as well as facilities and supplies) must care for him. Secondly, the sufferings of badly wounded victims tend to have greater demoralizing effect on the remaining population than the dead. Thus such weapons "build a deterrent capability into conventional ordnance."

Robert Crichton has described the treatment that is given to victims of antipersonnel bombs, when and if they are brought to hospitals:

CBU's (Cluster Bomb Units) have created a need for drastic new surgical techniques. Because there is neither time nor facilities for X-rays, a CBU victim, if hit in the stomach, is simply slit from the top of the stomach to the bottom and the contents of the stomach emptied out on a table and fingered through for "frags" as a dog is worked over for ticks. When the sorting is done the entrails are replaced and the stomach sewed back up like a football. This "football scar" had become the true badge of misery in South Vietnam.[5]

Referring to the pellets of the "pineapple bomb," an ex-Green Beret reported, "Because of their shape and/ or velocity, once they tear into the body they move in a complex path, doing great damage and complicating removal." Two French physicians added:

The trajectories in the body are long and often very irregular because of the ricocheting in the inner organs, which causes several deep wounds. . . . One single particle can cause several intestinal wounds, so that it becomes necessary to examine the whole abdomen. . . . It is sometimes necessary to X-ray the whole body to find certain particles, to start from the wound entrance to try to reconstruct the possible trajectory. . . . The wounds caused by these bombs are of a new type, which has never been described before in world literature.[6]

Finally, there are the incendiary weapons, the most famous being napalm. Developments in this area include new delivery systems to involve more people, and new incendiary agents which will not wash out of the flesh but will keep burning long after the attack.

Gas Warfare

The military has also resorted to gas warfare in Vietnam. As early as 1962, the United States began to supply the South Vietnamese with CN and CS. These riot control agents were initially intended for use in civilian disturbances or when NLF forces intermingled with civilians. By early 1965, the South Vietnamese army, guided by

U.S. advisers, was using CN, CS, and DM agents in military operations against the NLF. On February 22, 1966, the *New York Times* reported that large quantities of tear-gas grenades were being dropped from helicopters on NLF-infested areas. This was done to drive troops from their bunkers and tunnels to the surface where they would be more vulnerable to subsequent bombing attacks by B-52s using antipersonnel bombs. By mid-1966, according to national press news stories, U.S. planes were dropping tons of CS gas on NLF positions prior to ground assaults by gas-masked U.S. infantrymen. These actions constituted a significant escalation of the use of gas for military purposes.

The increased use of tear gas in Southeast Asia has been reflected in procurement and budget data. In 1964 the army procurement of CS was 183 tons; in 1967, 603 tons; in 1969, 3,032 tons. For the period 1964–69 the total is 6,868 tons; this is enough CS to achieve a battlefield concentration over an area twice the size of South Vietnam. Expenditures for riot control agents rose from $1 million in fiscal 1965 to $70 million in fiscal 1969. Little or no CN or DM has been used since 1965.[7]

CS is not really a gas; it is a powder which becomes dispersed into a fine cloud by explosive charges. Due to the increased interest in irritant chemicals stimulated by the Vietnam war, two new forms of CS have been developed since 1964. The first, CS1, is normal CS which has been finely pulverized. It has greater persistence in the air and is drawn more deeply into the lungs. This results in extensive coughing and nausea. The second, CS2, is finely pulverized and treated with silicone to render it moisture resistant. It may persist for many weeks after it has been released, and can be blown from the ground into the air by wind.

As the use of CS in Vietnam became routine, a wide range of devices for dispensing CS was developed. In April 1969, the army issued a new manual devoted to the use of riot-control gases. It described no less than eighteen weapons systems that can be used to disperse tear gas.

This includes rifle grenades; hand grenades; projectiles for automatic grenade launchers and multiple rocket launchers, for ground and aircraft use; 4.2-inch mortar bombs; 105-mm and 155-mm gun and howitzer projectiles; high-capacity dusting apparatus, both portable and for mounting on trucks and aircraft; aircraft bombs; cluster bombs and bomblet dispensers, of ratings from 50 to 1,000 pounds. Prior to these innovations grenades had been the standard means of delivery.

The chemical war in Vietnam has now been extended into Cambodia. In fact the use of persistent CS is an important part of the campaign there. By leaving the country well salted with this persistent chemical the military hopes to prevent the NLF, North Vietnamese, and Cambodians from returning for several weeks or months after the invasion has ended.

Development of the New Weaponry

Development of these new weapons dates from the first years of the Kennedy administration. Kennedy and his advisors were convinced that revolutionary warfare constituted a special kind of threat to United States interests; one that could not be effectively met because of overreliance on nuclear weapons for massive retaliation.

In his speech to the graduating class of West Point, 1962, Kennedy said:

> This [revolutionary war] is another type of war, new in its intensity, ancient in its origin—war by guerrillas, subversives, insurgents, assassins; war by ambush instead of by combat; by infiltration, instead of aggression, seeking victory by eroding and exhausting the enemy instead of engaging him . . . It requires in those situations where we must counter it . . . a whole new kind of strategy, a wholly different kind of force, and therefore a new and wholly different kind of military training.

Kennedy set up a "Special Group for Counterinsurgency" to devise tactics and weaponry for these wars. In his 1959 book *The Uncertain Trumpet,* General Maxwell Taylor, chairman of the Special Group and later ambassador to Vietnam, described how the role of ground forces as a shield behind which the U.S. could deliver blows from its "atomic sword" was shifted so that atomic forces would provide "a shield of protection warding off the threat of hostile attack while the forces of limited war provided the flexible sword for parry, riposte and attack." Vietnam was to be the proving ground for these new theories and weapons, as General Taylor himself explained to a congressional committee in 1963:

> . . . Here we have a going laboratory where we see subversive insurgency, the Ho Chi Minh doctrine, being applied in all its forms. This has been a challenge not just for the armed services, but for several of the agencies of government, as many of them are involved in one way or another in South Vietnam. On the military side, however, we have recognized the importance of the area as a laboratory. We have had teams out there looking at the equipment requirements of this kind of guerrilla warfare. We have rotated senior officers through there, spending several weeks just to talk to people and get the feel of the operation, so even though not regularly assigned to Vietnam, they are carrying their experience back to their own organizations.[8]

Third Generation: The Electronic Battlefield

Despite the new weapons, the Vietnamese have not been defeated. In General W. C. Westmoreland's terms, the American military force resembled a "giant without eyes" unable to find or engage an elusive enemy. This, coupled with increasing political demands within America for troop withdrawals, gave birth to the next and current generation of weapons. This is an effort to use advanced electronic systems to detect the enemy and to destroy him by remote control. This concept is called by the army the "electronic battlefield." Parts of the weapons systems are now being either used or tested in Vietnam, Cambodia, Laos, and Thailand.

The goal of the electronic battlefield program was described by General Westmoreland on October 14, 1969, when he said:

> I visualize the Army's job in land combat as:
> First, we must find the enemy.
> Second, we must destroy the enemy.
> And third, we must support the forces that perform the other two functions.
> By studying operations in Vietnam, one can better understand these functions.
> Large parts of the infantry, ground and air cavalry, and aviation are used in what I will now call "STANO" —surveillance, target acquisition and night observation, or function number one—finding the enemy. In this function large areas can be covered continuously by aerial surveillance, systems, unattended ground sensors, radars and other perfected means of finding the enemy. These systems can permit us to deploy our fires and forces more effectively in the most likely and most productive areas.
> The second function—destroying the enemy—is the role of our combat forces—artillery, air, armor and infantry, together with the helicopters needed to move the combat troops. Firepower can be concentrated without massing large numbers of troops. In Vietnam where artillery and tactical air forces inflict over two-thirds of the enemy casualties, firepower is responsive as never before. It can rain destruction anywhere on the battlefield within minutes . . . whether friendly troops are present or not. . . . On the battlefield of the future, enemy forces will be located, tracked, and targeted almost instantaneously through the use of data links, computer assisted intelligence evaluation, and automated fire control. With first round kill probabilities approaching certainty, and with surveillance devices that can continually track the enemy, the need

for large forces to fix the opposition physically will be less important.[9]

Westmoreland went on to say that advances in technology would certainly permit a tremendous "economy of manpower" in the future. In other words most of the combat troops could be withdrawn from Vietnam without decreasing the military's ability to rain death and destruction upon that country.

It is also clear from the speech that the goal of the third-generation weapons is to create an automated battlefield. The object of such a battlefield is not the protection or occupation of territory. It is simply to kill all those in an area judged to be the enemy.

Many of the components of this system are already being used in Vietnam. The E-63 personnel detector or "people sniffer," which detects the presence of ammonia and other chemicals given off by man, has seen considerable use in Vietnam. In practice it is mounted on a helicopter which skims over the countryside at treetop level looking for concentrations of enemy soldiers. When a "hot spot" has been located, the helicopter immediately rises and marks the location for future bombardment. The device does have its limitations; it cannot distinguish people from animals, one person from many, friend from foe. A *New York Times* article states "that degree of exactitude would be welcome, but that is not the way the war is fought today. War Zone C and large areas of South Vietnam have been designated as 'free bombing zones.' Anything that moves there is regarded as fair game. Previous high readings on the 'people sniffers' have brought B-52 raids from Guam."[10]

In its efforts to perfect new surveillance and detection systems, the military planners have studied the potential applications of space age technology. One of the army's major new projects is STANO, briefly described in Westmoreland's speech. Since 1966 over $2 billion has been spent on development and procurement of these new weapons under STANO. Programs under STANO include:

- Fopen: Radar base devices for detecting moving personnel in the jungle.
- LLLTV: Low light level television, which sees 85 percent better than the human eye and comes equipped with laser illumination.
- Aerially implanted geophones to detect sound made by people.
- Infrared target detectors which employ infrared light to detect people at night.
- Computer command controls to gather data from electronic spy equipment and direct U.S. firepower to the targets.[11]

In addition to sensing and spy devices, STANO also includes weapons which can be automatically triggered by these devices. These include land mines which can be dropped from the air and remain active for thirty days and mines which can be automatically triggered. All these devices and weapons share the same fault. They are indiscriminate. Like the people sniffer they draw no distinction between friend or foe, civilian or soldier, adult or child, and will impartially call down an automated death on all who cross their path.

CHAPTER 8

The Air War: Emptying
the Countryside

Intensity

The American policy of pacifying the countryside by emptying it has been closely integrated with the heaviest aerial bombardment in history. By bombing, the United States has attempted to destroy areas which it could not control, forcing the survivors into areas that it did control and thereby depriving the guerrilla forces of their help. In 1965, the first year of this operation, the U.S. dropped more than a ton of bombs for every "enemy soldier" in Vietnam. By 1968 it had dropped twelve tons of bombs for every square mile in all Vietnam, North as well as South. According to one account, "By March 1969 the total level of bombardment had reached 130,000 tons a month—nearly two Hiroshimas a week in South Vietnam and Laos, defenseless countries. And Melvin Laird's projection for the next twelve to eighteen months was the same."[1] By April 1969, it was estimated that bombings by B-52 raids alone had blasted some 3.5 million craters— 45 feet in diameter and 30 feet deep—in South Vietnam; these holes had filled with water to become breeding areas for malarial mosquitoes and other insects.[2] In North Vietnam, where the bombing was designed not only to destroy military objectives, but also to terrorize the people and break their will, official Pentagon sources cite some 100,000 B-52 missions between February 1965 and August 1968, with each mission dropping an average of seven tons of bombs. The enormity of this attack becomes clear when it is noted that in the entire course of World War II, a total of 500,000 tons of bombs was dropped in the Pacific theater.[3] In Laos, the American aerial attack has been even more intense. The number of U.S. Air Force bombing sorties per month in that small country ranges from 12,500 to over 20,000.

The results in Vietnam, as described by Tom Buckley in the *New York Times Magazine* of November 23, 1969, are grim indeed:

> [You see] bomb craters beyond counting, the dead gray and black fields, forests that have been defoliated and scorched by napalm, land that has been plowed flat to destroy Vietcong hiding places. And everywhere can be seen the piles of ashes forming the outlines of huts and houses, to show where hamlets once stood.

Depersonalization

As a journalist, Jonathan Schell witnessed the American effort in Quang Ngai Province in 1967 and later described the rationale for American aerial action there:

> I asked the major how he distinguished members of the Viet Cong from the rest of the population. "If they run is one way," he said. "There are a lot of ways. Sometimes, when you see a field of people, it looks like just a bunch of farmers. Now, you see, the Vietnamese people—they're not interested in the U.S. Air Force, and they don't look at the planes going over them. But down in that field you'll see *one guy* whose conical hat keeps bobbing up and down. He's looking because he wants to know where you're going. So you make a couple of passes over the field, and then one of them makes a break for it—it's the guy that was

lookin' up at you—and he's your VC. So you look
where he goes, and call in an air strike."[4]

Generally villages could be bombed if it was known that
they had been supporting the NLF by offering them food
and labor, or if American troops or planes had received
fire from the village.

In Indochina, the killing of the populace from the air
has become depersonalized, its individual American practitioners dehumanized. In *Air War: Vietnam,* Frank Harvey described a navy pilot being initiated into his task:

> He learns how it feels to drop bombs on human beings
> and watch huts go up in a boil of orange flame when
> his aluminum napalm tanks tumble into them. He gets
> hardened to pressing the firing button and cutting
> people down like little cloth dummies, as they sprint
> frantically under him. He gets his sword bloodied for
> the rougher things to come.[5]

Following an attack by American gunboats and helicopter
gunships, Asahi correspondent Katsuichi Honda, writing
from Quang Ngai Province, described the sporting atmosphere of the scene:

> They seemed to fire whimsically and in passing even
> though they were not being shot at from the ground
> nor could they identify the people as NLF. They did it
> impulsively for fun, using the farmers for targets as if
> in a hunting mood. They are hunting Asians.

Warnings

Sometimes the American planes first dropped warning
leaflets; Schell quotes extensively from a number of these.
They often show American planes destroying a village and
killing its inhabitants. In one, "a man lies on the earth,
clutching his chest. Streams of blood flow from his eyes,
nostrils, mouth, and ears. The rest of the pamphlet is in

black and white, but his blood is printed in red ink." The warning is that "your village will look like this." The text on the back includes the point that "many hamlets have been destroyed because these villages harbored the Viet- cong." Then the warning: "U.S. MARINES WILL NOT HESITATE TO DESTROY, IMMEDIATELY, ANY VILLAGE OR HAMLET HARBORING THE VIET- CONG. WE WILL NOT HESITATE TO DESTROY, IMMEDIATELY, ANY VILLAGE OR HAMLET USED AS A VIETCONG STRONGHOLD TO FIRE AT OUR TROOPS OR AIRCRAFT."[6] Once a village is destroyed, survivors are leafleted again. They are told that their village was destroyed because of the Vietcong, and that they should turn to the Saigon government and the allied forces, who will "help you to live in peace and to have a happy and prosperous life." Those who survive the destruction of their villages are then fed into the "pacification" or "refugee" programs.

Objectives

There are, of course, complicated policies to determine what types of areas are to be bombed with what in- tensity; but the basic scheme is to locate areas actively supporting the NLF and then to destroy those areas. The purpose is twofold: to deprive the NLF of its popular rural support by removing the population, and to destroy some villages in order to deter others from supporting the NLF.

The latter objective, viewed together with America's general destruction of the Vietnamese countryside and the antipersonnel effort directed at the Vietnamese popu- lation, suggests that what the U.S. is doing to Vietnam is meant in part as a deterrent to other nations who might be thinking of anti-American revolution. This is explicit in the statements of Dean Rusk and others that we must crush this "people's war" in order to prevent others in the future.

The Bombing of Laos and Cambodia

In Laos the same methods as in Vietnam are being used for the same purposes. On October 1, 1967, the *New York Times* reported that in Laos, "the rebel economy and social fabric" are now the main targets of America's attack. It is claimed that this attack has been successful:

> Refugees from the Plaine des Jarres area say that during recent months most open spaces have been evacuated. Both civilians and soldiers have retreated into the forests or hills and frequently spend most of the daylight hours in caves and tunnels. . . . The bombing, by creating refugees, deprives the Communists of their chief source of food and transport. The population of the Pathet Lao zone has been declining for several years and the Pathet Lao find it increasingly difficult to fight a "peoples' war" with fewer and fewer people.

Jacques Decornoy, *Le Monde*'s Southeast Asia expert, reported in July 1968 that—

> One of the officials of Sam-Neua district told us that between February, 1965 and March, 1968, 65 villages had been destroyed. A number impossible to verify in a short report, but it is a fact that between Sam-Neua and a place about 30 kilometres away where we stayed, no house in the village and hamlets had been spared. Bridges had been destroyed, fields up to the rivers had been holed with bomb craters.

Considering the volume of the bombing, and the sort of bombs that are used, it is easy to understand the terror that has driven the people away from the countryside and into the cities and refugee camps.

This process has now been extended with a fury to Cambodia. In May 1970, saturation bombing began.

B-52 raids, which marked the first week of the American invasion, have increased and present administration statements indicate neither a slowdown of B-52 raids nor of the massive aerial support for the South Vietnamese troops which remain.

CHAPTER 9

Military Ground Operations:

Extermination, Self–Preservation,

and Escape

America's ground operations in the war are more diffi-cult than her air activities. This is because the vast tech-nological advantage of the U.S. war machine is less suited to use on the ground, where contact is sought with an enemy who is constantly watchful, highly mobile, and quite indistinguishable from the people at large. In tra-ditional Western warfare, the objective of an infantry has been to kill or capture an enemy who has been located. But Vietnam is different. There the task of destruction is routinely easy, while the problem lies in "making con-tact" with the opposition. The NLF exacerbates the Ameri-cans' problem by tirelessly observing a fundamental prin-ciple of guerrilla warfare: never engage the enemy on any but your own terms.

Search and Destroy

Most offensive U.S. ground operations are "search and destroy" missions. (The name for these missions was changed in March 1968 to "reconnaissance in force," but the reality did not change.) These missions typically begin with B-52 saturation bombing of an "objective" area, a circle on the map which U.S. intelligence believes to be a haven for the NLF. If the "objective" is a town or hamlet, B-52 bombing is aimed to set it afire; if the "objective" is open jungle, the B-52s simply open craters in it in a gridlike pattern. Following the B-52 bombings, long-range artillery fire—175-mm and 8-inch howitzers, which can fire over twenty miles—continue to pound the "objective." Next comes aerial bombing by smaller, lower-flying attack bombers which are armed with half-ton bombs, 2.75-inch fire bombs, and huge canisters of gelatinous napalm. A good "hit" with napalm is one which "rolls" a long way, engulfing acres of land in instant flame. Last to arrive and devastate the "objective" from the air are helicopter gunships firing rockets and M-60 machine guns, largely at random. New "cobra" gunships fire M-75 grenades filled with steel wires which, while ineffective against most military targets, are designed specifically to maim and kill.

With destruction nearly complete, search begins. Troops move in by helicopter or in tanks and set up artillery bases. Actual "searching," which usually begins the second day, is supported by the entrenched artillery and, if necessary, by further air strikes. The objects of search are weapons, rice, shelters, clothing, and, in fact, any traces of civilization which could possibly be of use to the NLF. Booty captured is either evacuated or destroyed. When a village falls within an "objective" area, it is completely and utterly destroyed—houses are burned down, food poisoned, utensils smashed, livestock killed, banana trees severed, mattresses slashed, etc.[1]

Seal and Search

"Seal and search" operations, somewhat different from "search and destroy," involve surrounding a village at night or early in the morning and preventing anyone from entering or leaving while the village is searched door to door for NLF suspects and weapons, radios, and other instruments useful to the support of a people's war. One major defense of the NLF in these operations is, it turns out, the language barrier. U.S. troops seldom can locate an interpreter whose sympathies are more with them than with the villagers, and therefore interrogation, as designed, becomes impossible.[2] All in all, these operations tend to be even more frustrating to U.S. soldiers than are "search and destroy" missions, and, as a consequence, acts of impulsive violence (including murder and rape) on the part of individual GIs are frequent occurrences.[3]

Engaging the Enemy

While "search and destroy" and "seal and search" missions usually follow rather well-designed blueprints, there does not and cannot exist a U.S. blueprint for "engaging the enemy." The NLF fights only when it decides on its own to do so, and this may occur at any time, night or day, during any stage of any U.S. ground action. When an NLF engagement does occur, the U.S. response is to open fire with every weapon of every type (including 20-mm cannon which fire one hundred half-pound shells per *second*) and, if the NLF positions can be "located," to call in air strikes as well. The "battlefield" itself is from all appearances deserted—no one on either side shows his head lest it be blown off. Guns are "aimed" only on rough guesswork. The U.S. uses huge quantities of tear gas to drive people into the open, where, in pitched battle, the statistical chance of being shot is overwhelming. U.S. troops have been counted by Reuters news agency to fire the following in one month in Vietnam: 1 billion bullets of all calibers, 88 million aircraft machine-gun bullets, 10 million mortar shells, and 4.8 million rockets (an average of over seven thousand shells per second).[4] American troops also use flamethrowers, poison gases, and other weapons generally considered illegal in "civilized" warfare.[5]

From time to time during the history of the war American military instructions have shifted between two theoretical aims: (1) to maximize enemy casualties and (2) to minimize U.S. casualties. President Johnson's "maximum pressure" guideline is an example of the former and President Nixon's "protective reaction" an example of the latter. Vietnam veterans report, however, that regardless of high-level verbiage, the reaction to contact with an NLF fighting force is always the same—a fearsome, unaiming hail of firepower by whatever means possible.

Operation Junction City

Coordinated U.S. operations may be rather small (one or more companies of a few hundred men each) or very large (one or more divisions of over ten thousand men each). Consider, for example, the aims and accomplishments of a well-known large mission, Operation Junction City, which was executed in the spring of 1967 in Tay Ninh Province northwest of Saigon (a region called "War Zone C"). The operation was aimed at twenty-two different circular or oblong "objective" areas ranging in size from about 20 to about 40 square kilometers each. The "objectives," many near (and one actually crossing) the Cambodian border, were supposed areas of NLF concentration. Many of the areas had been tall, majestic teak forests until the huge trees were "defoliated" by American herbicides. This U.S. plan backfired, however, for when the shade of the large trees was gone, a dense undergrowth of elephant grass and "wait-a-minute" vines (so called because soldiers on foot get caught in them and have to "wait a minute") sprang up quickly in the tropical climate and made both air reconnaissance and ground movements even more difficult than before. Undaunted, the U.S. military went ahead with its destruction campaign, General Westmoreland predicting that Operation

Junction City would destroy the NLF's effectiveness in War Zone C and destroy his will to fight.

During the operation, twenty-one villages were annihilated, their populations either killed or moved into "pacification" camps. What the operation sought, i.e., "contact with the enemy," was (according to U.S. maps) made in only one of the twenty-two "objectives," and then only on its fringes. Instead, "contact" occurred around the U.S. base camps and artillery support bases, where the NLF recognized (quite properly, of course) the root of its problem to lie. Despite this obvious failure of Junction City to achieve anything but the vast wastage of rural society and the surrounding jungle, Westmoreland announced that the NLF was "through forever in War Zone C" and later, on November 23, 1967, that "there is no chance left for the foe."[6] Less than three months later the NLF launched the famous "Tet offensive"—their largest attack ever—whose main thrust came from War Zone C.

Indochina and the Individual GI

For the individual American soldier's morale, the psychological pressures of this kind of war are immense. Most 11-B riflemen, who do the actual fighting and dying, are nineteen- and twenty-year-olds. More than half are draftees.[7] A disproportionate number are black. They arrive in Vietnam with very little idea of what the war is all about, except that they had to come to it. If they are confused about why they are fighting, they become still more confused about whom they are fighting. They are told that the NLF uniform is black pajamas, only to discover that the everyday dress of the entire rural population is black pajamas. The Vietnamese who sell them oranges or cigarette lighters are indistinguishable from (in some cases the very same!)[8] Vietnamese who try to kill them. When American GIs manage to capture a village, they find Vietnamese tax gatherers and rich landlords following them with a view to reestablishing their exploitative hold on the peasantry.[9] Even the ARVN (South Vietnamese army), who generally refuse to devastate their own country with the same vigor that the American command advises, appear therefore to be unreliable and "poor fighters" in the eyes of a U.S. soldier.

For all these reasons, a feeling of constant fear and tension grows up among GIs in the field, who come to view all Vietnamese—all "gooks"—with suspicion. The army nurtures this psychology through its "troop topics" discussions, which play on racial fears and simplistic anticommunism ("If we don't kill them here, next thing they'll be in San Diego . . ."). The Vietnamese people come to be seen only as miniature threats which appear and disappear from the hostile landscape. The GI develops an aversion to his total environment, and his primary concern becomes to survive his ordeal until he can escape it.

The survival concern means that he will often accept the army's offer (and this is a standard army device)[10] to reenlist in order to avoid combat duty. In the field it means he will stick close to his commanding officer, since only the officer can call in the air strike which might save his life. It also means that the soldier will be more likely to kill a Vietnamese on the mere suspicion, however faint, that the Vietnamese is armed.

The escape concern means that the soldier counts the days until his five-day rest and recreation leave.[11] Still more does he count the days until—if he has not been lured to reenlist—his tour in Vietnam (normally twelve or thirteen months) is ended. In Vietnam itself his avenues of escape are the myriad bars, brothels, etc., which cluster around U.S. bases and as much as follow American units around the countryside. Cold soda and beer, and mail from home, are godsends to the GI, and GIs with their own radios can and frequently do listen to "Hanoi Hannah," who, in English-language broadcasts from Hanoi, plays American rock 'n' roll and gives more detailed news broadcasts than are available over U.S. Armed Forces radio.

Drug Abuse Within the American Military

Although Pentagon officials minimize the drug problem among American soldiers in Indochina, it is otherwise widely acknowledged that narcotics provide a widespread mode of escape from the tensions of the war. Dr. Joel H. Kaplan, who served as an army psychiatrist in Vietnam from November 1968 to October 1969 and helped set up the army's first formal drug-abuse program there, reports that 70 percent of all American outpatients and 50 percent of all inpatients treated by his psychiatric team in I and II Corps (the northern half of South Vietnam) proved to be drug abusers. The general process of addiction described by Dr. Kaplan is from "Js" (marijuana joints) to "OJs" (marijuana joints dipped in liquid opium) to "opium dens" in South Vietnamese cities where GIs begin by smoking opium pipes and proceed to maintaining liquid opium or a mixture of liquid opium and "speed" (Methedrine). Soldiers also get high by sniffing glue or popping barbiturates and amphetamines such as Dexedrine, Binoctal (a French headache preparation), and Darvon (an army-issue pain-killer). The irregularity of the soldier's life results in frequent cases of "OD" (overdose), and Dr. Kaplan's team saw "a number of OD's who were brought by buddies into the emergency room, comatose from drugs or dead on arrival." By his own experience, Dr. Kaplan estimates that between 10 and 20 percent of the GIs in Vietnam are serious drug abusers, and of this number half became addicted after their arrival in Vietnam.[12] Many returning Vietnam veterans regard these estimates as conservative.

While the GI is preoccupied with survival and modes

of escape, however, the NLF guerrilla is preoccupied with winning the war. Unlike the U.S. soldier, he cannot and does not want to leave Vietnam. His "tour of duty" is open-ended. He wants to save Vietnam and live there, and it is this simple fact that explains his tenacious dedication to ridding his country of destructive foreigners.

CHAPTER 10

Defoliation: The War Against
the Land and the Unborn

> . . . At first they felt sick and had some diarrhea, then they began to feel it hard to breathe and they had low blood pressure; some serious cases had trouble with their optic nerves and went blind. Pregnant women gave birth to stillborn or premature children. Most of the affected cattle died from serious diarrhea, and river fish floated on the surface of the water belly up, soon after the chemicals were spread.
>
> —Report of Cao Van Nguyen, M.D., following an American chemical attack on an area of 2,500 acres with approximately 1,000 inhabitants near Saigon on October 3, 1964.

Among the new weapons designed for waging war against an entire rural population, none shows its purpose quite so clearly as the defoliation program. It is a new kind of warfare. No longer is military technology used only to kill people; chemicals are also used to destroy the ecology that supports them.

Operation Hades: Migration, Starvation, and Exposure

Defoliation was begun on a test scale in 1961, and greatly expanded in the following years. The official name of this program is Operation Hades, or Operation Ranch Hand, as the military prefers to call it. The operation has destroyed much of the forest and cropland in South Vietnam, and to a lesser extent in Laos, Cambodia, and Thailand. To survive, after their land is ruined, the Vietnamese must go to the refugee camps and cities, which are under American control. Thus defoliation is one of the tactics used to deprive the rebel forces of support by forcing a "massive migration from countryside to city."[1] Donald Hornig, science adviser to President Johnson, has frankly described the purpose of crop destruction. In his words, "it's all geared to moving people."[2]

Starvation is being used as a military weapon against a population which is already undernourished. Jean Mayer, President Nixon's special adviser on nutrition, has pointed out that malnutrition is endemic to much of South Vietnam, and that diseases such as beriberi, anemia, kwashiorkor, and tuberculosis will increase if crop destruction is continued. He adds that the ultimate target of the crop destruction program is the weakest element of the civilian population, namely, women, children, and the elderly. Viet Cong soldiers may be expected to get the fighter's share of whatever food there is.

Officially, the army claims that herbicides are used only as a tactical weapon, to "deny the enemy concealment in forest areas."[3] The army denies that herbicides are used in populated areas. But there is ample documentary evidence to the contrary, even from government sources. In a speech delivered to the House Subcommittee on National Security Policy and Scientific Developments, Rear Admiral William E. Lemos listed five uses of herbicides. These were defoliation of base perimeters, defoliation of lines of communication, defoliation of infiltration routes, defoliation of enemy base camps, and—finally—crop destruction. A fuller explanation is given in Army Training Circular TC 3-6, entitled *Employment of Riot Control Agents, Flame, Smoke, Antiplant Agents, and Personnel Detectors in Counterguerrilla Operations*. It reads:

> Guerrilla operations rely heavily on locally produced crops for their food supply. Crop destruction can reduce the food supply and seriously affect the guerrilla's survival. Naturally dense vegetation in jungle areas is ideal for elusive hit-and-run tactics of guerrilla. Removal or reduction of this concealment limits the guerrilla's capability to operate in the defoliated area.

Defoliation of enemy base camps in Vietnam often means spraying the surroundings, including the fields, of suspected enemy villages. Destruction of croplands obviously involves spraying populated areas.

Until 1968 the air force followed up crop destruction missions by dropping leaflets urging those who had lost their crops to leave their homes for refugee camps where food was available. After the Tet offensive, the cities and refugee camps became, in the opinion of the military, overcrowded. The crop destruction program continued as before, but the leaflets no longer urged the Vietnamese to leave their homes.

By its own admission, as early as 1969 the air force had sprayed over 4 million acres of forests, at least one-fourth of all forested area, and almost 10 percent of all arable land. Others put the number of acres of cropland destroyed at a much higher figure. Yoichi Fukushima, head of the agronomy section of the Japan Science Council, claims that *by as early as 1967 American chemical attacks had already ruined more than 3.8 million acres, or almost one-half of the arable land in South Vietnam*.[4] It is not surprising that Vietnam has changed from a country that exported rice in 1960 to one which must now import at least half of its rice.

Orange, Blue, and White

The air force has been spraying four different chemicals in varying combinations. The three major combinations are called Orange, Blue, and White because of the coded stripe of color on each barrel. Other chemicals have also been used on a smaller scale. Agent Orange is used primarily against forests and broad-leaf crops such as beans, bananas, and manioc; it is a 50–50 mixture of 2,4-D (dichlorophenoxyacetic acid) and 2,4,5-T (trichlorophenoxyacetic acid). Agent Blue consists primarily of cacodylic acid which contains 54 percent arsenic by weight; it is used primarily against rice. Agent White is a blend of 2,4-D and picloram. Picloram is an unusually persistent herbicide which can kill vegetation and prevent reuse of the land for many years. Its use has recently been increasing in the fertile areas around Saigon.

Birth Abnormalities

Direct exposure of human beings to any of the herbicides is hazardous. Cacodylic acid, used in Agent Blue, bears the poison skull and crossbones when used as a laboratory reagent. The danger from 2,4-D and 2,4,5-T is more subtle. Recent tests conducted for the National Institute of Health have demonstrated that these chemicals and their associated impurities cause birth defects, and possibly cancer, in rats and mice; in the case of the latter chemical, fetal malformation occurs at a rate of over 90 percent. If the test results can be applied to people, it would take less than one-hundredth of an ounce to produce abnormal human fetuses, which means many women in the countryside who drink contaminated water or eat contaminated food may be in danger. Within the last two years there have been numerous reports of increasing birth abnormalities throughout South Vietnam, and photographs of grotesquely deformed babies have begun to appear in Vietnamese newspapers. Last April, Deputy Secretary of Defense David Packard ordered a suspension of the use of 2,4,5-T in Vietnam until genetic questions could be studied further.

Long-Range Effects

The long-range effects of the "defoliation" program on both the society and the ecology of Vietnam will be profound. Millions of people have been driven from their ancestral homes into refugee camps and cities. In many cases their fields have been rendered useless for years to come. The forests and swamps of Vietnam may never recover. Orians and Pfeiffer, on a recent trip to Vietnam, reported that many mangrove forests have been killed and may never regenerate.[5] Upland forests killed by repeated spraying are now being invaded by bamboo and grasses resistant to the sprays. The forests may become permanent grasslands. Destruction of all vegetation can lead to serious erosion and to irreversible laterization of the soil, a process in which rain washes away the humus and the soil bakes as hard as cement. This soil can never be used again. Thirty percent of Vietnamese soil has the potential to laterize. The effect on animal life may be equally disastrous. On their recent tour, Orians and Pfeiffer saw no frugivorous or insectivorous birds in defoliated areas. Insects and other animals which directly or indirectly depend upon vegetation for food will be decimated.

(Note: At the time of the Cambodian invasion, the C-123 planes used in crop destruction and defoliation were stripped of their nozzles and used to haul captured weapons out of Cambodia. According to the *New York Times* of June 23, 1970, it was anticipated that they would return to their original missions in due time.)

CHAPTER 11

Refugees: The Deliberate

Tragedy

Bombing, crop destruction, and forced "relocations" have changed the whole face of society in South Vietnam. Three million people were officially registered as refugees between 1965 and 1968, and of these, 1.5 million remained on the rolls in 1968. An estimated 2 to 3 million others had been displaced from their homes, but had not, for one reason or another, been registered as refugees.[1] Most of these persons have either been placed in refugee camps or have gone into the cities. Marine Lieutenant Colonel William R. Corson describes the unseen agony of one of the more "humane" instances of the American disruption of Vietnam's rural society, the forced evacuation of 13,000 civilians from an area near the DMZ named Trung Luong to a resettlement area at Cam Lo, twenty miles distant:

> The truth of the matter from the Vietnamese peasants' point of view was that a trip of twenty miles was more fearful than the trek of Steinbeck's 'Okies' to California during the 1930s. Over 90 percent of the residents of Trung Luong had never traveled farther than ten kilometers (about six miles) from their homes. They feared that Cam Lo would not be

'California' but rather a point of no return. Furthermore, the natives of Trung Luong were Buddhists who because of their religious beliefs were greatly concerned about dying in a strange place. They believe quite strongly in the necessity of being buried in their own family burial plots in order to achieve the Buddhist version of heaven. This fear, added to the loss of their fields and length of the trip, was sufficient to demolish the people. Without a shot being fired, we had conspired with the GVN (Government of [South] Vietnam) to literally destroy the hopes, aspirations, and emotional stability of 13,000 human beings. This was not and is not war—it is genocide.[2]

"Urbanization"

"Urbanization," the massive influx of peasants into the cities, has caused fundamental and traumatic dislocations in Vietnamese life. In the early 1960s, 85 percent of the South Vietnamese lived in the countryside. By early 1969 this figure had dropped to 50 percent, according to some estimates. Saigon has quintupled in size over the last decade and in 1969 had a density of 12,740 people per square mile, one of the highest in the world.[3] The tripling of the population of the cities has created huge labor surpluses. These have been largely absorbed by the needs of the Americans. Young boys shine shoes, wash cars, pick pockets, and pimp for their sisters. Girls become barmaids and prostitutes. Women do laundry for the Americans and those men not drawn into the war work as day laborers or pedicab drivers. The cities have become completely dependent, for their economic survival, on the prolongation of the war.[4]

More importantly, the social ecology of South Vietnam has been completely disrupted. Children often earn three or four times as much as their parents and, because they are young, are able to adapt better to life in the cities.[5] This has to a fair degree destroyed the traditional family structure, one mainstay of Vietnamese society. In fleeing to the cities, the other mainstay—village life—had to be abandoned. The traditional civilization has been destroyed in the cities and replaced by a social order catering largely to the needs of Americans.

Conditions in the Refugee Camps

Almost all the refugees not in the cities are in refugee camps. About half of these are children under fifteen and most of the rest are women and old men. The Kennedy subcommittee report found life in refugee camps to be deplorable.[6] Donald Duncan, a Green Beret, testified before the International War Crimes Tribunal:

> The conditions under which these people are forced to live are, by any standards, appalling. There is usually a grave shortage of water, perhaps one water point for two hundred people. In other cases water has to be brought in, if there is any water at all . . . the latrine facilities, if they exist at all, are of the worst order . . . there was over-crowding, in the number of people living in one cubicle, for instance in the provisions made for beds, which are usually nonexistent.[7]

According to David Tuck, an infantryman in the U.S. army,

> From what I could see from these people they looked just like they were starving . . . shortly after we got there [to the camp] I was on a work detail to dump some garbage . . . as soon as we dumped this these refugees—a whole lot, a horde of children, it seemed— literally jumped into this sump [hole full of garbage] and fought like animals for the garbage. They also had to be in their refugee camps at a certain time because if they showed up outside our perimeter or outside the South Vietnamese perimeter they were liable to be shot as VC.[8]

Shelter consists typically of long parallel rows of unwalled floorless frames made of poles.[9] The camps are usually built in barren areas, with little or no shelter from the sun, so they are stifling hot in the dry season and covered with several inches of mud in the rainy season. Because the people can't farm, they are completely dependent on the government for food. The official relief payment is ten piasters (about eight cents) a day per person—barely enough to live on. Because of the widespread corruption, most refugees get much less. Less than half the supplies intended for the camps ever get to the refugees.[10] Other facilities are also pitifully lacking. In Quang Ngai Province in 1967, there were sixty-eight refugee camps servicing 122,680 people. Fifty had no schools, forty-six had no latrines, and forty-two were without a medical dispensary.[11]

"Resettlement"

Officially, the number of refugees has been decreasing. The Kennedy subcommittee report states that 1.5 million people have been taken off the refugee rolls. This doesn't mean that 1.5 million peasants have returned to their farms, however. Many refugees leave the camps for the cities where they feel they have a better chance for survival. Many others lose their refugee status when their camps are declared permanent homes by the government. Ernest Hobson, civilian provincial adviser for refugees in Quang Ngai Province, is quoted in *The Military Half* by Jonathan Schell:

> "All that resettlement is just paperwork," he said, ". . . what we do is say 'O.K., this place we've built for you is now permanent, it's yours' . . . Another way of doing it is to put in a village chief and give the camp a name. Then it can be treated as a village or a hamlet."[12]

In the process, government officials pocket the $43 resettlement allowance intended to allow the family to build a new house. The Kennedy subcommittee report estimates that 75 percent of the money intended for resettlement allowances is siphoned off in graft.[13]

When the refugees are actually moved, they are generally taken to "resettlement areas," often no different from camps. Another reason for the drop in the number of official refugees, especially new refugees, is the policy of the American army and the Saigon regime of not creating more refugee camps. The army still forces Vietnamese from their villages and into areas around roads, cities, and army bases. In most cases, these people have no place to farm and so must be fed. However, because they aren't living in "refugee camps" they aren't considered refugees.

Refugees in Cambodia and Laos

Vietnam is not the only Indochinese country with a "refugee problem." The heavy American bombing in Laos has displaced hundreds of thousands of Laotians. As the war spread to Cambodia, tens of thousands of refugees were created there. Before the U.S.-Saigon invasion, however, the American airplanes had bombed and strafed repeatedly inside Cambodia leaving the inhabitants of many villages either dead or homeless. Up to May 1969, the Cambodians reported 7,178 border violations by American, ARVN ("Army of the Republic of Vietnam"), or Korean troops. The actual number of violations is probably much greater. Up to this time, 293 Cambodians were reported killed and 690 wounded.[14] Several villages have been heavily damaged or destroyed.[15] After the right-wing military coup and the U.S.-ARVN invasion of Cambodia, the number of refugees there has skyrocketed. Over a hundred thousand Cambodians, mostly the ethnic Vietnamese, have fled their homes, and numerous villages have been burned by the invading armies. At the end of May 1970, over 70,000 Cambodians were living in refugee camps.[16]

By the end of 1969 in Laos, six years of the most intensive aerial bombardment in history by the United States had created 600,000 refugees, more than twenty percent of the total Laotian population; 150,000 of these persons were driven from their homes in 1969 alone. For the past several years, as indicated in part I, a large percentage of the population has been forced to live in caves and tunnels, venturing out to farm only at night.[17] The Plain of Jars, once home to some 150,000 persons, has been virtually depopulated. As in Vietnam, the generation of refugees in Laos appears to be part of a deliberate policy. In the words of David Kales of the Hearst newspapers:

> . . . a nagging suspicion persists that the effects of bombing are not entirely unintended but derive in part from conscious policy. U.S. officials here [in Vientiane, Laos] appear to operate on a desperate assumption: that the only way to secure the people permanently from the Communists—and deprive the enemy of its manpower—is to remove them physically from Communist territory. From this point of view, the bombing is a broom, sweeping the refugees into the government safe towns.[18]

Not only is the population removed from enemy influence by this procedure, but it is also placed in an enervating environment which tends to kill the will—particularly the will to resist. Kales notes that the United States operates a continual air lift for the refugees from the war zones to the government-controlled cities, whereupon:

> Arriving in such places, the refugees are driven to camps that resemble the shantytowns of the Great Depression. There, a few women cook rice provided by AID. Children play tag or rummage for odd bits of sticks and stones on the ground. Most of the people either sit dozing, waiting listlessly—sometimes for months, sometimes for years—for jobs and new homes.[19]

For those Laotian refugees somehow caught between the refugee camps and the liberated areas, the United States, in the best American tradition of the quantity game, has combined its historic bombardment with "history's greatest rice drop."[20]

The Future

In the future, it is hard to see anything but a vast increase in the numbers of refugees, especially in Laos and Cambodia, where the process of concentrating a rural population into small areas around cities and military bases is still physically capable of being pushed further. In the war which seems to be approaching throughout Indochina, America's only viable strategy will be the one she has been using thus far: employing her enormous firepower to destroy the countryside and force the survivors to flee into American-controlled areas to escape death from the skies.

CHAPTER 12

War Crimes and Atrocities:
Three Approaches

The Nuremberg Precedent

The United States helped conduct the Nuremberg war crimes trials, sitting in the position of the victor in moral judgment over its defeated enemy. At that time this country laid down and pledged itself to a code of wartime conduct whose violation it considered to be grounds for criminal prosecution. The principles of Nuremberg were formulated by a UN-directed international law commission in 1950 with U.S. support. According to these principles, war crimes are defined as:

> Violations of the laws or customs of war which include, but are not limited to, murder, ill-treatment or deportation to slave labour or for any other purpose of civilian population of or in occupied territory, murder or ill-treatment of prisoners of war or persons on the high seas, killing of hostages, plunder of public or private property, wanton destruction of cities, towns or villages, or devastation not justified by military necessity.[1]

But within twenty years, the U.S. was itself conducting a war in which actions it had previously labeled as war crimes had become an accepted part of military strategy.

Let us examine some of the specific crimes which the Nuremberg principles label as war crimes.

Murder of the civilian population: The most blatant case of outright murder in this war has been the now publicly acknowledged massacre of up to five hundred unarmed Vietnamese civilians at Mylai in March 1968. But the massacre at Mylai was not just an isolated instance of criminal activity in the midst of war. On the contrary, it was just one outgrowth of a war policy that accepts the murder of civilians in massive numbers as a necessary and scarcely regrettable complication of anti-guerrilla warfare. Murder of civilians is the obvious result of such speeches to our troops as this statement by a high-ranking U.S. officer: "I want you to keep these Vietnamese on the run so much, so hard that I want to see Vietnamese blood flowing upon the earth."[2] One ex-GI, Sp/4 David Tuck, has told of the advice he received on reaching Vietnam with his infantry unit: ". . . before we got over there we were told to make friends because unless we win the hearts and minds of the people we will lose the war. But, once we got over there our officers told us otherwise: that the only good Vietnamese was a dead Vietnamese . . ."[3] Such incitement to indiscriminate murder is at the very heart of America's Vietnam policy. Given such official encouragement, American soldiers have adopted such practices as the "mad minute" in which a unit will shoot off all its weaponry against all houses in any village from which sniper fire has been received. "Mad minutes" are murder—nothing less.

Ill-treatment or deportation of civilian population: The war in Vietnam has generated over 3 million refugees. Most of these are peasants whose homes, fields, and livestock have been destroyed by American troops bent on depriving the Viet Cong of support. The peasants are herded into refugee camps which are indistinguishable from concentration camps—enclosed by barbed wire, minimal food and sanitation, nothing for the inmates to do but sit and await the end of the war when, if they survive the physical and spiritual devastation of enforced "liberation," they will return to the poisoned and cratered fields of their ravished country.

Every single refugee has been at the least the victim of criminal ill-treatment, for each has had his possessions plundered (villages are napalmed or put to the torch, livestock is disposed of before the refugees are removed) and his ancestral ties with the land violated, and all have been condemned to life in the physically destructive and morally degrading atmosphere of the concentration camp.

Murder or ill-treatment of prisoners of war: Prisoners of war are routinely ill treated and often tortured either directly by American soldiers or by the South Vietnamese to whom the U.S. turns them over, in violation of the U.S.-ratified Hague and Geneva conventions on the treatment of POWs. The milder forms of ill-treatment include beating, psychological pressure, physical degradations. Electric torture has been used frequently. A former U.S. Army interrogator of POWs, Peter Martinsen, has testified to such practices. He states, "I cannot think of an interrogation that I saw in Vietnam during which a war crime, as defined by the Geneva Convention was not committed. I cannot think of one without harassment or coercion . . . beating, torturing and harassment (such as screaming and yelling) was used. This was coercion, and it was specifically stated that one not do this."[4]

Sp/4 Tuck, mentioned above, has reported that in his experience wounded prisoners "were never left to die by themselves, they were always executed."[5] In one instance, which he claims was not unusual, a prisoner was killed by being thrown out of a helicopter.

These are not isolated instances. Such things are known to the commanding officers and are not discouraged, and this, in a rule-laden organization such as the army, is tantamount to outright support. While the combat soldiers who murder their prisoners out of rage and hatred may have no conception of what international laws govern the treatment of prisoners (this is not part of army training, though it should be) intelligence officers and commanding officers must be well aware that mistreatment of POWs is a crime under international law.

Wanton destruction of cities, towns, or villages, or devastation not justified by military necessity: The war in Vietnam has resulted in wanton destruction not only of cities and villages but of an entire country and its way of life. In South Vietnam most of the physical destruction is outside the cities. Hundreds of villages have been razed by U.S. firepower. Fields and jungles have been poisoned with chemical defoliants. The long-term ecological destruction wrought by these chemicals is as yet unknown, but the natural balance of the countryside has been destroyed over vast areas of the country. Water and fish are poisonous as a direct result of defoliant sprays. In the large areas of the country designated as free-fire zones anything is fair game—land, property, and most importantly people are all victims of the heavy artillery fire, napalm, gas, and antipersonnel bombs which constitute America's probably illegal arsenal in Vietnam [see chapter 7].

In the North, where the U.S. claimed to be bombing only military targets, disregard for internationally recognized limitations on bombing was blatant. According to the North Vietnamese, who invited international documentation of their charges, ninety-five hospitals and other health facilities, clearly marked with the red cross, were attacked from February 1965 through January 1967. Thirty-four of these devastated medical institutions were seen by an international investigating commission. Through December 1966, 391 schools were said to have been bombed.[6] These raids were not accidents, for many were repeated and many of the bombed institutions were far removed from any conceivable military targets. Maps with hospitals marked as targets on them have been found in the possession of U.S. pilots shot down over North Vietnam.[7]

The deliberate bombing of children at their schools and the destruction of medical facilities were cold-blooded calculations in an attempt to make the North Vietnamese people turn against their leadership. In terms of the principles the U.S. itself applied at Nuremberg, they are war crimes.

The guilty: Given the official encouragement to murder on a vast scale which is implicit in the indoctrination of American fighting men and in the weapons supplied to them, is it just or even honest for the army to point the finger of accusation at the particular murderers of civilians at Mylai? As the mother of one of the soldiers involved in this killing lamented, "I sent them a good boy, and they made him a murderer."[8] There is good reason to believe that American policy is making murderers of the majority of U.S. soldiers fighting in Vietnam, and the formulators of that policy—the country's highest civilian and military officials—are the ones who bear the ultimate responsibility for Mylai and its counterparts.

America, with all the devastating might that American know-how can muster, is waging a war in Indochina counter to all internationally recognized principles of humane warfare. Is it not time to consider whether good boys do indeed become murderers in this war and whether men who speak in terms of the highest principles of human freedom to justify their war policy are not in actuality committing crimes against humanity?

There will be no Nuremberg trial for Americans— America is too powerful for other nations to judge officially. But let it be recalled that at Nuremberg the United States accepted the principle that heads of state and high government officials should be held accountable for actions which international law defines as war crimes, and that all individuals are expected to adhere to a moral, not a criminal, code.[9]

The Myth of Mylai: A Soldier's View

Reporter Seymour Hersh's eloquent exposé of the massacre at Mylai of 502 "oriental human beings" produced a wave of general disbelief, followed (but only after the Pentagon owned up) by horrified shock. But for those of us who have served in Vietnam, there was no disbelief or shock, only mild surprise that Captain Medina and Lieutenant Calley (the officers accused by the army) could be so dumb as to murder so many in one place at one time. What the army was so quick to label "an isolated incident" is isolated for only two reasons: (1) the excessive number of civilian casualties, and (2) the amount of publicity generated.

Whether one is concerned with the deaths of a few innocent people such as are described in Daniel Lang's *Casualties of War,* or the destruction of an entire city and its inhabitants like Ben Tre which Air Force Major Chester L. Brown rationalized by saying, "It became necessary to destroy the town in order to save it," these acts must be examined in the context in which they occurred. What makes a Lieutenant Calley or a Major Brown believe that the killing of Vietnamese peasants is OK? What motivates the dozens of documented (and thousands of undocumented but just as real) cases of GI brutality and murder? The pattern is too widespread and regular to be explained by "battle stress" or "combat fatigue" of individual soldiers or units. The fact is that U.S. war crimes are an accepted and regularly used method of waging war in Indochina.

The following definition of war crimes has been adopted by the General Assembly of the United Nations: ". . . murder or ill-treatment of prisoners of war, killing of hostages, wanton destruction of cities, towns, or villages or other devastation." Obviously Mylai and Ben Tre violate this definition of international law, yet both events as well as many similar ones have had the official sanction of the Department of Defense. Indeed such operations are often a real source of pride.

The official encouragement and approval of murders of civilians can be seen in a policy which was begun several years ago at the time when it was becoming readily apparent that the U.S. was not going to win the war in Vietnam, at least not in the sense of capturing and securing vast objectives and "fronts." Since the traditional way of measuring battlefield success by territory captured was not valid for a guerrilla war, the Pentagon dreamed up a scheme called "the body count." Under this plan the army would release two sets of figures weekly. One would be U.S. KIA (killed in action), the other would be VC KIA. The idea was that if the U.S. could maintain a "kill ratio" of at least 10 to 1, the world would see how effective the American war machine was, and would know that we were winning. Never mind Tet of 1968 or Khe Sanh.

So the stage was set and the pressure was on. Washington demanded that Westmoreland start producing enemy bodies. Westmoreland passed on the word to all division commanders—"Bodies!" The division commanders put the pressure on their brigade commanders, who in turn leaned on the battalion commanding officers, who demanded that their company commanders and platoon leaders produce the necessary enemy KIAs to maintain that vital 10 to 1 ratio. The generals and colonels and majors don't pull triggers, so the entire burden of actually collecting the bodies falls on the Medinas and Calleys. And if the weight and obsession of the military hierarchy isn't enough, the units on the field come up with their own special inducements. Some have large scoreboards on which the enemy body count is kept. The April 7, 1970, *New York Times* carried a story about "ear boards," a brainchild of the Special Forces, who originated the idea by paying Cambodian and Montagnard mercenaries for each VC left ear they brought in. Units who report the highest body count get lavish commendation from the brass. The soldier who kills the most VC by himself during a certain period often gets a cash award or three days off to visit the seaside resort of Vung Tau, or even a five-day R and R (rest and recreation) to Hong Kong or Hawaii. Fistfights among GIs over who killed what VC are frequent, since the reward could be five days in Honolulu with the wife and kids.

Such pressure to produce more Vietnamese bodies is bound to lead to frequent murder of peasants who live near the field of action. GIs who are going to be rewarded for the number of corpses they can claim as "theirs" are naturally going to be less discriminating about who's a VC and who's not than soldiers under strict orders to protect the populace. Such overemphasis on body count also leads to frequent doubling, tripling, and quadrupling of the number of enemy killed. *Newsweek* on February 26, 1968, carried an article explaining how the Pentagon scaled down its count of VC KIA for Tet from the originally announced 30,000 to 7,000 after newsmen reported instances of widespread and deliberate overcounting of enemy and civilian bodies. Just as frequent is the counting of water buffalo and monkeys as enemy killed. And often bodies are added up where none of any kind exist at all.

Given the state of the military mind, then, what happened on March 16, 1968, in Mylai was just a blunder—an overdoing of an accepted way of dealing with the Vietnamese—although to those outside the military it was an atrocity.

The Myth of Mylai: Two Reporters' View[10]

Many Americans are justifiably horrified by reports of mass executions of civilians in Vietnam. The most recent incident at Songmy [Mylai], or "Pinkville," in Quang Ngai Province now centers around two servicemen, Lieutenant William Calley and Staff Sergeant David Mitchell, who stand accused of murder. Experience in Vietnam and Quang Ngai Province as journalists has led us to write this letter in hopes of dispelling two possible misapprehensions; that such executions are the fault of men like Calley and Mitchell alone, and that the tragedy of Songmy is an isolated atrocity.

We both spent several weeks in Quang Ngai some six months before the incident. We flew daily with the FACs (Forward Air Control). What we saw was a province utterly destroyed. In August 1967, during Operation Benton, the "pacification" camps became so full that army units in the field were ordered not to "generate" any more refugees. The army complied. But search-and-destroy operations continued.

Only now peasants were not warned before an air strike was called in on their village. They were killed in their villages because there was no room for them in the swamped pacification camps. The usual warnings by helicopter loudspeaker or air-dropped leaflets were stopped. Every civilian on the ground was assumed to be enemy by the pilots by nature of living in Quang Ngai, which was largely a free-fire zone.

Pilots, servicemen not unlike Calley and Mitchell, continued to carry out their orders. Village after village was destroyed from the air as a matter of de facto policy. Air strikes on civilians became a matter of routine. It was under these circumstances of official acquiescence to the destruction of the countryside and its people that the massacre of Songmy occurred.

Such atrocities were and are the logical consequences of a war directed against an enemy indistinguishable from the people.

CHAPTER 13

Vietnamization: New Rhetoric for

Old Objectives

In his November 3, 1969, speech President Nixon said, "In the previous Administration, we Americanized the war in Vietnam. In this Administration, we are Vietnamizing the search for peace." Nixon went on to define his Vietnamizing the search for peace as "a substantial increase in the training and equipment of South Vietnamese forces."

The Long History of "Vietnamization"

In fact, Nixon's Vietnamization program is neither as new as he claims it to be, nor is it a search for peace as he says. This is simply the old and discredited scheme of using Vietnamese to fight against Vietnamese. The French colonizers had used the very same plan and the very same terminology before—unsuccessfully. Since the Americans took over from the French colonizers, there have been continual attempts at Vietnamization. By 1954, when the United States tried to put Ngo Dinh Diem into power in the southern part of Vietnam (now known as South Vietnam), the total number of troops in this area was less than 50,000. They were the remnants of the defeated French

colonial force. By 1960 the United States had hel
build up the so-called South Vietnamese army of about
350,000 troops—armed, clothed, paid, and trained by
Americans. By 1965, the year that the United States decided to send American troops into Vietnam in great numbers, the size of the South Vietnamese army was at
500,000 men. Toward the end of the Johnson administration, the number went up to nearly 800,000. Now, under
the Nixon administration, the Saigon regime has 1 million
men under arms, in a country of about 14 million people.
In fact, the size of the Saigon army has always been listed
as three to four times larger than "enemy" forces.

ARVN's Unwillingness to Fight

In spite of this and in spite of the fact that the Saigon
army is much better equipped than "enemy" forces, American soldiers have had to do most of the fighting. This is
not because the South Vietnamese soldiers are not well-
trained and therefore cannot match the NLF forces without American assistance, but it is because they are simply
not willing to fight. On December 10, 1967, *Song* (a Saigon daily newspaper whose editor and staff were members
and leaders of the Rural Development Cadre Teams sponsored by the joint cooperation of the CIA and the USOM)
began a long article entitled "Looking at the Faces of the
Two Quang Provinces in War, Hunger, Misery, and Corruption" by saying:

> Not long ago newspapers [in the country] reported an
> attack on the province capital of Quang Ngai . . . The
> enemy forces did not exceed 100 men while in the
> province capital there were thousands of riflemen,
> many field-grade officers, and all kinds of brave-looking
> outfits. The police in white and striped clothes alone
> exceed the enemy forces by four times and *could have
> easily repulsed the enemy if they had wanted or cared
> to shoot.* [Emphasis added.]

A *New York Times* article on May 24, 1967, reported that—

> . . . Enemy forces overran Quang Tri city, the province capital, freed 250 guerrillas from jail and successfully attacked two regimental headquarters of the South Vietnamese First Infantry Division . . .
>
> A few days later, in a series of events that were not fully reported at that time, *they moved virtually unmolested in Hue, while the army and the national police fled.* [Emphasis added.]

Another example is the situation during the "Tet offensive" in the spring of 1968 when the Saigon army refused to engage NLF forces after the latter occupied most of the cities and towns in South Vietnam. Even General Thi, the South Vietnamese general in charge of the province of Vinh Long, when asked by an American adviser what he was going to do about the VC's invasion of the city of Vinh Long, was not willing to do anything at all, as he shrugged his shoulders and said: "If they succeed they succeed, and if they fail they fail."[1]

In the September 5, 1969, issue of *Quan Chung* (a Saigon magazine), Mr. Trinh Pho, a Vietnamese officer in the political warfare section of the South Vietnamese army, wrote a long article entitled "The Mobilization of Soldiers in a New Sweep" in which he demonstrated how terribly corrupt the Saigon army is and how the soldiers do not want to fight. In fact, he said that the only reason why the Saigon government drafts so many people into the army is to keep a check on them.

The Real Enemy in Vietnam

There are many reasons for the Saigon soldiers' unwillingness to fight. One of the most important reasons is the people that they are forced to fight against. In the words of an open letter from ninety-three South Vietnamese Catholic priests and intellectuals to American

Christians on the occasion of the first Moratorium Day, October 15, 1969: "Those whom the U.S.A. accuses in its ignorance as Communists, are in reality our relatives, our brothers, our sisters, our friends dispersed in villages and hamlets." Since most of the soldiers in the Saigon army are inducted by force from the villages and hamlets and since for the past six years or so American bombs, bullets, gas, chemical defoliants, etc., have been raining down upon the same villages and hamlets, the real enemies of the Saigon soldiers are not the so-called Communists but the Americans and the leaders in the Saigon government who are known to be accomplices in the slaughter of the Vietnamese people and the destruction of their country.

Another important reason for the Saigon soldiers' unwillingness to fight lies in the fact that the Saigon government is so corrupt that it does not want to pay its fighting men even enough for subsistence. A Saigon soldier receives 3,500 piasters a month (or about $10 at the black-market price). With this money, the soldier can buy about 100 pounds of rice at the official price, or only about 6 to 8 pounds of meat. If the soldier only buys rice and nothing else, then he will have enough to eat. But if he were to buy meat with his monthly salary it might last him for only two to three days. What about his wife, his children, and his parents who have to be fed and clothed?

The appallingly low salary of the soldiers, the hyperinflation caused by foreign spending, and the lack of food caused by the destructiveness of the war have forced many of the South Vietnamese soldiers' wives to become prostitutes and bar girls for the Americans. Saigon daily newspapers are full of stories of Vietnamese soldiers stealing to feed their families or committing suicide or homicide because their wives sleep with Americans or because the soldiers cannot feed their families. The Saigon leaders and generals, meanwhile, profit from the prolongation of the war. The June 23, 1970, *Newsweek* was confiscated in Saigon because it had an article on how Saigon leaders (including Thieu and Ky) had their wives transfer money abroad. An indication of how much Saigon generals and leaders can make from the war can be seen in the words of General Nguyen Khanh, who bragged to both the Vietnamese and American press that he had earned $10 million after becoming premier for only a few months.[2] The South Vietnamese soldiers do not see why they should fight and therefore cause destruction of their villages and hamlets and death and casualties of their brothers and sisters, their relatives and friends in order to protect the interest of a few leaders who are making merry in the cities.

If the United States insists on propping up the Saigon government against the Vietnamese people, it will have to keep its armies in Vietnam for a long time—in spite of Nixon's repeated use of the "Vietnamization" slogan and of his token withdrawal of American troops.

The Deception of Vietnamization

The use of the "Vietnamization" slogan has been effective here in the United States since its pleasant sound misleads the American public into thinking that President Nixon proposes to give Vietnam back to the people who live in it or that he will turn over the fighting to Vietnamese. The withdrawal of some American troops (250,000 by April 1971, provided that the Vietnamization program is going well) furthermore misleads the American people into believing that the Vietnamization program is successful, and that American troops will be withdrawn completely from South Vietnam in the near future. In reality, however, the withdrawal of American troops at the present rate is a ploy to lengthen the war instead of shortening it. The Nixon administration knows very well that after six years of wanton destruction of the Vietnamese land and Vietnamese society, it does not need a large force of 540,000 men to carry on the job. The Vietnamese capacity to resist ought to be less now, and therefore a smaller American force ought to be enough to keep the Saigon government in power, however precariously. Hence

Nixon's decision to withdraw some American troops.

The withdrawal of American troops, especially of the infantry (which is composed mostly of draftees) will first of all substantially decrease the amount of money spent. It now costs the United States about $40,000 to train and send an American boy to Vietnam to fight for a year. The reduction of about 250,000 troops will save the United States about $10 billion annually, which could then be spent in the production of more sophisticated and more destructive weapons to be used by the more than 200,000 professional soldiers left in Vietnam after April 1971. Secondly, the withdrawal of the draftees from the war will decrease the rate of American casualties in Vietnam, since most of the casualties are now suffered by these people.

By spending less money and by having fewer American casualties in Vietnam, Nixon hopes that opposition to the war in the United States will also be less, thus giving him a freer hand in carrying on the war for a much longer time. He thinks that perhaps with more time and more destructive weapons the Vietnamese will to resist and their capacity to resist will be worn out. On this score, the Nixon administration's Vietnamization program is exactly the same as the Johnson administration program, save for the terminology.

Nixon, however, went much farther than Johnson when he declared in his November 3 speech and repeatedly afterward that progress at the Paris peace talks depends on the progress of the Vietnamization program. Washington's decision in 1969 to downgrade the Paris peace talks, to launch an offensive in Laos, and recently, to invade Cambodia signify the failure of the Vietnamization program in Vietnam. What lies ahead is a longer and a wider war, with continued American involvement. President Thieu declared in a speech which was reported in *Dan Toc* and other Saigon newspapers on November 20, 1968, that he would make it impossible for the United States to withdraw its support. "Vietnamization" means that American policies are being dictated by the South Vietnamese generals.

CHAPTER 14

Mercenaries: Buying "Allies" for America's War

To most Americans, raised on schoolbook stories of the British attempt to suppress the American Revolution with Hessian hirelings, the word *mercenary* has distasteful, even shameful overtones. Indeed, America began its history as a nation by denouncing the tyranny of George III in the Declaration of Independence, accusing the British sovereign of these among other crimes:

> He has plundered our seas, ravaged our coasts, burnt our towns, and destroyed the lives of our people.
> He is, at this time, transporting large armies of foreign mercenaries to complete the works of death, desolation, and tyranny, already begun, with circumstances of cruelty and perfidy scarcely paralleled in the most barbarous ages, and totally unworthy the head of a civilized nation.

"Let Asians fight their own wars" seems at first glance a worthy sentiment, but the record of recent years reveals that it is not Asian freedom for which these "allies" are fighting, but Washington's paycheck.

Lacking conviction in the "domino theory," Southeast Asia's disinterest in fighting America's war against an "international Communist menace" is by now proverbial. As a result, for political and public relations reasons, the U.S. has felt compelled to offer financial inducement to susceptible segments of Asian society in order to create the impression that the U.S. is not alone in the Indochina war. Beginning with its patronage of the irregular tribal guerrillas inherited from the French colonial army, the U.S. has increasingly turned to mercenaries of all sorts and most recently has sought to institutionalize and legitimize the practice by the so-called "Vietnamization" process and in its policy toward Cambodia.

The "Irregular" Mercenary

Apparently from the outset of its involvement in Indochina, Washington recognized the possibilities of capitalizing upon traditional ethnic and religious animosities in encouraging Asians to fight Asians. The French army, frustrated by the pacifist outlook of the Buddhist Lao, Khmer, and Vietnamese people, had set the precedent by recruiting the animist hill tribes of Indochina into commando units which could be relied upon for bellicose behavior; these included the Meo, Nung, T'ai, and other "Montagnards" who for centuries have felt little affection for the culturally dominant Buddhist lowlanders.[1] Washington soon followed suit. As early as 1960, the U.S. was paying Meo mercenaries to fight in Laos, where defense of their profitable opium trade gave them added incentive. The mercenary tribesmen's usefulness as purveyors of terror under U.S. direction was evident and recruitment widened. In 1965, *New York Herald Tribune* reporter Jimmy Breslin described the behavior of the U.S.-paid guerrillas called Nungs:

> "We just rode Nungs, you can tell by the wire here," a Marine helicopter crewman told Breslin. "They get a VC and make him hold his hands against his cheeks. Then they take this wire and run it right through the one hand and right through his cheek and into his

mouth. Then they pull the wire out through the other cheek and stick in through the other hand. They knot both ends around sticks . . . Oh you ought to see how quiet them gooks sit in a helicopter when we get them wrapped up like that."

Although U.S. utilization of such mercenaries has grown apace, the public was kept in the dark until 1970, when congressional investigations finally dug out the truth about America's involvement in Laos. There our allies—the opium magnates, the Meos—now have taken over virtually the entire burden of the war from the hapless 25,000-man Royal Lao army, itself wholly created and financed by the State Department to function (at the cost of about $100 million a year) as "a military trip wire" to dramatize Communist encroachment so as to permit U.S. intervention if desired.[2] The absurdity of Washington's efforts to keep secret its patronage of the Meo *armée clandestine* was revealed in a recent interview by an American reporter of General Vang Pao, the Meo commander: Vang Pao denied he received even indirect American aid, but—

> as he was speaking, American F-4 Phantom jets roared overhead, several American observation planes were parked nearby and three cargo-laden American transport planes landed in quick succession at his official Sam Thong base. [Then Vang Pao] climbed into his unmarked American helicopter guarded by Laotians carrying American-made M-16 automatic rifles and was flown back to his secret headquarters by a three man American crew.[3]

On varying scales, U.S.-directed irregular mercenaries now ply their trade in all of Indochina. In South Vietnam, in at least sixty camps, Thai, Cambodian, and Vietnamese "Montagnards" are being integrated into the "Vietnamization" program.[4] In Cambodia, the U.S. Green Berets have long been working with the right-wing Khmer Serai, who share at least some of the responsibility for the overthrow of the neutral Sihanouk government.[5] And in the haven of Thailand, CIA camps now train Lao and Thai hill peo-

ples for long-range guerrilla forays into Laos and North
Vietnam. In fact, in Thailand the U.S. pays Thai troops to
fight a Meo insurrection, while in Laos it pays Meos to
fight a Lao insurrection.

"Regular" Foreign Troops as Mercenaries

The popularity of the mercenary concept at the Pentagon made it inevitable that the practice would not be
limited to tribal "irregulars." Among the first "regular"
forces to be utilized in mercenary roles were soldiers of
the army of Thailand, whose services have been purchased
by the U.S. for several years to fight in Laos in unmarked
uniforms or disguised as Royal Lao troops.[6] Such masque-
rading was soon impossible as Washington became increasingly desirous of employing foreign armies on a large
scale in Vietnam.

When American troops were committed to battle in
Vietnam in 1965, Washington felt keenly the lack of international support for its intervention. Despite verbal bel-
licosity on the part of Thailand and other SEATO governments, the U.S. found its Southeast Asian allies deeply
reluctant to join the effort to shore up the tottering Saigon
regime. After prolonged urgings apparently failed, Washington resorted to monetary rewards to tempt its "part-
ners" into participation. On September 16, 1966, substantial increases in U.S. economic aid to the Philippines
were announced. On the very next day, the first contingent
of Filipino forces was sent to Vietnam. According to Senate Foreign Relations Committee testimony, the Philippine
government's price was in the neighborhood of $38 mil-
lion.

A similar process, although more protracted, was involved in Washington's purchase of regular forces from
Thailand. Although the dispatch of Thai expeditionary
forces was announced in Bangkok in January 1967, none
arrived until nine months later—after an apparently pain-

ful bargaining process. That the U.S. bought Thai involvement was obvious, but the details of the deal were kept secret from the American people until June 1970, when Senate testimony was released revealing that the Thais were induced to join the fight against communism in South Vietnam for the price of $50 million a year— $200 million so far since their arrival in September 1967. The U.S. pays Thai soldiers an "overseas allowance" far in excess of their regular pay and provides quarters, rations, transport, equipment, and entertainment. In addition, supplemental bonuses are provided which can amount to as much as $6,000 per soldier.

Washington acquired another "free world partner" in the form of South Korean (ROK) army divisions which proved to be especially adept at the kind of terrorist tactics which U.S. forces have only sporadically been moved to utilize, such as the execution of every tenth person in a village.[7] In the wake of the Korean troops' arrival in South Vietnam, no one was surprised when, in January 1968, Washington granted Seoul a "special" military aid package of $100 million. Apparently this was not sufficient, for it was later revealed that at the Honolulu meeting between President Johnson and Korean President Chung Hee Park, the latter made Korea's continued participation in the war contingent upon a number of additional financial concessions—notably that the U.S. pay for the creation of an entirely new ROK division, wholly finance all ROK logistic personnel in Vietnam (approximately 16,000 men in support of 50,000 troops), and guarantee U.S. military intervention on behalf of South Korea in the event of a second Korean war.[8] Although driving a hard bargain, Korea, like other American "allies," has an overriding interest in the continued prosecution of the war. Just as Japan's postwar economy was given a boost by the apparently unending flow of U.S. "procurement" orders, so the Philippines, Thailand, Taiwan, and South Korea have come to rely heavily upon Washington's war-related spending on matériel and R and R (rest and recreation). Korea is said to receive $150–200 million annually (or up to one-fifth of her total foreign currency revenue) from the war—enough to finance her Five-Year Plan.

The Impact of Cambodia

The mercenary concept has been given added vigor as a consequence of the U.S. invasion of Cambodia. Among the first troops to penetrate beyond the twenty-one-mile limit imposed on U.S. forces were Khmer units, which for years had been fighting in Vietnam in the pay of the U.S. Green Berets. The Saigon army, which is entirely clothed, fed, armed, moved, and protected at U.S. expense and under U.S. direction, has now been given the hegemony of eastern Cambodia, a job they have taken on with unaccustomed zeal due to Saigon's territorial designs on certain portions of Cambodia. In the west, the Thais have agreed to send "volunteer" forces into western Cambodia. Untypically, Bangkok's announcement straightforwardly admitted that these troops would be armed and supplied by the U.S. Considering Thailand's centuries-old irredentist ambitions toward the westernmost provinces of Cambodia, Bangkok may have asked a lower price than when troops were dispatched to South Vietnam.

Washington's newest acquisition, of course, is the Cambodian army itself. Indeed, some observers have concluded that it was their envy of the Saigon army's officer corps—living high off U.S. salaries and PX supplies—that led the Cambodian army to overthrow the Sihanouk government and call for American aid. If so, their belief was well founded, for the Nixon administration quickly responded with a pledge of $7.9 million for the period April 22–June 30, 1970, and estimates are that the bill for the succeeding twelve months will come to $50–70 million.[9]

Thus has Washington given a new twist to the age-old mercenary profession. The U.S. not only pays Asians to fight Asians of other countries, but now, via the institution of "Vietnamization" (and soon, presumably, "Cambodianization"), hires Asian soldiers to fight in their own land against their own people—not for liberty or patriotism, but to defend the privilege, wealth, and power which Washington has bestowed upon the local military hierarchy.

CHAPTER 15

Elections in South Vietnam
and Laos: Facade for
Client Governments

To most Americans, Vietnam and Laos are obscure nations halfway around the world into which the U.S. every year pours massive amounts of her human and material treasure. Were it not for the image, constantly put before them by their leaders, of two small, democratic nations struggling nobly to defend themselves against external aggression and internal subversion by Communist forces, many of these Americans would find it difficult to justify so much of their money and so many of their sons being sacrificed in Southeast Asia. This point has not been lost on successive administrations in Washington who have flaunted elections before the American public to convey the impression that the U.S. effort in Indochina is in support of popularly elected governments and in defense of self-determination against an opposition that is portrayed as attempting to subvert true national self-expression.

Not only have elections in Vietnam and Laos been flagrantly abusive of anything that might remotely be called democratic, but, more basically, elections have been manipulated to ensure American political control through puppet or client governments. Far from helping to ensure that the will of the Vietnamese or Laotian peoples is carried out, the American-endorsed electoral record in the two countries is, in fact, one which has fairly consistently prevented any possibility of establishing indigenous, popular, genuinely representative governments. The pattern of American use of elections as tools for her own political ends becomes clearer when one turns to the recent electoral history of the two countries.

South Vietnam

In expounding its version of recent elections in Vietnam, the administration generally offers a threefold argument which holds that (1) in 1955 the South Vietnamese people voted not to reunite with the North but rather to become a separate nation under Ngo Dinh Diem; (2) in 1967 the current regime of Generals Thieu and Ky was popularly elected; and (3) the United States has consistently offered to allow a free and open election for settlement of the war, but the other side has consistently rejected this offer. A look at the historical record helps put these arguments in perspective.

The election of 1955: The French defeat at Dienbienphu left the Viet Minh in almost total control of Vietnam. Yet, even with complete victory throughout the country imminent, the Viet Minh agreed to withdraw its military forces to the North pending nationwide elections in 1956 in accord with the solution worked out at Geneva. The U.S., justifiably fearful that the national hero, Ho Chi Minh, would sweep the elections, moved almost immediately to undermine the Geneva accords and to set up an illegal, independent state in the South. President Eisenhower later admitted that there was no one he knew who was informed on Vietnam who did not agree that "possibly 80 percent" of the Vietnamese people would have chosen Ho Chi Minh in a free election.[1] With U.S. support, Ngo Dinh Diem returned to Vietnam from self-imposed exile in the U.S., was appointed premier by Head of State Bao Dai, and closed off the DMZ to turn it into a border between two countries, a clear violation of the Geneva treaty, which stated that the division line was provisional and "should not in any way be interpreted as constituting a political or territorial boundary." After rejecting the North's invitation to discuss arrangements for the 1956 elections as provided for at Geneva, and thus blocking the legal reunification of Vietnam, an elaborate election was staged between Diem and Bao Dai, who had already been ejected from the country. Ballot gimmickry prevented secrecy in voting, and reprisals for "wrong" voting were widespread. *Life* magazine reported on May 13, 1957, that American advisers had told Diem that a 60 percent "success" would have been quite sufficient, but Diem "insisted on 98%." That the election was something short of credible is evident by examining the returns. In Saigon, for example, Diem got 605,025 votes from a total of 450,000 registered voters.[2]

Three days after the election, a Republic of South Vietnam was declared by Diem with himself as the first president. The subversion of the Geneva agreement, a solution that would have spared the U.S. its costly involvement and saved the Vietnamese people the unimaginable suffering this involvement has brought about, was complete. Despite continued appeals to Saigon by the North to discuss plans for the 1956 elections, July 20, 1956, the agreed-upon date for national reunification, passed uneventfully.

The election of 1967: This election, upon which President Thieu and Vice-President Ky base their claim to legitimacy, was prevented from being a true contest between the various political forces that exist in South Vietnam. Although a convenient fiction for the attempt to justify the U.S. government's preference in South Vietnam, and despite the wide publicity they have been given by Saigon and Washington, these elections were carefully organized and controlled by the military men who were themselves theoretically mere candidates. The National Assembly (which was itself elected on September 11, 1966, under an electoral law which barred all those who "work directly or indirectly for Communism or Neutralism"[3]) was given the task of establishing the basis for the elections. A committee of the Assembly decided to exclude Thieu and Ky from the ballot because they had not answered a summons to explain why they had not resigned their military offices as required by the Constitution. At the full Assembly's "first reading," General Duong Van "Big" Minh, hero of the coup which overthrew Diem and living in exile in Thailand, and Au Truong Thanh, former finance minister under Ky who had announced that he would campaign on a straight peace platform, were included on the ballot. Marshal Ky immediately announced that Minh could not return from exile and that police had discovered that Thanh was a Communist. The Assembly then met for a second time "in an atmosphere of tension heightened by the discovery that the head of the National Police, the notorious General Nguyen Ngoc Loan, and two of his lieutenants, armed with automatic rifles, were leaning over the balcony rail above them observing loudly that those who did not heed their words would hear their guns." Not surprisingly, the Assembly quickly reversed its own committee and itself by including Thieu and Ky on the ballot and excluding Minh and Thanh.[4]

Not content to settle for a sure thing, the Thieu–Ky regime continued its manipulation. Rules to restrict campaigning to one month before the election were flagrantly violated by Ky, while he insisted that other candidates adhere to them. Opposition candidates were harassed, detained, and transported by the regime's vehicles to places often miles from their waiting audiences. Parties advocating a neutralist solution were at times prohibited, and the press was heavily censored, an act which violated the Constitution and embarrassed the American embassy. Excluded as voters were all those living in "insecure" areas, which meant those areas controlled all or part of the time —usually at night—by the NLF, and those voters con-

sidered "unreliable," which in South Vietnam means people believed to be sympathetic to the NLF, peace, or
neutralism, all of which are considered synonymous with
communism.[5] When the balloting finally took place, many
army men voted the Thieu–Ky ticket twice (where stationed and at home), and there were frequent reports of
ballot frauds and miscounts by the senior election officials, who were often Ky appointees.

Even with this massive American-sanctioned effort, the
Thieu–Ky ticket managed only 34.8 percent of the vote;
the opposing candidates totaled 65 percent. (Thieu himself had estimated before the election that he would receive 40 to 50 percent and observed that it would be
impossible to govern with less than 40 percent.) Fraud
and intimidation on a massive scale had failed, but Thieu
and Ky had been elected. Even Ambassador Ellsworth
Bunker, when the returns were in, admitted that "it represents the desire of the country, of everyone, for peace."[6]
But peace would have meant, at the very least, the full
participation of the various political elements in the struggle for Vietnam. And this the Americans and the ruling
junta in Saigon could not and would not allow. The NLF,
which U.S. policy supporter Douglas Pike has described
as the only "truly mass-based political party in South Vietnam,"[7] was automatically excluded from participation. So
too were those candidates and voters who might favor a
neutralist solution, or, at the very least, negotiations with
the other side. Indeed, the surprising runner-up in the
election, Truong Dinh Dzu, was put in prison for talking
about "peace" and "neutrality" in his campaign. Thus,
much like the Vietnamization program today, the election
of 1967 shored up the hold on power of a narrowly based
clique of generals, and made sure that the war would continue. The losers were the Vietnamese people, many of
whom must have shared the feelings of Binh Kien, then
vice-president in charge of current affairs of the 25,000-
member General Association of Saigon Students, who declared at a meeting six days after the election to which
the presidential candidates had been invited (three, in-

cluding Dzu, went): "The elections of September 3 were nothing but a farce conducted by foreigners."[8]

Thus the elections of 1955 and 1967, as well as the consistent actions of the U.S. and the generals in Saigon, stand as chilling rebukes to the American contention that it has consistently offered to allow free and open elections to end the war. Perhaps the war would end if all political groups were honestly allowed to participate, but the results would probably not make Washington happy. But all this is not to say that if only fairly honest elections could be carried out in Vietnam, then all would be well again in that fractured nation. For the elections that have taken place in South Vietnam, despite all the fanfare that U.S. presidents and Vietnamese military men have surrounded them with, are largely peripheral to the lives and struggle of the great majority of Vietnamese. What makes them important is the way they have been staged and used by a small clique of power-hungry men in Saigon as well as by the U.S. government to deny peace and social progress to Vietnam. Each, for its own reasons, desperately needs an electoral mantle of legitimacy no matter how spurious: Thieu and Ky, so that the Americans will continue to provide them with the means without which they could not stay in power; the U.S., to try and convince its own citizens and the world that its cause in Vietnam is just. Until this unholy alliance is ended, there can be neither a truly popular, representative government nor peace in Vietnam.

Laos

As in Vietnam, U.S. money and influence have been used in Laos to manipulate elections. While useful to certain cliques in Vientiane as well as the U.S., these electoral charades have been largely irrelevant to the unsolved social problems of the majority of Laotians. They have, in fact, played an almost negligible role in the political life of the nation, only serving to further polarize the contending forces in its civil conflict. The U.S. role in the Laotian electoral process has been either to undermine the results of a reasonably fair attempt to bring different elements into the government, or to attempt to legitimize a rightist seizure of power that has come about by more direct means. U.S. manipulation of Laotian elections can be seen by briefly examining the three elections since the Geneva agreement of 1954, those of 1955, 1958, and 1960.

The election of 1955 was a rather inconclusive affair. The government in Vientiane under the leadership of Katay, who was partly of Vietnamese origin, used strong-arm tactics in talks with the Pathet Lao over terms for national reconciliation. This heightened the sense of distrust on both sides and led to the breakdown of discussions. Katay was undoubtedly emboldened by a new economic agreement with the U.S. in July 1955 which provided for increased direct military aid.[9] The Pathet Lao did not participate in the December election, rendering the results, which indicated a majority for none of the four parties which took part anyway, meaningless.

The election of May 1958 was the only one which even deserves the name. Leftist candidates were allowed on the ballot, and, despite U.S. attempts to influence the outcome, they won thirteen of the twenty-one seats contested. With such results, Pathet Lao leaders should have been invited to join the government, but the U.S. was alarmed at the prospect of their success. Thus the U.S. suspended economic aid, which now amounted to all but a fraction of the Laotian budget.[10] Souvanna Phouma, then prime minister, knew as well as anyone that his country had become a client state; he made a series of concessions to the right in an attempt to keep the Americans from destroying the delicate hope for national reconciliation that the elections had brought about. But the U.S. was now determined to overthrow Souvanna in favor of someone more pliable and more militantly anti-Pathet Lao. They wanted to "install a reliably pro-Western regime," in the words of Arthur Schlesinger, Jr.[11] To the withholding of aid, the U.S. added

bribery. In the maneuverings that followed the inaugura-
tion of the new Assembly, "allegedly with the enticement
of monetary bribes distributed by the P.E.O. [Programs
Evaluation Office, staffed by soldiers out of uniform and
set up in 1958 to administer U.S. military aid] and C.I.A.,
a sufficient number of deputies were persuaded to block
Souvanna's reappointment."[12] Through such machinations,
the U.S. succeeded in bringing down Souvanna. On August 18 a new government was formed under the more
right-wing Phoui Sananikone, from which the Pathet Lao
was excluded.

The election of 1960 was blatantly rigged. The Phoui
government, after dismissing certain right-wing ministers
from the cabinet in December 1959, was brought down
by right-wing military elements, led by General Phoumi
Nosavan and backed by the CIA and PEO.[13] The ensuing election of April 1960, meant to legitimize the military coup, has not been taken seriously in diplomatic cir-
cles. General Phoumi and his compatriots so rigged things
that defeat was impossible. The CIA felt it again necessary to engage in open monetary bribes.[14] The fourteen
Pathet Lao and Peace candidates, of course, all failed.
One hapless man voted for himself along with a dozen
members of his family and still polled no votes![15]

Although elections have not been very meaningful in
Laos, the pattern of U.S. manipulation of their results is
perfectly consistent with the U.S. involvement in the political life of the country in general. By preventing the
national reconciliation that alone can bring peace to the
Laotian people, blatantly evident in such actions as the undermining of the neutralist Souvanna after the 1958 election, the U.S., as in Vietnam, continues cynically to prolong
the war in Indochina in the name of anticommunism.
Those who benefit from this U.S. intervention are not the
citizens of democratically elected governments; rather,
they are a handful of military and civilian clients in Saigon
and Vientiane who themselves manipulate the U.S. aid, on
which they depend for survival, toward their personal ends.

CHAPTER 16

Military Censorship in Vietnam:

Nonnews and False Views

Military censorship in Vietnam comes in two forms: the "nonnews," or subjects *never* to be mentioned, and the more subtle method of contriving information, rearranging facts, and disseminating false statistics.

Nonnews Taboos

The "nonnews" taboos are explicitly stated, usually verbally, by officials from the information offices in Saigon: MACOI (Military Advisory Command Office of Information); MACV (Military Advisory Command Vietnam); and JUSPAO (Joint United States Public Affairs Office). Military censorship directives usually come from MACOI, MACV, or the various subordinate commanders and chiefs of staff in the field. Matters concerning U.S. policy, foreign affairs, Special Forces, or the CIA usually fall under the jurisdiction of JUSPAO.

The "nonnews" list is long, and constantly increasing in size. But a partial list would include:

1. Ineffectiveness or mistakes of ARVN (Army of the Republic of Vietnam)

2. Handling, processing, interrogation, or treatment of POWs
3. Shotguns, flamethrowers, lethal or nonlethal gas, napalm
4. Female or very young VC
5. Malfunctions of the M-16 rifle
6. The CIA or Air America
7. Ambushes or defeats of U.S. units
8. The term NLF (National Liberation Front)
9. Enemy tenacity, courage, or ingenuity
10. Marriage of U.S. personnel and Vietnamese
11. GI use of marijuana, hashish, or opium

It should be noted, however, that this "nonnews" is self-imposed and that enterprising civilian reporters like Don Webster of CBS or AP's Peter Arnett often bypass military information channels and get the stories directly from the individuals concerned, thus end-running the army's attempt to muffle certain subjects. The military, of course, goes to great pains in order to discourage this sort of honesty, from direct presidential pressure in the case of Arnett,[1] to carefully staged attempts by the Pentagon to discredit network TV news of the war.[2]

The Censorship of Deception

However, most war correspondents depend a great deal on military information channels, and even if they become quite adept at reading between the lines for the "nonnews," it is still quite easy for them to fall prey to the censorship of deception.

This form of underhanded news control is widespread in Indochina, and takes a variety of forms. One of these is the *use of semantics*. Prior to 1968 most U.S. operations were known as search and destroy. But as world opinion and antiwar campaigns began to scrutinize American methods of conducting the war, search and destroy was replaced by search and clear, a much less offensive term.[3]

Another frequent method is the *juggling of figures,* especially in regards to enemy "body count." It is official MACV policy that no matter how little contact occurs, VC losses will always be at least two thousand per week. To meet this figure, each combat division is given a minimum quota of enemy to *report* killed. This pressure to produce "tangible results" frequently *results* in civilian murders or a greatly distorted kill count.[4]

There is also a *military information double standard.* In November 1967, the Information Office of the Twenty-fifth Infantry Division submitted a story on female VC to MACV and MACOI for clearance. The story related an incident in which an enemy "point girl" was killed by an American ambush patrol. MACV cleared the story for release, but MACOI nixed it, saying "stories of U.S. troops killing women draws a bad light on our forces. A girl killed in an ambush at night doesn't help our image." The effect of this split decision was to deny the story to civilian news media, but release it for use by military publications.[5]

Harassment of Reporters

Harassment, intimidation, and prosecution are all directed at military information personnel who try to tell the whole truth about the war. A USARV directive, the *Colonel's Kernals,* dated December 1967, says:

> . . . there are a few military IOs (Information Officers) out here who are not playing on the team. On occasion these guys have downgraded one or another of the programs the U.S. is trying so hard to make work in Vietnam—and have done their sounding off to the press yet! . . . To argue your case in the press is not to show the courage of your convictions; it's a betrayal of a trust. It's disloyal.

To ferret out these "disloyal" soldiers, MACOI sends out army spies armed with fake press cards to act as reporters.

These "newsmen" visit various suspected information offices and try to trick information personnel into speaking "disloyal words."[6] Even civilian reporters can get into hot water over certain taboo news. Merton Perry of *Newsweek* did an exposé on Vietnamization in 1967 entitled "Their Lions—Our Rabbits." Perry's critical appraisal of ARVN almost cost him, and his bureau chief, Everett Martin, their jobs—and the October 8, 1967, issue of the magazine in which the article appeared was banned and confiscated in Vietnam.[7] The most recent blatant persecution of GIs for honest reporting revolves around the AFVN (Armed Forces Vietnam Radio and TV Network) newscasters. Sp/5 Robert Lawrence, Sp/5 Michael Maxwell, and Sergeant Hugh Morgan were all transferred to combat duty and charged with violation of military regulations after making open charges of censorship over the air.[8]

And even the ordinary soldier in Vietnam is told what he can and cannot say in letters home, or speeches after he gets back. MACV and USARV Command Information channels direct a constant barrage of intimidating and threatening instructions regarding what can be said. The directives make it plain that the army can and would and has taken action against anyone they feel is violating the rules of information disclosure. One such directive states: "It's just common sense to avoid getting into matters involving our country's foreign policy."[9]

These examples represent only a fraction of the kind and extent of censorship in Indochina. But they illustrate the all-out efforts of the Pentagon to keep the truth about the war from the American people and the GIs serving in Vietnam. Army censorship is not an antiwar slogan. It is a military fact.

CHAPTER 17

Executive Deception: Brainwashing the United States

Like most wars, the Indochina conflict has been a two-front struggle, requiring support at home as well as success abroad. As escalation and lack of success abroad have intensified the war's unpopularity at home, the home front has increasingly held center stage. Little wonder, then, that President Johnson's charge to Vice-President Humphrey, bound for Asia on a sudden mission in February 1966, was to return to Washington with a report that would "nail, once and for all, Fulbright, Mansfield, and the editorial board of the *New York Times.*" Little wonder, too, that the genial and trusting Governor George Romney later complained of having been "brainwashed" by his own countrymen on his 1967 fact-finding tour of Vietnam.

Intentional Deception

Executive branch deception of the American public is a highly complex phenomenon. In part, the deception has been coolly *intentional*—as in the White House decision to demand a long-desired congressional resolution in Au-

157

gust 1964 on the pretext of the Tonkin Gulf incidents, despite grave internal doubts as to whether the attacks had really happened at all. Here, as is frequently the case, critically significant information was consciously withheld from the Congress and the public. To cite another example, persistent denial of America's actual massive military involvement in Laos was intentional under three administrations until the press and Congress forced belated disclosures in 1969–70.

Indeed, Americans have been intentionally deceived— or more bluntly, lied to—at almost every step of the war's escalation: on the facts and figures of U.S. involvement throughout Indochina, on the true nature of the war (foreign "aggression"? foreign "subversion"? international Communist conspiracy? internal revolution?), on the pretexts for bombing the North, on the hiring of Asian mercenaries (Koreans, Thais, and symbolic Filipinos), on the results of "pacification," on the content and actual consequences of U.S. "peace overtures," on the nature of the South Vietnamese regimes we have supported, and on North Vietnamese and NLF intentions.

Self-Deception

In part, however, the process of deception has also been *unintentional*. Much of the rhetoric and many of the actions that have accompanied our Indochina involvement have been ad hoc responses to situations of stress: a cumulative series of reflex moves and lunges produced by deepening executive anxiety, defensiveness, alarm, desperation, and even (in the late Johnson era and perhaps today) a sensed state of siege. Kennedy's "adviser" increase of 1961, Johnson's decision to bomb the North, Nixon's invasion of Cambodia have all been produced by such states of mind—and have all required a simplified (and hence grossly distorted) rationale. Similarly, in rhetoric, Johnson on our "national honor," Humphrey on "a billion Chinese . . . with nuclear weapons," Nixon on Hanoi's alleged unwillingness to negotiate, and both administrations on the goal of "peace with honor"—all have misled the public more out of exasperation and ignorance rather than intent. At the root of executive deception, it must be said, is a vast amount of executive self-deception—or, again to put it bluntly, stupidity.

Executive deception is also, in part, *personal*—the outgrowth, in Mr. Johnson, of an obsession with secrecy and manipulation; and in Mr. Nixon, of a bent for the selling of policy as television personalities sell detergents. The result, in both cases, is a highly selective airing of the truth.

Institutional Deception

Finally, and perhaps most important, such deception is heavily *institutional*. Here the root cause is what C. P. Snow has termed the "closed politics" of policy making—the tendency of decision makers to narrow the circle of those consulted as issues become critical. In Washington the "need to know" criterion for access to classified papers has systematically excluded from major decisions those specialists best equipped to evaluate vital data and recommendations; and the result has been decisions based—and publicly defended—on inadequate and misleading information. The external manifestation of "closed politics" is, of course, the perennial assurance, "We have the facts; trust *us*."

One further cause of institutional deception is the hydra-headed pluralism of the government itself. As one highly placed State Department executive put it in the autumn of 1969, "The problem is not so much that the President and Secretary of State lie to the people about what is going on in Laos; it is rather that the President and Secretary are *lied to* by the component parts of government in Washington and the field." It was ironic but predictable, he added, that Nixon would finally learn exactly how many Americans were at work in Laos not from the executive agencies involved, no matter how hard he pressed the question, but from the shrewd staff investigators of the Symington subcommittee.

The True Believers

There is, of course, an additional aspect of executive deception that cannot be ignored: the presence in each post-World War II administration of a handful of "true believers"—men who practice neither intentional nor unintentional deception about Southeast Asia but instead relentlessly adhere to a rigid ideological overview. To Foster Dulles, Rusk, and Rostow, and to a number of lesser lights, Vietnam and Indochina scarcely existed except as pawns in a grander struggle: between good and evil, the right and the wrong, freedom and servitude. Such men cannot be accused of deception: only of grandiosity and ignorance. But such men, though powerful at times, have been rare. The Indochina war is more the product of self-styled pragmatists than of true believers.

Given the complexity and persistence of executive deception—of governmental "brainwashing," in George Romney's term—it is little surprise that the "credibility gap" remains so painfully difficult to close.

The Executive Approach to Indochina

The sad fact of the matter is that each American president who has fallen heir to the Indochina crisis—in 1953, 1961, 1963, and 1969—has believed himself to be confronted by one constant and intractable set of problems:

1. He must, he believes, achieve "success" in Indochina. Thanks to the "loss" of China and its impact upon the Democrats, success to each president has meant a non-Communist outcome in South Vietnam; otherwise, the dominoes may start falling—and the one significant domino is clearly his own administration. From the beginning,

then, Indochina becomes a domestic issue; its "loss" will cause defeat at home.

2. He must therefore keep funds flowing to achieve the necessary success; and this means maintaining strong congressional and public support for the Indochina involvement. Hence the careful solicitude toward key committee chairmen—notably Armed Services and Appropriations, in both houses.

3. He must also therefore produce, or at least strongly emphasize, good news and progress from the war. Hence the stress on inflated "body counts" and indexes of "pacification." So Johnson sought (and bought) "more flags" and invented "the allies" to cover our singular aloneness; so Johnson saw the Tet offensive in 1968 as a major U.S. victory. So Nixon seeks "Vietnamization" to cover our continuing aloneness; so Nixon sees the dismemberment of Cambodia in 1970 as a major U.S. victory.

4. To guard against the inevitability of bad news and setbacks (loss of American lives, for instance), it becomes necessary to keep before the American public—and to escalate, if necessary—the significance of the conflict. Hence the striking tendency toward oversell: the spiraling assertions that our "prestige," our "word," our "national honor," our "will"—indeed, the American Experiment itself—are all at stake in the Indochina outcome. In the process, of course, Indochina becomes vital to our national security quite simply (and solely) because four American presidents have *said* that it is vital to our security.

5. In this regard, those who focus on the bad news, and those who question the very significance of the region to U.S. national security—whether journalists, newscasters, congressmen, scholars, or others—should be countered, if not muzzled. This, too, can become an escalating process, with repressive consequences ever drawing nearer. Kennedy found our Saigon press corps a dangerous nuisance; Johnson turned against his two doubting secretaries of defense; Agnew comes close to calling Fulbright and Harriman traitors.

6. Those most dependable (and, in the past, quite effective) in countering the critics are high officials with classified "inside information" and especially the post-World War II "professionals" in national security matters, notably the generals and admirals. Such military officers, who have their own special stake in the war [see chapter 29], are regularly paraded before the Congress, the press, and the public. Hence the Pentagon's vast annual budget of over $40 million for public relations. Hence, too, the very early militarization of American involvement in Vietnam.

7. Most effective, however, as a way to avert criticism and opposition, is to bypass entirely close scrutiny by the Congress, the press, and even substantial portions of the bureaucracy, who might leak their doubts to the press or Capitol Hill. This is best done through use of covert (and therefore "deniable") instruments to achieve success without raising obstructive questions—hence such disparate moves as large-scale CIA operations throughout Indochina, bypassing Congress, and planning for the Cambodian invasion through a specially constituted high-level interagency unit, bypassing specialists and critics within the bureaucracy.

Consequences of the Flight from Candor

Such, then, are the dimensions of the problem each president has inherited, perceived, and enlarged. In each case he has had a fleeting opportunity to reexamine and disinvest. In each case, out of ignorance, momentum, or most likely fear of the domestic consequences (in the past ten years each president has judged that his real problem lies with "the hawks," "the right-wing backlash," "neo-isolationism"), the chief executive has embarked on a tragic flight from candor in dealing with his own countrymen. The result, time and again, has been distortion of reality, escalation of rhetoric, intensification of secrecy, circumvention of Congress, manipulation of the press, and hoodwinking of the public—and increasing death and destruction for the people of Indochina.

At the root of the process of executive deception is a persistent and destructive effort to simplify, for the nation's consumption, three things: an inordinately complex geopolitical situation in Southeast Asia, a cumulative policy blunder, and a cumulative American failure. Whatever the temporary successes, this effort at simplification seems, in the long run, disastrously self-defeating. Lack of candor on the home front promises to compound the terrible harm done to Indochina by inflicting deep and abiding harm on American society itself.

CHAPTER 18

The Indochina War and
International Law

One comparison often made by Westerners between the "West" and the "East" is that the "East" is somehow morally inferior because it has not developed the concept of "law," and the corollary concepts of legality and illegality. Westerners pride themselves on their legal systems and institutions, and on the resultant order these have allegedly imparted to their society. The United States, moreover, has attempted to justify its actions in Indochina on the grounds of international law. In fact, in the view of innumerable law scholars, American actions in Indochina have on the contrary been characterized by an appalling disregard of established law.

The United Nations Charter

Article 2, Section 3, states: "All members shall settle their international disputes by peaceful means in such a manner that international peace and security, and justice, are not endangered." Section 4 states: "All members shall refrain in their international relations from the threat or use of force against the territorial integrity or political independence of any state . . ."

The record is overwhelmingly clear that the U.S. has not abided by this provision of the UN Charter, of which it was one of the principal architects. The administration has commonly attempted to justify its actions by citing Article 51 of the UN Charter, which reads, "Nothing in the present Charter shall impair the inherent right of individual or collective self-defense if an armed attack occurs against a member of the United Nations, until the Security Council has taken the measures necessary to maintain international peace and security. . . ."

This article does not mitigate the illegality of U.S. actions in any way. It is invalid as a justification for two reasons: (1) No "armed attack" had occurred when the U.S. radically escalated the conflict by bombing North Vietnam in February 1965 [See Chapter 22.] An armed attack refers specifically to a situation such as Germany's attack on Poland in 1939. This phrase was used to guard against precisely what has happened, that is, any provocation being termed sufficient ground for massive reprisal. The SEATO Treaty makes explicit this distinction when, in Article 2, it refers to "armed attack" *and* "subversive activity." Even if, contrary to fact, it is assumed that North and South Vietnam are separate and discrete political entities, the protagonists prior to our entry into the conflict were the government of South Vietnam and South Vietnamese insurgents outraged by the oppression of the Diem regime. Subversion there was, but it was led and executed by native elements, with minimal aid and direction from anyone else. (2) Using the term *self-defense* to refer to the military efforts of the government of South Vietnam and hence U.S. aid to them assumes that there is a "self," that is, the government of South Vietnam, and an "other," that is, North Vietnam. But Vietnam is one country, divided into *temporary zones* in 1954 as a practical measure to allow defeated French troops to withdraw in an orderly manner. Any actions by any Vietnamese against the government of South Vietnam then constitute civil conflict, within the "self," and not the "self" against some "other" force.

The Geneva Accords of 1954

At the Geneva conference to settle the first Indochinese war, the French admitted defeat at the hands of the Viet Minh forces led by Ho Chi Minh. Ho agreed, however, at the insistence of China and Russia, to temporarily remove his forces from areas which in fact his troops already controlled, in order to allow for the orderly disengagement of the two forces. [See Part I] The accords further stated that elections would be held in two years to choose a government for all of Vietnam. In the intervening two years, there would be two zones in Vietnam, the South, administered by the French, and the North, administered by Ho. No foreign country was allowed to subvert these arrangements by introducing any war personnel or matériel. The United States Final Declaration explicitly stated that "the Government of the United States . . . will refrain from the threat or the use of force to disturb [the agreements] . . . in accordance with Article 2 [Section 4] of the Charter of the United Nations dealing with the obligation of Members to refrain in their international relations from the threat or use of force."

The U.S. then proceeded to install and support Diem, giving him $325 million in 1955 alone. The U.S. supported his obstinate refusal to even discuss arrangements for the stipulated elections. U.S. commitment to the government of South Vietnam increased in the form of military advisers (10,000 by 1962), in direct violation of its own Declaration, and the bombing in 1965 followed.

SEATO and "Past Commitments"

It has been stated by the administration that the SEATO Treaty (Article 4, Section 1) creates an "obligation . . . to meet the common danger in the event of armed aggression." It has also argued that the "assurances" of Presidents Eisenhower and Kennedy have very nearly obligated the U.S. to act as it has. The attempt of both these arguments is to make it seem as though the U.S. really had no choice in the matter—its actions have been predetermined by events in the past, it was "locked in" by previous arrangements. It is apparently hoped that by shifting the responsibility to seemingly impersonal factors, U.S. escalations will somehow be more palatable. The fact is, however, that SEATO places the U.S. under no "obligation" in this situation, and the "assurances" of Presidents Eisenhower and Kennedy were much more limited than the administration presents them.

The SEATO Treaty, first of all, explicitly states that its provisions are subordinate to the UN Charter: "This Treaty does not affect and shall not be interpreted as affecting in any way the rights and obligations of any of the Parties under the Charter of the United Nations . . ." Since U.S. actions have violated the UN Charter, they have clearly violated the SEATO Treaty as well. Secondly, while the provisions of SEATO give the United States the *right* to intervene militarily in case of an armed attack, they create no *obligation* to do so. But the crucial fact is that no armed attack had occurred when the U.S. entered the war. In fact, two leading members of SEATO—Pakistan and France—have publicly denounced the United States' claim that it is legally bound by SEATO to intervene, and are opposed to American policy entirely.

With regard to the "assurances" of former administrations, President Eisenhower stated that his administration had made no commitments to South Vietnam "in terms of military support or programs whatsoever." And President Kennedy, although he sent advisers, made clear that the war in Vietnam was "their war": "We can help them, we can give them equipment, we can send our men out there as advisors, but they have to win it, the people of Vietnam." These quite limited "assurances" by no means made the decisions to start bombing North Vietnam and to send combat troops to Vietnam in 1965 inevitable.

The United States Constitution

In summary then, the United States government, by its actions in Vietnam, has violated three solemn international agreements. Since these treaties have all been ratified by the government they thus become the law of the land, and any violation of them by any branch of the government constitutes a violation of the Constitution.

CHAPTER 19

The Vietnamese–American

Negotiations

The issue of negotiations has been prominently debated in the U.S. since the American escalation of the Vietnam war. The various administrations involved at first rejected negotiations altogether. Then, at intervals after April 1965, they have tried to give the impression that the U.S. government is anxious to negotiate and is flexible about terms, while the "other side" is unreasonably obstructing a peaceful settlement. The facts suggest quite a different picture.

The government of the Democratic Republic of Vietnam (Hanoi) and the NLF have indeed presented firm negotiating positions and have altered them only cautiously. But firmness and caution do not spell unreasonableness. The "other side" is engaged in the defense of its own country and people against the intrusion of the world's most powerful military machine. For them, national independence and survival are at stake. There is no room for flamboyant gestures, designed to dazzle distant observers unfamiliar with the situation at the price of national sovereignty. The irreducible minimum of their position is that Vietnamese alone should determine Vietnamese affairs. About this, there is no room for fundamental

169

compromise. Nevertheless, despite the limits within which they must operate, the NLF and Hanoi have consistently shown an interest in negotiations and have taken a series of concrete moves designed to facilitate a negotiated settlement.

From 1955 to 1965 the American government rejected the idea of negotiating with "the enemy," and even after 1965 added all sorts of obstructive qualifications to its expressions of interest. It has tried to create the appearance of flexibility, while maintaining throughout an unrelenting commitment to one particular resolution of the war. Though it attempts to paper over the fact, its position has always been and still is that the present Saigon government, or some twin emerging from the next military coup or from carefully controlled elections, must dominate the future of South Vietnam. In the context of a civil war, this is the equivalent of insisting on military victory. In the politics of Vietnam, it is the equivalent of insisting on a continuing American voice in the affairs of Vietnam. This is not movement toward a negotiated settlement. It is not being flexible. For a totally external, alien force, intervening without legal or moral basis in the vital affairs of another country, it is not reasonable.

Let us look at the circumstances which bear upon the state of the Vietnamese-American negotiations, and consider (1) some features of the historical and military context of the negotiations which are often ignored; (2) the history of efforts to negotiate, as they reveal the interest of the two sides in negotiations; and (3) the negotiating positions as they have emerged since the start of full-scale negotiations in January 1969.

The Context

It used to be part of American conventional wisdom to believe that "Communists always betray agreements." In the complexity of international relations, the number of agreements which have been fully kept by any sort of government is probably a minority of the total. But there is no special disposition on the part of Communist governments (which in any case differ one from another on all sorts of matters) to ignore their international pledges. The old myth lingers on, however, and prevents Americans from taking the risks for peace that they do for war.

Ironically, in the actual history of negotiations over the fate of Vietnam, the "other side" has much more reason to complain of betrayed agreements. When Ho Chi Minh established an independent government for all Vietnam in 1945, the French agreed the next year to recognize it in return for major concessions from Ho, but immediately set about violating that agreement and sabotaging the Vietnamese government. After a long war for Vietnamese independence, the Geneva accords of 1954 established conditions and procedures for the re-creation of a single Vietnamese government over all Vietnam, within two years from the date of the accords. The United States undermined the accords by supporting and encouraging the separatist Saigon government in its noncooperation. The aftermath of the Geneva agreements of 1962 over Laos, which the U.S. government cites as an example of Communist perfidy, is actually a case of American violation of her public pledges.[1] So those whom the U.S. government has taken as its enemies in Indochina have more reason to wonder how much to risk for peace. If the U.S. government is cautious about entering an agreement with the NLF or Hanoi, how much more wary *they* must be of rushing into a settlement before American intentions are absolutely clear.

There is another difference between the two sides which bears upon their attitude toward negotiations. The NLF forces and the North Vietnamese units fighting with them in South Vietnam (the point applies to situations in Laos and Cambodia as well) are extremely dependent upon morale. In order to endure the hardships and suffering which are a part of resisting the world's richest and most highly developed arsenal of destruction, they must be

continually fortified in their sense of the clarity and right-
ness of their objectives, and in their certain progress
toward them. These forces have demonstrated a high level
(though not a perfect one) of discipline and coordination.
But these qualities must to a great degree be achieved
through individual commitment and sense of purpose.
Their style of fighting, the relative inferiority of their lo-
gistics and weaponry, and the material inducements for
defection require it. Hence, their representatives in Paris
must forgo the luxury of public maneuver and vacillation
to secure a debater's advantage, for fear of dispiriting a
fighting force whose main advantage is spirit (or
"politics," as they might say). For example, if, in order
to appear accommodating and to test the U.S. proposal of
mutual withdrawal, they accepted the American view that
North Vietnamese soldiers are alien intrusions in South
Vietnam and therefore equivalent with the American
presence, then, despite some brief international plaudits
which would follow, they would have abandoned their
premise of the ultimate oneness of Vietnam. As the negotiations dragged on, the moral position and the morale of
their fighting forces in Vietnam would be undermined.

By contrast, verbal concessions masking actual intransigeance, in a way that looks good in the headlines, are
an inexpensive maneuvers for the U.S. government. The
American military style is technological. Men on patrols
or sweeps serve to spot the enemy, who, if he offers serious
resistance, is then attacked by gunship, jet bomber, or
artillery. The morale of the troops in that situation is
comparatively a minor factor. As Saigon's troops have
been integrated tactically into this technological machine,
the state of their morale also means less. Of course, a
change in the conditions of their fighting might reveal the
poor morale, as it would that of the U.S. troops—
something we know in any case from desertion rates.

As long as America is confident of its control over the
course of the negotiations, it can seem, for propaganda
effect, to make concessions. This matters, not to Saigon's
soldiers, but only to their governmental leaders, who in a

now familiar pattern fear that the U.S. may really mean it this time and often publicly undermine the American maneuver by their nervous reassertions of intransigeance.

The "other side," then, is disposed toward a cautious, firm posture because it is in an elemental battle on its own soil for national survival (not just some imagined extension far from one's borders of "national security"); because of its experience with previous international "settlements" of Indochinese affairs; and because of its peculiar military needs. Ignoring the vast differences in their situations, some commentators have ascribed flexibility and reason to the U.S. government and a lack of interest in peace ("they want to humiliate us") to America's opponents in Indochina. The record tells us otherwise.

The Record on Seeking Negotiations

Both sides have expressed an interest in a negotiated settlement, but it is not difficult to see how the commitment of the NLF and North Vietnam to its necessity has been and will remain greater. With the power equation so much to America's advantage, they cannot hope to throw her out bodily. They know she will leave only when the costs (physical and political, international and domestic) become too great. Exactly what constitutes too great a cost will be determined by an American government. At the moment when it decides it can no longer bear the cost, it will proceed to negotiate a cessation of hostilities and the departure of its troops, extracting whatever concessions it may. This sequence of events describes the best that can be expected by Hanoi and the NLF. Even if the Saigon government disappeared utterly (which is unlikely, since what American power created and sustained it can re-create), attacks on Vietnam could continue from Thailand or Okinawa, or from American bases within Vietnam. So their maximum expectations necessarily *include* negotiations. Having been burned in previous settlements, they approach negotiations very cautiously but know they must eventually negotiate.

The U.S. government's maximum expectations, however, do not require negotiations. If the "other side" would negotiate its own surrender, the maximum American aims would apparently have been attained. But in the absence of that inconceivable event, the U.S. government hopes, and has hoped for a long time, to conclude the war without negotiations on the basis of full military victory. The words "military victory" may not be used, may even be denied, but the meaning is there. The formula was enunciated by Ambassador Henry Cabot Lodge in December 1966: the enemy "just might fade," as they did in the Malaysian and the Philippine revolts, leaving the Saigon government in charge.[2] The idea is kept alive in occasional background discussions by American generals, who have recently revived talk of a Saigon invasion of North Vietnam.[3] It is inherent in Nixon's hopes for Vietnamization, a policy which, if successful, obviates all negotiations, since the "insurgency" will have been defeated. Hence optimism about Vietnamization and downgrading the Paris talks go together. In contrast to the Vietnamese against whom the U.S. battles, then, American dependence upon negotiations as a final instrument of achieving peace is more tentative, until she decides that her maximum expectations are unreachable, or undesirable.

For several years after the American military presence in Vietnam began to grow, the U.S. government ruled all negotiations out of court. The NLF offered to talk (for example, in a formal statement broadcast in January 1964), but the U.S. supported Saigon in its position that there was nothing to talk about. The "rebels" merely had to give themselves up and the "outside agitators" go home.[4] Then in April 1965, after having enormously increased and widened the level of American intervention in the war (regular bombing of North and South Vietnam, American combat units entering the battle), President Johnson abruptly switched his position and declared himself ready to negotiate. There followed over the next three-and-one-half years the most intricate of dances, where Johnson's administration dispatched emissaries around the world to arrange negotiations and at the moment of success acted—whether inadvertently or intentionally ceased to matter, since the pattern was so consistent—in a way guaranteed to sabotage its own efforts. Bombing was escalated just as preparations for negotiations were coming to a head in December 1965.

The leading students of these episodes, two *Los Angeles Times* correspondents, refer to the view that "in the balance of forces in Washington, those who were urging the waging of an intense—if limited—war far outweighed those in favor of seeking a negotiated, compromise peace."[5] This sums up the American position since 1965 and could not but reinforce Vietnamese caution toward our public stance of seemingly favoring negotiations. *Not just the Vietnamese, but many Americans as well, came to the conclusion that the U.S. government was using the prospect of negotiations in order to pacify popular desires for peace rather than as a serious route toward achieving it.*

After the first several "feelers" about negotiations and their undercutting by American military thrusts at a crucial moment, Hanoi adopted a firm position that it would refuse to negotiate until the U.S. ceased bombing North Vietnam. It was apparent that the U.S. hoped to decide the balance of political forces in South Vietnam by taking the war beyond South Vietnam—in other words, she envisaged a settlement based on her power generally to widen the war, rather than on what she could achieve militarily and politically in South Vietnam itself. For Hanoi to accept this approach would have been to accept defeat on behalf of the NLF. So, in order to reject the American definition of the war and to deal with American vacillation about the idea of negotiations, Hanoi insisted on the precondition of no bombing in the North and on the participation of the NLF at any full-scale negotiations about a settlement for South Vietnam.

In practice, however, Hanoi and the NLF responded to any concrete American initiative toward scaling down the war. They rejected the idea that the presence of North Vietnamese troops in South Vietnam was "equivalent" for negotiating purposes with either the bombing of the North or the huge military buildup in the South. Even to date, they have acknowledged only in guarded ways that regular northern forces are in the South at all, since this admission would tend to grant the equivalency which they reject. At no point before or since the 1965 escalation have North Vietnamese forces in the South come anywhere near the American military presence in numbers, let alone in firepower. And in any case, they would insist that Vietnam is ultimately one and they have as much right to be in South Vietnam as do the many North Vietnamese who play leading roles in the Saigon government. (The proportion of Vietnamese from the North in Saigon cabinets and in Saigon's national assembly is consistently 20 percent or more.) *All this is the formal position. But when the U.S. has taken some concrete step in a direction that suggested deescalation, or even when it has not but seemed interested in doing so, the response from the "other side" has been concrete and real, though underreported in this country.*

For example, during the thirty-six-day bombing pause of December 1965 and January 1966 (a pause applied only to North Vietnam, while bombing continued in the South), American military contact with North Vietnamese units virtually ceased (though NLF activity continued at a reduced level).[6] On March 31, 1968, in the face of defections from his policy in America's foreign policy establishment after the Tet offensive and in the midst of Senator Eugene McCarthy's strong showing in the Democratic primaries, Johnson announced the cessation of bombing over part of North Vietnam and his own retirement at the end of his term of office. Shortly thereafter the long siege of U.S. marines at Khe Sanh was lifted. An American military success was claimed, but the timing was to say the least an extraordinary coincidence. Preliminary discussions to arrange full negotiations began in Paris in May 1968. When the American delegate Averell Harriman called for signs of restraint, shellings of Saigon ceased for two months (and did not resume except sporadically), ground activity sharply declined, and North Vietnamese troop levels in South Vietnam decreased by a quarter to a third.[7] The American president refused to interpret these developments as positive responses, despite Harriman's urgent identification of them as just that. Johnson nevertheless later agreed to complete cessation of the bombing of North Vietnam and to negotiations with delegations of both Hanoi and the NLF, thereby meeting Hanoi's conditions for full-scale negotiations. He did so in late October 1968—a desperate but belated attempt to assist the election of Hubert Humphrey to the presidency. Out of this decision—to which Hanoi responded by virtually ceasing movement across the DMZ, something that Washington had particularly urged on Hanoi but about which there was no formal agreement—emerged the four-delegation talks in Paris beginning January 1969.

As the records shows, it is a myth that it is primarily the U.S. which has made concessions to bring about negotiations. One must wonder about the morality of the American demand for reciprocal actions in return for moderating but not ceasing her aggression against another country. But the fact of the matter is, she has been given them. Even as they denounce Nixon's Vietnamization policy as a fraud, Hanoi and the NLF have responded to actual American troop withdrawals by a reduced level of military activity since withdrawals began in the summer of 1969. Nixon noted on April 20, 1970: "There has been an over-all decline in enemy force levels in South Vietnam since December," the date of his announcement of another small reduction in U.S. forces. While American commanders kept predicting another "major Communist offensive," nothing had come up until the moves of Saigon and the U.S. into Cambodia at the end of April 1970 and the consequent escalation of the war. It is apparent that the Vietnamese would like to see the U.S. out of their country

and they stand ready to respond to any gesture which
leads in that direction.

Negotiating Positions

The clarity with which the issue of nationalism relates
to the struggle in Vietnam has varied according to the
different situations facing the country since 1945. But an
understanding of developments hinges on realizing that
most of the time nationalism has worked in favor of
America's opponents and against her clients in Vietnam.
How could men who fought *for* French colonial authority
and *against* the independence of their own country—and
this describes almost all the top leaders in Saigon—how
could they be considered nationalists or nation builders?
In the absence of strong organization among the unarmed
neutralist opponents of the Saigon regime—e.g., the Buddhists—the chief defenders of national sovereignty in South
Vietnam are the NLF and their North Vietnamese allies.

Being guardians of nationalism is both a strength and a
burden for the "other side." It has a remarkably powerful
appeal to the people of the country and, along with the
response to social needs and aspirations, helps explain the
NLF's continuing ability to recruit soldiers despite its fearsome casualties. But nationalism is also a demanding
emotion. It requires of its leaders constant evidence of
their uncompromising devotion to its principles. This is
especially so with a nationalism backed against a wall,
struggling for survival against an overwhelming external
enemy. Herein rests the hardness of the NLF position.
Hanoi, invoking in its Four Points the 1954 Geneva
accords with reference to the general principle of Vietnamese self-determination without foreign interference,
defers to the NLF for the expression of what constitutes a
proper settlement for South Vietnam.

The NLF in its negotiating proposals at Paris (the Ten
Points of May 1969) has declared its readiness to enter
a provisional coalition government with "the political

forces representing the various social strata and political tendencies in South Viet Nam, that stand for peace, independence and neutrality. . . ." In press conferences, the NLF negotiators have indicated that, although the present top three men in the Saigon government are unacceptable national traitors (compounding their service to the French by serving as present agents of American schemes in Vietnam), the Saigon government as a whole is one of the "political forces," once it turns toward peace, and prominent figures from past Saigon regimes, such as Duong Van Minh, might be leaders in the coalition. Their position describes the provisional coalition government as implementing the withdrawal of foreign troops; assuring freedoms of speech, press, political organization; prohibiting reprisals against collaborators with either side in the preceding struggle; and holding general elections in South Vietnam. Before the election, "neither party shall impose its political regime on the people of South Viet Nam." And it is anticipated in the proposals that the elections will produce, not a one-party government but another coalition of varying groups.[8] There is nothing remarkable about these proposals, except their moderation. Although we can expect that the NLF will be the leading element in any postwar situation, there is much room for negotiation within the terms of this outline of a political settlement—which are the "political tendencies," and what proportion of the provisional coalition government each should occupy. This is where real bargaining may take place as an accompaniment to America's agreement to depart. A State Department official publicly hinted on June 30, 1970, that the U.S. might after all enter into such bargaining, although Nixon promptly and on his own initiative disavowed the suggestion.[9]

The hard core of the NLF proposals emerges in issues relating to national sovereignty. The United States must withdraw all its military personnel and matériel and remove all its military bases. The disposition of Vietnamese armed forces (presumably including North Vietnamese as well as Saigon units) shall be decided by Vietnamese. The arrangement of South Vietnamese affairs shall exclude foreign interference. These firm words are abrasive to American sensibilities. As foreigners in the situation, Americans prefer to think of these matters as international rather than as nonnegotiable positions resting on ideas of national rights.

The American proposals at the negotiations, announced by Nixon in May 1969, suggested that an international body should supervise the elections and that an un-specified number of American and other outside forces would remain an unspecified period in restricted areas of Vietnam, after "major portions" of all "non-South Viet-namese forces" had been withdrawn over a twelve-month period. How apparently conciliatory for the world's great-est power, but how insensitive to the nationalism of the Vietnamese! It was too much even for the Saigon govern-ment, which amended the U.S. proposals to stress what Nixon's statement did not contradict, that is, that any elections would be organized by Saigon, not by foreigners —thereby declaring that "supervision" meant "observa-tion," not "organization" or "control." Saigon's position is that the NLF would first have to disarm and abjure communism before being allowed to participate in the elections and in their "supervision."[10] In a further round of clarifications of the U.S.-Saigon negotiating position at the end of July 1970, Thieu declared that neither Com-munists nor advocates of coalition government could par-ticipate in the elections. Nixon (though absurdly arguing that these qualifications would not exclude the NLF) backed up his Saigon client: "President Thieu's position with regard to negotiation is on all fours with ours."[11] An election organized by the Saigon government (or for that matter by any single political faction in South Vietnam), even with "international supervision," is not a prospect that inspires confidence. Aside from the crippling condi-tions that it prescribes for future elections, the record of previous Saigon-run elections, including that of August and September 1967 which had high-level American ob-servers, is a bleak one.[12] Nor have the Vietnamese forgotten the promises of internationally supervised elections in 1954: in accordance with the Geneva agreements, Viet Minh military forces went to the North; the remaining political workers, whose political rights were guaranteed by the agreements, were instead slaughtered; and the elections did not occur.

The principal American stress in its public explanations has been on the old issue of reciprocity: if the Americans are to withdraw, then so must the North Vietnamese. As in the past, the NLF is unwilling to accept the equivalency between American (and Korean, Thai, and Australian) troops and Vietnamese troops from the North. Especially now, after frantic American infusions of money, training, and weaponry into the Saigon army, the NLF can hardly accept as reasonable being left to Thieu's tender mercies without the right to call on help from all Vietnamese. *But also as in the past, practical understandings can probably be reached whereby U.S. withdrawal and the "disappearance" of North Vietnamese units from South Vietnam can occur along with the explicit creation of a provisional coalition government, in which the artificially inflated Saigon regime is reduced to its natural size within the South Vietnamese political scene.*

The bitter pill, which the American government has yet to swallow, is that the Saigon government cannot be maintained in any settlement. Declarations of American willingness to see it go have always been qualified in such a way as to nullify their effect. The social and political forces it represents can play a role, but these forces, as distinct from the reluctant population over which it has police control, have never been great and diminish as the war continues. The importance of the Saigon regime lies in its being a conduit of American wealth and power. Once the flow ceases, the regime will deflate to the size of its very limited social base. It will no longer be a regime, but only a faction. Having spilled so much blood—some American, more Vietnamese—in defending this regime, Americans have difficulty facing these facts. *The play of political forces within South Vietnam, without foreign intervention, under the sorts of conditions that could be negotiated, may very well produce a government committed to communism and union with the North. But there is no likely conclusion to the war which can preclude this possibility.*

So the negotiations have been stalemated, and the U.S. government declared its lack of interest by neglecting for half a year (until July 1970) to reappoint a chief negotiator for its team after Lodge's departure. It is sometimes said that, having promised negotiations if the bombing of the North were halted, Hanoi now refuses to negotiate. The assertion implies that if they do not agree with the American-Saigon position, they are not seriously negotiating. Negotiating is meeting regularly and exchanging views. This has gone on since January 1969 and survived even the invasion of Cambodia. Whether the negotiations progress or not depends on whether common ground is discovered. The irreducible difference that has emerged is that the U.S. still contemplates the continuance of the Saigon regime or some similar substitute and is uninterested in negotiating a coalition government. This is the content of Nixon's definition of the war, reiterated June 30, 1970: "Winning a just peace" is "saving 17 million people in South Vietnam from a Communist take-over." These words, translated into the real circumstances of South Vietnam, mean the endless American protection of the Saigon operation. The U.S. talks of accepting a coalition government if elections produce one—but since in this plan the Saigon government would run the elections, this is only apparently a concession and would in effect perpetuate the Saigon government. (The scenario is from *Catch-22:* The U.S. will accept a coalition government resulting from elections, but advocates of coalition government may not run in the elections.) The NLF, with Hanoi's support, will not accept a settlement where they are forced to accept the perpetuation of what they rightly regard as an instrument of American power.

Even if the situation in Indochina had not been complicated by the escalation and extension of the war into Laos and Cambodia, the prospects were not good for a breakthrough in the talks. With the war's enlargement, they seem quite remote. The U.S.-Saigon invasion of Cambodia was analogous to the bombing of North Vietnam. It attempted to treat issues local to South Vietnam by carrying the war to other areas; and like the bombing of the North, the move backfired. *Success in any talks, whether two-, four-, or multi-sided, depends on the U.S. recognizing that it cannot determine the fate of the Vietnamese, even if that determination is clothed in the rhetoric of defending them. Once this is recognized, a settlement will come handily.*

PART III

Why Is the
United States
Fighting in Indochina?

CHAPTER 20

Is Communism the Enemy in Indochina?

To many Americans the U.S. is fighting in Indochina against an international Communist conspiracy directed from Moscow or Peking. People support the government's war policies because they believe that they'll be in worse trouble "if we don't stop them there." Is there any basis to this widespread idea?

Communist Divisions

People are as reluctant to give up old, worn-out ideas as they are to part with worn-out but comfortable clothes. The clothes may not fit anymore but one keeps them hanging in the closet or tucked away in a drawer. Ideas may not correspond to reality, but deep down one still believes in them. The concept of world communism is one such idea.

When Russia was the only Communist state it was the center of an international Communist movement which was held together through the Communist International and dominated by the Soviet dictator Stalin. When Communist parties came to power after World War II in

Eastern Europe as well as in China and parts of Korea and Vietnam, this spelled the beginning of the end of an international Communist movement dominated from a single center such as Moscow. In 1948 Tito's Yugoslavia successfully defied Russia. After Stalin's death in 1953, Eastern Europe began to acquire greater independence vis-à-vis Russia. The brutal Russian invasion of Hungary in 1956 and of Czechoslovakia in 1968 showed the Russian rulers afraid of democratic changes in Eastern Europe. But many foreign Communist parties actually condemned the Russians for their action. This proved once again that communism is no longer an orchestra responding to the direction of a Russian conductor. Despite Moscow's suspicions, Poland is negotiating with West Germany, and Rumania continues its maverick policies. Even in Czechoslovakia, trampled beneath the Russian boot, the spirit of independence survives. The Russians are accumulating a burden of hatred with the Czechs may one day repay. The breakup of the "Communist camp" continues.

The Sino-Soviet Split

The clearest proof of the absence of a unified world Communist movement is provided by the conflict between Russia and China. This conflict has progressed from subtle arguments over ideology to outright warfare over territorial issues. Russia has called on the Chinese people to overthrow Mao Tse-tung's government. The Chinese leaders have called on the Russian people to throw out Brezhnev and Kosygin. In the wake of the Czech invasion, Moscow declared that it had a right to intervene militarily to protect other Communist countries. China called a spade a spade. Charging that the Kremlin leaders were "new tsars" and a "bunch of hypocrites," Peking said that this new doctrine really meant that "you have the right to order other countries about, whereas they have no right to oppose you; you have the right to ravage other countries, but they have no right to resist you . . . This is nothing but a synonym for a colonial empire." On the occasion of Lenin's hundredth birthday in April 1970, the Chinese charged that the Soviet leaders were on a level with Hitler and the Nazis. Moscow replied that Mao was a power-mad despot who dreamed of becoming a new emperor. *Pravda* said that "the people in Peking emulate the ringleaders of the Nazi Reich."

Throughout the spring and summer of 1969, Chinese and Russian troops clashed repeatedly in bloody battles along their lengthy border with heavy casualties on both sides. It is reliably estimated that 650,000 Russians and 815,000 Chinese troops armed with the latest in weaponry including tanks, jets, and rockets are positioned on both sides of the border. The Russians have threatened to use nuclear weapons in the event of a war with China. What can "world communism" mean when the two most powerful Communist states stand ready to tear each other apart?

In the case of Indochina, Moscow and Peking are also at loggerheads. Although both China and Russia have supplied Hanoi with aid it has been in competition with each other rather than in cooperation. From the very beginning of the American escalation, the Chinese Communists pointedly rejected Russian overtures to coordinate military aid to North Vietnam. As a result Hanoi was placed in the difficult position of having to balance carefully between the two powers. In his last testament, Ho Chi Minh, who died in September 1969, pleaded for the reconciliation of the two hostile Communist giants. It seems a vain hope for the foreseeable future.

Communism in Asia

In Asia, with the exception of Korea, the various Communist movements (notably in China and Vietnam) owed almost nothing to Moscow in their struggles for power. But has Peking replaced Moscow as the center of a new "Asian communism" with expansionist tendencies?

It is true that in recent years China has encouraged revolutionary guerrilla warfare—wars of national liberation—in a number of Asian countries. This has been part of her effort to eliminate American influence along her borders and thereby increase her own security. But the Chinese have not sought to control these movements nor have they committed military personnel or significant amounts of material aid. The Chinese message to the national liberation movements, based on their own experience, has been "Do it yourself."

However much he may desire the success of revolutionary guerrilla warfare, Mao Tse-tung possesses no magic recipe for victory. In fact successful guerrilla-led revolutions have been rare because all of the conditions necessary for their success seldom occur at the same time. Guerrilla revolutionaries have succeeded only where they appear both as social reformers (or revolutionaries) and as nationalists who heroically rid their country of the foreigner. Significantly, in the case of both China and Vietnam it was the ability of the Communist parties to identify themselves with the deep-seated aspiration for national independence that was the key factor in their success.

Where Communist parties have gained political and military control, they have retained strong national identities and have been as defensive of their nation's autonomy as non-Communist governments. For this reason if more Communist-led revolutionary movements come to power in Asia there is no reason to believe they will accept domination from China or anywhere else. Both North Vietnam and North Korea, for example, have maintained their independence from both Moscow and Peking. In short, there is no such thing as a Peking-directed Asian communism.

Communism as a Viable Alternative

Beyond the question of power lies the far deeper question of what the Communist movements offer to Asian peoples. Democracy versus communism is not the issue, for in Asia Communist movements are often opposing corrupt and oppressive dictatorships which offer neither freedom nor real hope for a better future to their people. South Vietnam is a case in point. Where Communist parties have come to power (in China, North Korea, and North Vietnam), the evidence is that they have begun to harness the resources and human energy necessary for national development. They have addressed themselves with notable success to the fundamental problems of eliminating the vast gulf between rich and poor, expanding educational opportunities, improving health facilities, and the like. The human costs have sometimes been great, but this must be seen in the context of the grinding misery of the past, the terror and oppression suffered under pro-American counterrevolutionary regimes, and the extraordinary death and destruction which the United States has shown itself capable of indiscriminately inflicting upon these peoples in the name of "democracy." The fact remains that as a system of political, social, and economic organization, communism has generally proven itself dynamic and viable in developing nations—far more responsive to the needs of the majority of people than are those ruling elites which the United States has consistently supported.

CHAPTER 21

Is China a Threat to Peace in Asia?

U.S. policy in Southeast Asia has been based on the alleged need to halt "Communist aggression" directed by Peking. Does China's record in the international arena support the view that her behavior is aggressive and expansionist? There is no evidence that China is inherently more aggressive than any other nation. In fact if one compares China's military record with that of the United States, Russia, France, England, Israel, Syria, Egypt, India, or Pakistan, it becomes clear that China has distinguished itself by its relative lack of military involvements. The several cases invariably cited as examples of Chinese aggression are examined in the sections which follow.

The Case of Korea

All available evidence indicates that China was caught unawares by the outbreak of the Korean War in June 1950. In fact, she probably felt angry because she was not informed in advance of North Korean moves. Russia was North Korea's initial ally and adviser.

China became involved in the Korean War as a result of a clear threat to her own security. The Allied operation in Korea had become an effort to overthrow the government of North Korea and replace it with a pro-Western government. As one of a series of diplomatic warnings, Chinese Premier Chou En-lai on October 1, 1950, warned the U.S. that Chinese troops would be forced to intervene if American troops crossed the thirty-eighth parallel. The American government disregarded this. While the Chinese showed great restraint, the U.S. showed none. The Chinese sent a delegation to the UN to explain their case, but on the eve of their presentation General MacArthur, commanding the UN forces in Korea, launched a raid on the hydroelectric plants (in Korean territory) on the Yalu River which separates China from North Korea. These plants supplied China with power. U.S. troops were on China's doorstep. The Chinese recalled their delegation from the UN and sent their troops into Korea. By acting to preserve her North Korean buffer China was simply attempting to protect her borders against an enemy advance, just as the United States would under similar circumstances. By 1958, with this task accomplished China withdrew all her troops from Korean soil, despite the fact that over 50,000 American troops remain in South Korea to this day.

From her actions and attitudes before and after the Korean War one can conclude that China acted reluctantly in Korea to protect her own interests. She had made no master plans with Russia and North Korea. In fact Russia billed her for more than $2 billion of military equipment which China used during the war. This is more than all the economic aid that the Soviets gave to China during that period. The Chinese actions in Korea hardly constitute aggression.

The Case of Tibet

The Chinese have been accused of invading and conquering Tibet in 1951 and putting down a rebellion there
in 1959. Two points must be made clear.

1. In modern times Tibet has not been an independent
state nor recognized as such by any country. Until the
overthrow of the Manchu dynasty in 1911, Tibet enjoyed
internal autonomy within the Chinese Empire while Peking
controlled her foreign relations and her military affairs.
During the following decades China was convulsed in
civil war and exerted little control over Tibet. The region,
however, did not become an independent state.

When the Communists came to power in 1949 they
began to reimpose Chinese control over outlying areas of
the old Chinese Empire such as Tibet, and retained the
Dalai Lama, Tibet's religious leader, as the nominal head
of the regional government. This restoration of the Chinese
control is by no means the same thing as aggression.
Significantly the Chinese Communists and the Nationalists
both agree that Tibet is part of China. Even Chiang Kai-
shek does not consider Peking an aggressor there!

2. Tibetans are one of many minority groups within
the multinational Chinese state, and possess their own
culture and forms of social and political organization.
Unfortunately, the dominant nationality in such states
often persecutes the minorities and such has been the case
in Tibet. The Chinese Communists were determined to
introduce revolutionary changes in Tibetan society over
the opposition of the traditional ruling class (the landlords
and religious leaders) and a sizable portion of the Tibetan
people. In 1959 these Tibetans took to arms and China
reacted by suppressing their rebellion in short order. The
Dalai Lama, who had supported the rebellion, fled to
India. What the Chinese did in Tibet in 1959, in fact,
has been closely paralleled by India's quiet suppression
of a similar rebellion by natives of Tibetan stock—the

Nagas—with the world hardly aware of it. The suppression of such internal rebellions by central governments does not raise the question of aggression. It should be noted, moreover, that the severity of the Chinese response was also conditioned by a very real concern over Indian and American involvement in the Tibetan rebellion.

The Case of India

The border conflict with India has been the result of basic disagreements over boundaries which were drawn by the British around the turn of the century and which were never accepted by any legitimate Chinese government. For several years minor skirmishes took place along the Sino-Indian border and numerous diplomatic exchanges failed to resolve the conflict. In 1957 the Chinese built a strategic road through the disputed Aksai Chin wasteland on the western edge of the border. The true status of this territory is perhaps indicated by the fact that India apparently did not even become aware of the existence of this road until some years later!

However, in 1962, responding to domestic pressures, the Indian government took the military initiative in this sector and attempted to expel Chinese forces from parts of the disputed territory. They failed. In the Eastern Sector, Chinese forces took the initiative and humiliated the Indian army by driving south of the disputed McMahon line against weak Indian resistance. After flexing their military muscles in a show of strength the Chinese forces unilaterally withdrew to their previous positions while Peking resumed efforts to negotiate a boundary settlement with India. The Chinese seemed ready to accept the status quo in the Eastern Sector in return for Indian recognition of Chinese claims in the Aksai Chin region where China's strategic interests were at stake. (It should be noted that China peacefully negotiated on generous terms the settlement of similar border issues with Burma and Pakistan.) The only solution to the border problem seems to be accommodation through mutual concessions. However, the Indian government has resisted substantive talks concerning the border question, and in the years since 1962 relations between the two countries have further deteriorated.[1]

The Case of Taiwan

China refuses to renounce the use of force in its efforts to recover Taiwan because it considers Taiwan to be Chinese territory. On this issue both the Nationalists and the Communists agree. The disagreement is over who should rule China—Chiang Kai-shek or Mao Tse-tung. Taiwan is thus the last outpost of the 1945–49 Chinese civil war. Taiwan is moreover the staging area for Nationalist attacks on the Chinese mainland and houses an American base containing the largest CIA complex in the Far East and three B-52 runways. In short Taiwan is a constant threat to China's security.

China's Defensive Military Strategy

The military record over the past twenty years does not support the idea that China has been an expansionist or aggressive power. China's leaders have developed her armed forces in order to protect China rather than engage in military adventures beyond her borders. A study commissioned by the American government shows that although the Chinese army is large, it has virtually no offensive force and the navy is "small and defensively oriented."[2] Alone among the great powers, China has no regular forces permanently stationed outside of her own borders. China has no overseas bases, no long-range bombers, aircraft carriers, or heavy troop-lift capacity. The Chinese armies are a shield for protection not a dagger for aggression. Peking's nuclear capacity, including development of an ICBM delivery system, doesn't begin to compare with American or Soviet power, and has been developed as a deterrent to an attack by the U.S. or the USSR. It is also a symbol of China's great-power status. Peking's leaders have frequently repeated their pledge not to use nuclear weapons unless first attacked with them. The U.S. has rejected Chinese pleas to engage in a mutual pledge of this kind. Of course China's possession of the bomb does not increase her neighbors' sense of security. Despite the nuclear nonproliferation treaty other Asian nations (Japan, India) may in the future decide to join the nuclear club. Such is the deadly illogic of the nuclear arms race.

China and Revolutionary Warfare

From the time of the French Revolution till the present, revolutionary leaders have believed that their experience and doctrine of revolution had meaning for peoples in other lands. For years Stalin sought to manipulate the Chinese Revolution for his own ends. Partly from this bitter experience Mao Tse-tung became convinced of the difficulty of exporting revolutions or administering them from afar. Nevertheless, the Chinese leaders themselves have not been immune from the idea that the Chinese Revolution could serve as a model for revolutionary struggles in other lands. In certain cases (Africa in the mid-sixties for example) the Chinese have tried to accelerate revolutionary progress. Where they tried this they have been rebuffed.

In 1965, Mao's strategy for people's wars, as enunciated by Defense Minister Lin Piao, clearly reflected this lesson:

> If one does not operate by one's own efforts, does not independently ponder and solve the problems of the revolution in one's own country and does not rely on the strength of the masses but leans wholly on foreign aid—even though this be aid from Socialist countries which persist in revolution—no victory can be won,

or be consolidated even it it is won . . . revolution cannot be imported.

In keeping with this strategy China has refrained from
sending combat forces to Vietnam or military advisers to
the NLF. So far in Indochina she has engaged only in
the battle of propaganda, and in providing small arms,
ammunition, and food supplies. Her total aid to North
Vietnam has been only a fraction of what the U.S. has
supplied to Saigon.

What are China's interests in Southeast Asia? Primarily
China seeks a neutralized friendly rim around her
southern borders. She is greatly concerned about protecting her weak underbelly. One evidence of her fears
is that in 1966 China printed maps pinpointing forty-two
major American air, naval, and army bases surrounding
China. Each base was depicted as a weapon pointing
directly at the mainland. Over one-fourth of the bases
were in Southeast Asia. China's fears of a U.S. invasion
of southern China were heightened by the American decision in the previous year to introduce troops into South
Vietnam and to bomb North Vietnam. Reacting to this
threat, China evacuated large sections of the south and
engaged in an intensive campaign of civil defense and
propaganda against the U.S.

China's relations with Southeast Asia have been marked
by realistic caution. Since the eighteenth century, when
an imperial edict proclaimed that Vietnam was "not . . .
worth an occupation," China has refrained from any
military adventures there. The Vietnamese for their part,
conscious of their vulnerable proximity to China, seek accommodation with her in an effort to preserve their
independence. Their traditional enmity and fear of the
Chinese has prevented them from calling on Chinese
volunteers in the present conflict. However, if the North
Vietnamese feel their national existence is at stake, and
if the Chinese feel their security is threatened, the Chinese
will intercede in Vietnam. The Chinese have a saying that
their relations with their border states are like those be-

tween the teeth and the lips. When the lips are gone the teeth will get cold. In other words, the Chinese will protect their borders and their buffers.

Over the years China has sought to protect the neutrality and independence of Cambodia. Prince Sihanouk sought close ties with China as a means of protection against Cambodia's traditional enemies—Thailand and Vietnam. The American and South Vietnamese invasion of Cambodia has once more challenged Chinese interests. China has already responded by recognizing and supporting Sihanouk's government-in-exile.

Conclusion: The facts do not support the American charge that China has been aggressive and expansionist. On balance, Peking's actions have been remarkably restrained in view of the magnitude of the provocations which it faces. For in fact it has been the United States which has encircled China with a ring of military bases, fought two wars on China's doorstep, and aided most of China's enemies.

CHAPTER 22

Is North Vietnam the Aggressor

in Indochina?

Another attempt to justify the massive U.S. intervention in Southeast Asia has been the argument that North Vietnam is a militantly aggressive, expansionist nation that must be prevented by force from gobbling up its neighbors. Such a distorted image of who the aggressor really is in Southeast Asia can be corrected by looking briefly at the three areas in which the North Vietnamese have been accused of aggression by the United States— South Vietnam, Laos, and Cambodia.

The Case of South Vietnam

In its White Paper of 1965 the U.S. argued that "South Vietnam is fighting for its life against a brutal campaign of terror and armed attack inspired, directed, supplied and controlled by the Communist regime in Hanoi. . . . In Vietnam a Communist government has set out deliberately to conquer a sovereign people in a neighboring state."[1] This argument stands the truth on its head. The core of this argument, that North and South Vietnam are two separate countries, has no basis in fact. As noted in part

I the names "North" and "South" were given to the two halves of Vietnam during the Geneva conference of 1954 and were meant to designate temporary *zones* to which the belligerents could withdraw pending elections in 1956 which would reunify the country. The Final Declaration of the Geneva conference stated bluntly that the demarcation "is provisional and should not in any way be interpreted as constituting a political or territorial boundary."[2]

South Vietnam as a political entity was created by Ngo Dinh Diem with U.S. assistance and encouragement in defiance of the settlement worked out at Geneva. The U.S. further undermined the Geneva accords when it backed Diem in his refusal to participate in the discussions for working out election arrangements which were scheduled to begin in 1955 between the representatives of the two zones. Thus rather than North Vietnamese aggression being responsible for the renewal of civil warfare in Vietnam in the years after Geneva, it was the conscious subversion of the 1954 agreements by the U.S. and Diem which blocked the reunification which would have prevented the outbreak of hostilities.

Even if one were to accept, for the sake of argument, the claim that the northern and southern zones of Vietnam are indeed two separate nations, the facts do not support the U.S. contention that its actions have been provoked by the "invasion" of South Vietnam by regular units of the North Vietnamese army. Before 1964, virtually all sources agree that the opponents of the Saigon regime were overwhelmingly southerners; and even as late as January 28, 1966, after the initiation of the bombing of the North and the massive increase in U.S. troop levels ordered by President Johnson, no less an architect of U.S. Vietnam policy than Secretary of State Dean Rusk was willing to concede to the Senate Foreign Relations Committee that "80 percent of those who are called Vietcong are or have been Southerners."[3] Not only were the fighters in the South largely southern before the huge U.S. escalation of 1965, but their support came mainly from the South, not the North or other Communist nations. The

State Department's director of intelligence, Thomas L. Hughes, declared in Panama on June 8, 1964, that "by far the greater part of the Vietcong forces in South Vietnam are South Vietnamese, the preponderance of Vietcong weapons come not from Communist countries but from capture, purchase, and local manufacture."[4] Three months later, Bernard B. Fall stated that "90 percent of the weapons being used by the Vietcong are captured American weapons."[5]

The U.S. buildup from early 1965, which saw the decision to bomb the North and to introduce some 200,000 more troops to combat in Vietnam during the course of that year, was taken ostensibly because North Vietnam had been forced to commit its regular troops to combat at the end of 1964. Yet on April 27, 1965, almost exactly two months after Lyndon Johnson ordered the continuous bombing of the North, Secretary of Defense Robert S. McNamara "confirmed" the presence in South Vietnam of only one North Vietnamese battalion numbering 400 to 500 men, a figure that was repeated by Senator Mansfield on June 16, 1966, and again confirmed by the Pentagon.[6] The question of just who was committing aggression is made clearer by comparing the figure of 400 to 500 North Vietnamese in the South when the bombing began to the number of U.S. "advisers" there at the time—some 23,000, a number which was destined to grow to well over 200,000 by the end of 1965.

The Case of Laos

As indicated in part I the conflict in Laos has been an integral part of the struggle in Indochina for a good many years. What are the interests and what has been the role of North Vietnam in Laos?

Hanoi's position: From the time of its formation in 1950, the Communist-led Pathet Lao has had close ties with the present-day leaders of North Vietnam who support its revolutionary program and would undoubtedly welcome its ultimate triumph. But the Pathet Lao is by no means merely an extension of the North Vietnamese Workers (Communist) Party.[7] A more pressing concern than expanding the scope of revolution in Indochina has lain at the base of Hanoi's interest in Laos. Like the U.S. itself in areas along its borders, the North Vietnamese are understandably reluctant to see an unfriendly regime in Laos that is dependent for its very existence on a great power (the U.S.) that is Hanoi's open enemy. For this reason North Vietnam has been willing to back the various neutralist solutions that have been worked out in Laos (whereby the Pathet Lao would obtain a share of the power). Such a solution represents an acceptable balance of the indigenous political forces in that country. Over the years U.S. support for right-wing groups in Laotian politics has undermined the chances for such a solution. North Vietnam's direct participation in Laotian affairs has largely been a response to such U.S.-backed right-wing attempts to exclude the Pathet Lao from legitimate participation in government to which their numbers, territory, and popular base entitle them.[8]

Upsetting the balance: One good example of such U.S. interference occurred in 1958 after an election in which the Pathet Lao and their allies received 32 percent of the vote and thirteen of the twenty-one contested seats. As Arthur Schlesinger reports in *A Thousand Days,* the U.S. was worried about the growing popularity of the Pathet Lao and decided to install a reliably pro-Western regime. In the new cabinet, which followed a CIA-backed coup, the Pathet Lao were excluded and forced increasingly to rely on North Vietnamese support. Moreover, the government that the coup ousted was that of the then neutralist Souvanna Phouma, whose military supporters were driven to the north in a temporary alliance with the Pathet Lao. Faced with U.S. encouragement of a rebellion against him, Souvanna Phouma invited in North Vietnamese "advisers," the first known North Vietnamese presence in Laos since the 1954 Geneva agreements.

During the ensuing conflict the CIA and its private airline, Air America, armed, trained, and supplied the so-called Clandestine Army of Meo hill tribesmen in northeastern Laos, and established a large secret headquarters for this army staffed with Americans. Until American reporters laid bare the story of U.S. efforts, the Nixon administration had consistently hushed up the "secret war" in Laos.

Escalation in Laos: In his statement on Laos of March 6, 1970, President Nixon claimed the U.S. bombing missions over northeastern Laos, which began in May 1964 and signaled a direct combat role there for the U.S. for the first time, were necessary because of an increasing violation of Laotian neutrality by North Vietnamese "invaders." Yet the president's statement conceded that the U.S. assumed a direct combat role in Laos. What Mr. Nixon also failed to mention was the attempted right-wing coup of April 1964 which preceded by one month the new outbreak of fighting. The attempted coup was headed by a faction whose cadres had received training from the CIA, which operates in Laos under the cover of AID, the Agency for International Development. The prior assassinations of two of the Pathet Lao's supporters in the cabinet (including the foreign minister)—apparently by one of the assassination squads which the CIA is known to have been training at that time—caused the final collapse of the tripartite coalition government and a restructuring of the neutralist cabinet toward the right. Unable to secure a share of power through the political process in Laos, the Pathet Lao retreated to its bases in eastern Laos and sought aid from North Vietnam.

Thus the first substantial reports of North Vietnamese infiltration followed the newest right-wing power play in Vientiane and the bombing by U.S. planes of an area of Laos—the northeast—that borders on North Vietnam; this bombing was unrelated to U.S. air strikes against the

Ho Chi Minh Trail further to the south. Moreover, as the Symington subcommittee of the Senate Foreign Relations Committee discovered in October 1969, the U.S. had established bases such as the one in northeastern Laos some seventeen miles from the North Vietnamese border complete with advanced navigational equipment to aid the all-weather bombing of North Vietnam.

Ho Chi Minh Trail: Outside of the Northeast, the only substantial commitment of North Vietnamese troops in Laos is to guard the Ho Chi Minh Trail. Several tens of thousands of troops are positioned there for this purpose. The charge that this is an indication of North Vietnamese aggression against "neutral" Laos is an indication of the double standards which the U.S. applies in Asia. The North Vietnamese have been forced increasingly to rely on the trail through parts of Laos because of U.S. escalation of the war in South Vietnam and in 1965 into North Vietnam. The U.S., of course, has its own bases and secure supply routes to conduct the war in the Philippines, Thailand, Okinawa, Guam, etc., as well as in the form of the Seventh Fleet.

North Vietnamese presence in Laos and support of the Pathet Lao forces is undeniable. But the crucial point is that it was American support and continuing sustenance of the right-wing forces there which opened the door for the internationalization of the internal conflict in Laos.

The Case of Cambodia

The Cambodian sanctuaries: The charge that North Vietnamese "sanctuaries" across the border from South Vietnam are clear cases of aggression is further proof of an American double standard. The U.S. condemns the Vietnamese who take refuge in sparsely inhabited areas of eastern Cambodia from the American ground sweeps and aerial devastation in South Vietnam, while condoning U.S. "sanctuaries" throughout East Asia. Moreover, before the coup that overthrew Sihanouk, the North Vietnamese posture in Cambodia was a low one. One reporter described the Vietnamese in Cambodia as—

> . . . lying low in the border regions and causing little trouble . . . the communists have not been sending their troops to attack government-controlled territory . . . the arrangement has meant the presence of foreign troops on Cambodian soil, but it has also allowed Cambodia, alone among its neighbors, to pass through the dangers of the Vietnam war without having its countryside ravaged and its population brutalized.[9]

Who violated Cambodian neutrality?: The hope that Cambodia might escape the ravages of war that have so destroyed parts of Vietnam and Laos was the motivation behind many of the actions of Chief of State Norodom Sihanouk, who in a most skillful manner played off the North Vietnamese and the Americans. One of his moves, an action that undercuts U.S. assertions that the North Vietnamese presence in Cambodia is one of pure aggression, was a series of agreements concluded with North Vietnam and the NLF as early as 1965 whereby the latter's forces would be allowed to pass through Cambodian territory en route to South Vietnam, and Vietnamese supplies could be unloaded at the Cambodian port of Sihanoukville. As Sihanouk moved to reach agreements with the Vietnamese, he also reacted strongly against repeated incursions on Cambodian territory by U.S. and South Vietnamese forces as well as subversion against his government by the same allies. Despite Nixon's statement that U.S. policy since 1954 has been to "scrupulously respect the neutrality of the Cambodian people," official Cambodian statistics up to May 1969 charge 1,864 border violations and 5,149 air violations by the U.S. and its allies which were responsible for 293 Cambodian deaths and 690 wounded.[10] In addition, in 1969 U.S. aircraft systematically defoliated large areas of Cambodia including the economically vital rubber plantations, damaging in the process over one-third of the productive trees. A U.S. State Department mission investigated and confirmed the Cambodian charges. Tens of thousands of Cambodian peasants witnessed their own food crops wither and die as a result of the spraying of American herbicides.[11] In May 1963 Sihanouk demanded the termination of U.S. economic and military aid; in May 1965 his government broke off diplomatic relations with the U.S. Such dramatic action was no charade on the part of the plucky prince. On top of U.S. incursions into Cambodian territory, the CIA and Green Berets recruited in Cambodia and paid and trained in Thailand and South Vietnam a Cambodian mercenary force (the Khmer Serai) which was dedicated to the overthrow of Sihanouk. One of the early instances of Khmer Serai provocations was the "Bangkok plot" of 1958–59, which called for an anti-Sihanouk invasion from Thailand by Khmer Serai forces. The United States, Thailand, and South Vietnam were implicated in the plot.[12] This undoubtedly encouraged the forces of Lon Nol and Sirik Matak to think that the U.S. might react favorably to a more right-wing regime.

Into the caldron: The coup of March 18, 1970, destroyed not only the Sihanouk government, but also the hope that Cambodia might be spared the massive aerial destruction, the thousands of homeless refugees, and the barbarous defoliation that are synonymous with the American way of war in Southeast Asia. That Cambodia must suffer so is not the fault of the North Vietnamese and the Viet Cong, who had used Cambodian sanctuaries with a minimum of disruption of the life of the people in a limited area. Rather it is because of the U.S.-South Vietnamese invasion. Another by-product of this invasion has been to drive the North Vietnamese and the Viet Cong further into Cambodia than they had ever been before. As of July 1970 it was estimated that they and the Cambodian resistance in forces loyal to Sihanouk controlled close to two-thirds of Cambodia.

In short the possibility for Cambodian neutrality and noninvolvement in the Indochina War has been destroyed as a result of the coup and the combined U.S.-South Vietnamese invasion. Neutralists like Sihanouk have therefore formed a new alliance with the Khmer Rouge, the Pathet Lao, the NLF, and North Vietnam in the struggle to preserve Cambodia's independence.

CHAPTER 23

The Bloodbath and

the Whitewash*

The lastest weapon in the Nixon arsenal is the psychological warfare technique of scaring the American people into believing that an American pullout from Vietnam will result in the slaughter of millions of people. This so-called bloodbath theory has in fact become an important excuse for prolonging U.S. involvement in the war. One spills blood today to save blood tomorrow. That this argument has been manufactured in the U.S. for American consumption is obvious from the fact that neither the government nor the press of South Vietnam stressed it until President Nixon trotted it out on November 3, 1969.

The North Vietnamese Record

In his speech of April 30, 1970, the president said that immediate American withdrawal from Vietnam would result in exposing the South Vietnamese people "to the slaughter and savagery which the leaders of North Viet-

*Senator Edward Kennedy read an exhaustive list of articles available in print on the bloodbath theory into the *Congressional Record,* Vol. 116, No. 85, p. S7805, May 26, 1970.

nam inflicted on hundreds of thousands of North Vietnamese who chose freedom when the Communists took
over North Vietnam in 1954." The facts do not support
him. It is undeniable that the leaders of North Vietnam
are experienced revolutionaries who do not shrink from
violence to pursue their ends. Nor of course does the U.S.
In the course of their struggles against the French and
their own Vietnamese opposition, the Viet Minh leaders
also resorted to violence.

But in regard to the question of political reprisals after
1954, Hanoi has a much better record than Saigon. The
proceedings of the International Control Commission,
established to supervise the Geneva accords of 1954,
provide the most reliable records on political reprisals in
Vietnam after 1954. The ICC reported only 19
complaints of political reprisals and only 1 political murder in North Vietnam from 1954 through 1956. During
the same period, 214 complaints were lodged against the
South Vietnamese government. In 1957, when the Diem
regime prevented the ICC from conducting further
investigations, there were 1,047 complaints lodged against
it. The Diem government, moreover, admitted that it
jailed over 48,000 political prisoners between 1954 and
1960. Untold numbers were killed by Diem's "guillotine
on wheels" which traveled to every village and hamlet.

What did occur in North Vietnam was a crudely carried
out land reform program which gave rise to a peasant
rebellion in 1956. Many deaths occurrred. A frequently
cited estimate is ten to fifteen thousand, but there is no
firm basis for determining the actual statistics. In any case
there is absolutely no basis for the assertion that hundreds
of thousands were slaughtered. Furthermore these were
not political reprisals of the kind President Nixon has
been scaring Americans with. It is a fact that revolutionary change involves violence and death. But the costs of
revolution are far less in human terms than the costs of
an open-ended war.

The Tet Offensive

In his November 3 speech the president revived the charge that as many as 3,000 Vietnamese were "eliminated" by the Viet Cong in Hue during the 1968 Tet offensive. According to the former chief information officer of the Saigon regime, while his government officially claimed that the inhabitants of Hue were killed by the Viet Cong, he knew in fact that many of the victims were killed by Allied and American bombings and buried in mass graves. Conveniently, the U.S. does not list civilian casualties, so the dead in Hue are either listed as VC or civilians killed by the VC.

Undoubtedly some outright executions were committed by the Viet Cong. According to the director of Hue's special police, the VC brought a list of all the "enemies of the people" into the Gia Hoi area of Hue. Gia Hoi consists of 25,000 residents; the list consisted of five names! What is clear now is that most of the dead at Hue were killed during the massive U.S. bombardments during the climax of an extremely hard-fought battle. They did not occur after a cease-fire, the time Nixon advertises as the hour of the bloodbath. The real bloodbath was caused by the Americans, not by Viet Cong "terrorists."

The Catholic Minority

Playing to his American audience, President Nixon has stressed the fate of the "million and a half Catholic refugees who fled to South Vietnam when the Communists took over the North." In fact UN statistics place the number of these refugees at about 750,000. Do the Catholics want the war to continue? Let them speak for themselves. The most anti-Communist Catholic leader in South Vietnam, Father Hoang Quynh, who led a guerrilla army against the Viet Minh in 1954, has expressed his willingness to make his peace with the Communists if they come to power. He has aligned himself with the Venerable Thich Tri Quang, a militant Buddhist leader considered by the U.S. as a pro-Communist, to bring about a settlement. Soon after Nixon's November 3 speech, ninety-three prominent Vietnamese Catholics called for an *immediate* withdrawal of U.S. troops. Finally, the Catholic priest in the Gia Hoi section of Hue has testified that during the Viet Cong occupation during the Tet offensive, "none of his clergy or parishioners were harmed by the NLF."

Who Will Suffer?

The question remains: Who will suffer if we withdraw rapidly? Not the South Vietnamese leaders. Ten thousand wealthy Vietnamese emigrated during the first year of the peace talks. An exit visa cost as much as $5,000 and a "certificate of French citizenship" about $2,000. A Swiss journalist reports that about $2 billion has been deposited in European banks. Many Vietnamese have bought into European banks and invested in European real estate. President Thieu himself has a home in Rome (where his brother is ambassador) and his wife owns more real estate in Europe. Clearly, these Vietnamese, who would be the most obvious targets should any political settling of accounts occur, have the means to flee in time to a life of safety and comfort.

Strangely enough the proponents of the bloodbath theory seem to be more worried about the fate of South Vietnamese civilians than the civilians are themselves. For civilians it is the continuation of the war, not its end, which results in an ongoing bloodbath. Ly Chanh Trung, an outstanding Catholic teacher in Saigon, voiced a widely held sentiment when he said that "I can no longer bear the spectacle of foreigners rudely destroying my country with the most up-to-date and horrible methods . . . [it is] the Americans who have the slogan of protecting freedom but who really are protecting the systems which trample down freedom." But there are Vietnamese in the South who fear an NLF victory for whatever reason. The U.S. could even provide political asylum and aid in resettlement to such people who may have compromised their future by collaborating with it in the war.

The Real Bloodbath

The real bloodbath and the real persecution in Vietnam are the ongoing ones caused by the war. The people who suffer are the thousands upon thousands of political prisoners, the students, the neutralist Buddhists and Catholics, the peasants, and anyone caught in a free-fire zone. As America's most respected and experienced diplomat, Averell Harriman, said in November 1969: "I have very little patience with the people who talk about the massacre that may happen at some future date if we withdraw, because there's a massacre going on now."

Richard Nixon's bloodbath is totally an American production. By raising the specter of oriental hordes and the supposed oriental disregard for human life, the president hopes to exploit old racist images and channel support for his own political purposes. A decision for immediate withdrawal should not be put off because of this projected fear. Historically the fear is without foundation. Presently the U.S. is immersed in a bloodbath of its own making. On January 8, 1968, the Conference of Catholic Bishops in Vietnam appealed for peace: "In the name of the Lord, we cry STOP."

CHAPTER 24

Protecting Our Boys

There is increasing agreement among most Americans that it was a national tragedy for the U.S. to get involved in Vietnam. But like the passenger who suddenly finds himself at the controls of an airplane, the question has not been "How did it happen?" but rather "What do we do now?"

Tunnel Without End

One of the most frequently used arguments for backing the war policy has been the need to "protect our boys" already in Vietnam. Congressmen regularly vote appropriations for the war lest they be accused of letting down America's fighting men. Opponents of the war, whether they be unkempt, bearded college students or button-down, close-shaven Wall Street lawyers, are labeled as something less than patriotic if not outright treasonable because they allegedly threaten the men in the front lines.

This argument is a red herring if there ever was one. It is simply an excuse for prolonging the war. Implicit in it is the idea that the U.S. cannot withdraw from Vietnam until it wins a military victory. If it is necessary to support the war in order to "protect our boys," the U.S.

can never get out until the enemy is completely defeated. But it should be quite clear by now that short of pulling out all the stops and running the real risk of a nuclear war, the chances of gaining a military victory in Indochina are slim indeed.

The Cambodian Gambit

President Nixon justified his Cambodian venture in part by pleading this need to protect U.S. forces now in Vietnam against a Communist attack which was supposed to be in the offing. In fact Communist forces in their Cambodian sanctuaries were not massing for an attack against U.S. forces as the president alleged.[1] What the president did was to use an emotional but phony argument to justify an act of escalation. The only sure means of protecting men now in Indochina is to bring them home as quickly as possible. Apart from the career officers for whom the war is a means of professional advancement, there was little if any enthusiasm for the Cambodian invasion among the American forces in Vietnam. The average "grunt" (foot soldier) is concerned only with the number of days he has left to serve. He knows where his safety lies. If continuing a war in Vietnam and escalating it into Cambodia is a means of protecting the GIs, why do they feel about it the way they do?

The Way Out

Clearly the more men the U.S. sends to Vietnam and Indochina, the more it exposes to death and injury. It is a strange logic which sees withdrawal rather than the war itself as the thing which destroys lives. It is the same strange logic which believers in the bloodbath theory cling to. No one has argued that the men in Indochina should be denied the weapons with which to defend themselves. What has been argued is that they should not be there.

It is said that as Nixon's program of phased withdrawal of combat troops proceeds, the remaining Americans are exposed to greater dangers and thus need redoubled support. The only answer is to bring them all out—combat troops, support troops, naval and air forces, advisers, everybody. The U.S. has the means to do so in short order. Furthermore, when U.S. determination to effect a complete withdrawal from Indochina is made known, there is no doubt that North Vietnam and the NLF will not act to hamper or harass but rather to facilitate our departure.

Continued war in Indochina will protect neither Asian nor American lives.

CHAPTER 25

Self-Determination—for Whom?

"We want nothing for ourselves, only that the people of South Vietnam be allowed to guide their own country in their own way." In 1965 President Johnson spoke these words to justify American policy. Recently President Nixon repeated this theme: "We seek the opportunity for the South Vietnamese people to determine their own political future without outside interference" (May 14, 1969).

The principle of self-determination is a popular one in the speeches of American leaders, who tend to use it in two ways when discussing other countries. On the one hand, it is used as a synonym for independence and national sovereignty, the freedom of a nation from outside domination and foreign control. In its second meaning it suggests a standard by which to analyze the internal political process, namely the access to power of various political groups. In this second usage the concept of self-determination overlaps with that of democracy.

Emphasis upon defense of these principles has been a consistent part of the justification offered for the Indochina war by administration spokesmen, particularly insofar as Vietnam is concerned. In practice, however, the record reveals that American actions throughout most of

Asia have in fact belied such ideals—on the levels of both national independence and internal access to power.

Dependence and Independence

There is an Alice in Wonderland character to the American government's use of self-determination in the first sense. The U.S. clearly suggests that "dependent" countries are the "satellite" nations either in or affiliated with the "Communist bloc." Conversely, if a country is non-Communist and economically, militarily, or diplomatically influenced by the U.S. to any substantial degree, it is automatically described as "independent" and cited as an example of self-determination at work. In American parlance, such Asian countries comprise "free Asia." For example, South Korea, with over 60,000 American troops on its soil, a standing army of 600,000 men paid and equipped chiefly by the U.S., and heavily dependent upon U.S. aid, continues to be cited as a prime case of an "independent" country. North Korea, with no Chinese or Russian troops on its soil, with a smaller army, and with far less assistance from foreign powers, is a "dependency." Clearly the American definition transmutes the notion of national independence from the category of description to that of a moral judgment bordering on the theological.

Even more striking is the Vietnamese example. The DRV has been consistently described by U.S. policy makers as a "Communist satellite," a pawn of the Communist camp. In fact, North Vietnamese have fought for independence for generations and have consistently opposed the introduction of foreign troops into their country. And though the war has necessitated extensive military assistance from the Soviet Union and China, there has been a notable effort to balance off the two great powers in order to preserve national independence. Even the most anti-Communist commentators on Vietnamese policy have attested to this maneuverability in Hanoi.

South Vietnam, on the other hand, presents a remarkable contrast. The Saigon government permits the involvement of a massive number of American troops, and sanctions an increasing number of massive military installations. The military junta in the South is almost totally dependent upon continued American assistance—economically, militarily, and politically. President Thieu's desire to remain in power requires continued U.S. assistance and opposition to any coalition government. Many of the men who make up the Saigon regime have a long record of collaboration with foreigners—first the French and now the Americans—in opposition to the independence struggle of their own country.

Indeed, a general feature of those "independent" governments supporting American policy in Asia—South Korea, Taiwan, Thailand, and South Vietnam—is that they are all military dictatorships with little reformist zeal even though they exist in countries with pressing economic and social problems. This last consideration may explain why they permit the massive intrusion of a foreign military establishment: if one is incapable of winning mass domestic support, subordination to a foreign power may be the only means of preserving some vestiges of minority power.

In Vietnam over the last twenty years the United States has ranged itself against the forces which are fighting to protect and secure Vietnamese independence free from outside control. First the Viet Minh and now the NLF have been the most effective fighters—both politically and militarily—for national independence, and this of course is one potent reason why the NLF has been able to survive American military might. If in Vietnam today it is impossible for the people "to determine their own political future without outside interference," it is precisely because the U.S. itself has intervened from the outside.

U.S. Goals and Minority Rule

American policy in Vietnam has not been shaped by the desire to promote the national independence and self-determination of the Vietnamese people but rather by the needs of an inflexible devotion to the successful prosecution of the war. In fact the prime effect of the American intervention in Vietnam has been to prolong the war long past the time when Vietnamese groups would have reached a political settlement. American support therefore has gone to those elements in the South which support the continuance of the war. These political elements, most hostile to communism and willing to fight it, have always constituted a distinct minority of the South Vietnamese population. In most cases, the U.S.-backed leaders have been Catholics, previous supporters of French colonialism, and defenders of entrenched property interests. Their regimes have been urban-based with only nominal control over the densely populated countryside. The Saigon regime which is the servant of a foreign power—the U.S.—cannot but repress its own people's quest for national self-determinatiion and democratic expression.

Saigon's Sham Democracy

U.S. intervention in South Vietnam has done nothing to increase the participation of the people in choosing their government. In fact, as the war has proceeded, the military character of succeeding regimes in the South has become more apparent. Given U.S. war aims, a strong military regime was most desirable from an American point of view.

Diem's military inefficiency was a key factor by 1963 in the American acquiescence to his overthrow.[1] The subsequent Duong Van Minh regime began to lose favor with the Americans—especially the U.S. general staff in Saigon—as the war effort began losing steam and as peace clouds rose on the horizon. Minh himself was suspected of favoring a neutralist solution to the war. The following regimes—those of Khanh, Ky, and Thieu, whose policies were strongly anti-Communist and intransigeant—were more to the American liking.

Under enormous pressure from the Buddhists and other dissidents, Thieu and Ky agreed to hold elections in 1967. By severely limiting both the electorate and the candidates, excluding all those who espoused neutralism, and using their control of military and political power in South Vietnam to the fullest extent, Thieu and Ky managed to garner approximately one-third of the vote—hardly a landslide. Only the government's control of the army, the support of the Catholics, and the fragmentation of the opposition permitted Thieu and Ky to win. Several months after the election Vice-President Ky himself admitted to an Italian journalist, "Our last elections were a loss of time and money, a mockery."[2]

Since then, the Thieu–Ky regime has made little effort to broaden its support. In May 1969, for example, Thieu assumed personal leadership of a newly formed progovernment political alliance, the National Social Democratic Front. Rather than being a broad-based popular group, however, this was merely a collection of the narrow interests which already supported the regime and it has never become a real political force in the South.

Other Forces

A central fact of South Vietnamese politics since 1954 has been the continuing conflict for power. This conflict has not simply been between the Saigon governments and the NLF. It has involved other forces as well—Catholics, Buddhists, the Mekong Delta politico-religious sects, various political splinter groups, students and intellectuals.

Some of these groups are organized and some are not. Perhaps the most significant of these groups is the Buddhists, who toppled the Diem regime in 1963 and nearly overthrew Ky in the winter of 1965 and the spring of 1966 when they held huge demonstrations calling for free elections and a civilian government. Only U.S. logistical and financial support saved the tottering Ky regime. Subsequent government efforts to quash the Buddhist opposition have included attempts to drive a wedge between the moderate and more activist wings of the movement. In addition the government has resorted to the imprisonment of Buddhist leaders under the charge of being "Communists" or "neutralists," terms applied to any critic of the Saigon duumvirate. Despite this repression the Buddhists and other groups remain a powerful non-Communist opposition to Saigon.

The political objectives of the various above-mentioned groups are quite diverse, yet despite these differences, most of these elements share a significant objective: accommodation and political settlement to end the war. The nonaligned factions thus pose a serious dilemma to the Thieu–Ky regime, which jealously guards its political prerogatives. Unable to appease these groups because of its own devotion to the prolongation of the war, the Saigon military leadership has resorted to increasingly repressive means of isolating and even silencing their spokesmen.

Revolutionary Warfare and Self-Determination

The war in Vietnam has been both a political and a military struggle. The NLF has fought basically a political war in South Vietnam against the superior military power of Saigon and the U.S. Appealing to wide sections of the population on the basis of both self-interest and patriotism, the NLF has rallied many to its banner. Even Thieu and Ky do not dispute that the NLF is the only popularly supported, effective political organization now operating in South Vietnam. Saigon's efforts to duplicate NLF success in political terms have been futile. The discipline and sense of commitment of the NLF political officials and soldiers have been striking when compared to the apathy and venality of their Saigon counterparts. The continued vitality of this revolutionary political-military organization in the face of the massed military might of the U.S. and its Saigon collaborators is striking evidence of the NLF's political success in South Vietnam.

In the context of a civil war in Vietnam where American influence is so omnipresent, it is impossible to gauge the political feelings of the population through Western-style procedures like elections. It is rather the process of revolutionary warfare itself which brings to the fore organizations like the NLF which will wield power in the postwar period.

But the process of war itself has led to a certain type of political action in South Vietnam. Because the struggle for power has been carried on through military as well as political means, only those groups which are armed have been able to compete effectively for political power. In a civil conflict such as the one in Vietnam, tremendous pressures exist to force people to choose one side or the other. Politics becomes the servant of war. Those groups which oppose the war and seek accommodation and a political settlement are left without a strong voice in determining the future of their country. Since the NLF—not the Saigon regime—welcomes accommodation and a political settlement, the unarmed opponents of Thieu–Ky probably lean to the side of the NLF if forced to make a choice. (But the relationship between groups like the militant Buddhists and the NLF is by no means clear.) It would be wrong, therefore, to assert that the NLF alone represents the will of the people of South Vietnam, although it is undoubtedly the major group which stands for self-determination and genuine national independence. But whatever the situation, the future of Vietnam should be determined only by the Vietnamese themselves. The

American intervention stands as an enemy to Vietnamese national self-determination, prohibits the expression of political forces in the South, and prolongs the agony of war.

CHAPTER 26

National Security and National Prestige

The Postwar World: Four Epochal Events

American attitudes and involvement in Indochina today can only be understood in the context of the great, revolutionary developments which occurred in the wake of the Second World War. Without exaggeration it can be said that these marked one of the monumental turning points in the history of mankind—a turning point to which man has as yet been unable to adjust. In this, at least four developments stand out as having been of particular significance to the postwar era of international relations in Asia:

1. The swift and easy destruction by the Japanese of the Western enclaves in China and the European colonial position in Southeast Asia: although the colonial powers attempted to resume their positions as overlords in Asia after the war, they were unable to do so.

2. Their failure was due partly to the revealed rot of the colonial system, but also to a great development of the postwar era: the rise of popular revolutionary movements throughout the world, but particularly in Asia.

Indigenous anticolonial and anti-imperialist movements which had gained strength in resistance to the Japanese conquest of Asia emerged from the Pacific War as the most popular, viable, and dynamic forces in many societies. The major examples of this, of course, were the Chinese Communists (who formally established the People's Republic of China in October 1949) and the Viet Minh.

3. Another significant global development was the breakup of the wartime Allied alliance and emergence of the cold war. Orthodox American historians have tended to interpret this in red-white-and-blue terms as a matter of Soviet provocations and American responses; recent revisionist scholars have begun to see the confrontation between the Soviet Union and the United States in the immediate postwar years as a more complex problem of interaction and mutual distrust. Insofar as American attitudes toward Asia are concerned, two facts might be noted here. First, just as the Soviet Union quickly proceeded to secure a sphere of influence for itself in Eastern Europe, so the United States at the same time was establishing its own sphere of influence in the Pacific (by taking over the former mandated islands: the Marianas, Carolines, and Marshalls) and in Asia itself (assuming control over Japan and Okinawa; reestablishing itself in the Philippines; continuing the role of dominant Western power in China which it had acquired during the war; and lending moral and material support to the attempts of the European powers to reimpose their oppressive colonial regimes).[1] And secondly, it should be kept in mind that the American response to Soviet communism in Europe conditioned its understanding of and response to popular and Communist movements in Asia.

4. Finally, the unprecedented revolutionary development of the postwar era: the nuclear age. In retrospect, Hiroshima must be seen as a beginning rather than an end, for the bomb and its potential and its subsequent proliferation have made the post-1945 period fundamentally unlike any other in history.

NSC-68 and the Commitment to Globalism

The American response to these momentous events was fundamentally a simple one, which became formalized in the spring of 1950. The Soviet Union did not test its first atomic bomb until late 1949, long after the cold war had entered a stage beyond any real hope of reconciliation. This, coupled with the Communist victory in China, prompted a thoroughgoing reevaluation of foreign policy in the upper echelons of the U.S. government beginning in late 1949. In April 1950—two months before the Korean War—this was approved by the President and National Security Council (NSC) and formulated as NSC-68, one of the key documents in the cold war. The document remains classified, but its general contents are known. As described by Dean Acheson, "The paper began with a statement of the conflicting aims and purposes of the two superpowers: the priority given by the Soviet rulers to the Kremlin design, world domination, contrasted with the American aim, an environment in which free societies could exist and flourish." Or again, in Acheson's words, the U.S. analysis of the world situation found that the Soviet threat "combined the ideology of communist doctrine and the power of the Russian state into an aggressive expansionist drive, which found its chief opponent and, therefore, target in the antithetic ideas and power of our own country. . . . While our own society felt no compulsion to bring all societies into conformity with it, the Kremlin hierarchy was not content merely to entrench its regime but wished to expand its control directly and indirectly over other people within its reach."[2] The American historian Walter LaFeber has described the contents of NSC-68 as follows:

> The overall picture was one of "an indefinite period of tension and danger." The study urged the United

States to undertake "a bold and massive program" of rebuilding the West until it far surpassed the Soviet bloc, and to meet "each fresh challenge promptly and unequivocally." In these efforts, the United States must stand at the "political and material center with other free nations in variable orbits around it." No longer, the study warned, could the United States ask " 'How much security can we afford?" nor should it any longer attempt to "distinguish between national and global security." The United States could survive only in a world at peace and free from Communist expansion.[3]

In this manner, NSC-68 boiled life down into a clear broth. America's strategic interests were everywhere. National security had become synonymous with global security. The world was polarized into good and evil, free and slave, and it was no longer necessary to make fine distinctions between, say, the Soviet Union, China, Korea, and Indochina. Because communism was seen as monolithic, with the Soviet Union its unchallenged suzerain, bent on "world domination," the situation in Asia was interpreted only through the lenses of a perverted Kremlinology.

- Thus the Chinese revolution was stripped of its rich history and the People's Republic of China became "a Slavic Manchukuo" in Dean Rusk's classic expression.
- Thus the Korean War (which broke out on June 25, 1950) was interpreted in a context which deprived it of its most fundamental aspect—that of a civil war— and seen instead as a thrust emanating straight from the Kremlin, or from a smoothly coordinated Moscow-Peking axis. Here was one early manifestation of the "domino" outlook, for as Truman told British Prime Minister Attlee in early December 1950, "In my opinion the Chinese Communists were Russian satellites. The problem we were facing was part of a pattern. After Korea, it would be Indo-China, then Hong Kong, then Malaya."[4] In fact, the Soviet role in

the Korean War was secondary at best, while China was probably caught entirely by surprise by the outbreak of hostilities, and only intervened in the well-founded belief that her own territory was threated by the American advance toward the Yalu.

- Thus the struggle in Indochina was wrenched from its profound origins as a struggle against colonialism and injustice and contorted to fit the neat moral universe of the American policy planners. Indeed, within days after the outbreak of the Korean War, President Truman announced:

> The attack upon Korea makes it plain beyond all doubt that communism has passed beyond the use of subversion to conquer independent nations and will now use armed invasion and war. . . . Accordingly . . . I have . . . directed acceleration in the furnishing of military assistance to the forces of France and the Associated States in Indochina and the dispatch of a military mission to provide close working relations with those forces.[5]

Beyond its formulation of Manichaeism as official policy, several other aspects of NSC-68 should be stressed: (1) It is important to note that it preceded the Korean War, for the chronology is often obscured and later American actions are generally interpreted as a response to that war. Quite to the contrary, it is more correct to see subsequent developments as a consequence of an ideological position on the part of the United States into which the Korean War itself was fitted. The war, as it turned out, simply made it easier for America's security managers to sell Congress and the public on their view. (2) At the time the document was formalized, the U.S. defense budget stood at $13.5 billion; NSC-68 called for this to be quadrupled to a sum in the neighborhood of $50 billion. Here was the seed of that military-industrial complex which now represents the American economy's kiss of death. And (3) NSC-68 paved the way for the war games of subsequent decades.

War Games

American strategic planning, like American detergents and automobiles, has relied on catchphrases. Under the Eisenhower administration, a nuclear-oriented policy of "massive retaliation" was followed, with the huge bombers of the Strategic Air Command (SAC) playing the decisive role. This was coupled with Dulles's "brinksmanship" and the attractive Republican concept of "a bigger bang for a buck." The massive buildup of the pax atomica continued into the missile age under the Kennedy and Johnson administrations, and shows no signs of abating. As Secretary Melvin Laird explained in presenting the Defense Department's budget request for fiscal 1971:

> The strategic offensive forces we plan to maintain in FY 1971 include 552 B-52 and FB-111 bombers; 1,000 Minuteman and 54 Titan II ICBM launchers, and 656 Polaris and Poseidon SLBM [Submarine Launched Ballistic Missiles] launchers; the strategic defensive forces will include about 650 manned interceptors, and about 1,400 surface-to-air missiles on site.[6]

As the decade of the 1970s opens, the nuclear spiral continues in the form of the MIRV (Multiple Independently Targeted Reentry Vehicles), ABM (Anti-ballistic Missile System), ULMS (Undersea Long-Range Missile System), new B-1 intercontinental jet bomber, and so on. At the same time, the Nixon administration has announced it is shifting from a "two-and-a-half-war" strategy to a "one-and-a-half-war" strategy. To guide one through these twisting and ever ascending paths, a new class of strategy specialist has emerged in the universities and semiofficial think tanks whose self-described task of "international systems maintenance" indicates that the goal is nuclear stalemate—or maintenance of the international status quo.

While the arms race accelerated under the Democrats, the Kennedy administration also introduced a modification in U.S. strategic planning by formulating the concept of "flexible response." Based to a considerable extent upon ideas advanced by General Maxwell Taylor in his 1959 book *An Uncertain Trumpet,* the concepts of "flexible response" or "gradualism" or "brushfire wars" were emphasized from around 1961, as fear of a global nuclear confrontation gave way to concern over Communist expansion through guerrilla warfare or local insurgencies. With this new focus, the army emerged somewhat from the shadows into which it had been cast by the dominant postwar role of the air force to that date. "Counter-insurgency" planning became fashionable among the intellectuals in the Kennedy entourage, and the way was paved for advancing into Indochina. Important in this situation was the development of technologies and strategies within the General Purpose Forces. As described in part II, Vietnam became the "laboratory" for the "new sciences" of warfare—heavier-than-ever-before bombing, defoliation, antipersonnel weaponry, "pacification," Special Forces, computerized decision making, and the like. And legitimizing the military concept of flexible response was the supposedly intellectual concept of geopolitical dominoes.

Dominoes

The domino theory was a logical outcome of NSC-68 and America's global moralism, but offered its own touches of sophistication. One of the earliest and best-known uses of the metaphor was by President Eisenhower during the Indochina crisis of 1954. In discussing why it was necessary to defend Dienbienphu, the president explained:

> You had a row of dominoes set up, and you knocked over the first one, and what would happen to the last one was the certainty that it would go over

very quickly. So you could have a beginning of a disintegration that would have the most profound in-
fluences.[7]

President Nixon, a stalwart bearer of the traditions of the
1950s, informed a television audience on July 2, 1970,
that he had personally talked to the dominoes, and the
situation was indeed unsteady. But what are the standards
for determining if one is really dealing with dominoes or
not?

Like the game itself, the business of geopolitical
dominoes has several versions. These may be delineated
as follows:

1. *Microcosmic dominoes:* In this approach, each
Asian nation becomes the world writ small, and internal
struggles become the personification of good vs. evil, "free
world" vs. "Communist," them vs. us, etc. Most domino
games currently in vogue draw heavily upon this particular
version.

2. *Geographical-propinquity dominoes:* According to
this version, if Vietnam falls, then Cambodia, Thailand,
et cetera, et cetera, fall too. In the case of Cambodia,
there is strong suspicion that the United States has rigged
the game. If players have a great deal of time or imagination, the line of dominoes may be extended to the Philippines, Hawaii, San Francisco, and points east, in which
case the game is usually known either as *Globe-girdling
dominoes* or *Apocalyptic dominoes.*

3. *Maoist-measles dominoes:* A variation named by
the former U.S. ambassador to Thailand, Kenneth Young,
this version is actually a bastardized rendition of the
Maoist concept of "wars of national liberation." The
general concept is that a successful war of national liberation in one country will have infectious results upon
another. The Maoist interpretation holds that the second
country must have some pizazz to start with. [See chapter
21.] The American version does not.

4. *Moscow and/or Peking pipeline dominoes:* In this
version, which goes in and out of style at regular intervals,

the game is dominated by others and Americans can only sit back and watch. Or blow up the table.

5. *Overall rules:* No matter which version of dominoes is played, it is a general rule that the markings on individual dominoes are irrelevant. It is also assumed, a priori, that it is bad for the dominoes to fall.

True Honor

It is often argued that the United States has committed its honor and prestige to the conflict in Indochina, and were it to pull out now its reputation would be besmirched, its credibility would be impaired, and its potential for effective action in the future would be undercut. This view, itself a kind of domino theory, rests upon the extraordinary notion that the type of actions described in this book, notably in part II, can in any way be equated with honor and are indeed seen as such throughout the world. Thus Mr. Johnson spoke of "national honor" while unleashing the most terrible bombardment known to history upon a small country and its people. And Mr. Nixon emphasized the necessity of avoiding "national humiliation" while almost as he spoke the military juggernaut he had released was systematically obliterating a Cambodian village named Snoul. True honor lies elsewhere.

Tom Wicker of the *New York Times* expressed America's dilemma with eloquence in his essay on the occasion of the 194th Independence Day of the land:

> Honor America Day could not attract men and women who believe little honor is due a nation, whatever its history and power, that persists in a brutal and destructive war long after its purpose can be discerned—a war that has uprooted the society of South Vietnam, blasted its cities and countryside, slaughtered and made homeless its bewildered people by the hundreds of thousands, all in the name of saving their right to self-determination, and America's right to "free-world"

leadership—a war entered by stealth in South Vietnam, fought by subterfuge in Laos, extended for unacknowledged reasons to Cambodia, and for the pursuit of which the President has said he may even have to resume the bombing of North Vietnam, a brand of warfare that already has brought America not the honor but the condemnation of the world.

On this July 4, the time has plainly come to put an end to a war that brings nothing but devastation to those it is supposed to save, and nothing but disunity and a waste of lives, energy and resources to those who call themselves saviors. Where is the glory, in such circumstances, in insistence that an end may be negotiated only on American terms? Where lies the real humiliation for the American giant? In courageously facing the limits and limitations of power, or in vain, costly pursuit of military or diplomatic victory over North Vietnam?[8]

The answer is not far to seek.

CHAPTER 27

The Logic of Escalation

In announcing the first U.S. incursion into Cambodia, President Nixon stated: "We take this action not for the purpose of expanding the war into Cambodia but for the purpose of ending the war in Vietnam." By going that extra twenty-one miles across the Cambodian border, Nixon contended, the enemy's jungle Pentagon could be engulfed, the troops brought home, and the victory bagged. Just a few weeks and many bags of rice later, however, it had become evident that the effect of this quick diversionary tactic was to open up a whole new front. No enemy headquarters had been found, 30,000 Saigon troops remained in Cambodia's backyard and were reluctant to leave. The NLF and the North Vietnamese were reinforcing their supply routes in northern Cambodia, the Lon Nol regime in Cambodia was threatened with peasant unrest as never before, and Thailand had entered the fray.

Once more the U.S. was going up the down staircase. This has become a familiar story by now. Five years ago President Johnson proclaimed that his latest step of escalation was designed to get the U.S. out of the war. LBJ's "best and prayerful judgment" was that the air attacks over North Vietnam "are a necessary part of the surest road to peace" (July 28, 1965). The United States has still not come very far along that road. If President Nixon's strategy fails, can one expect further escalation on the part of the United States?

If at First You Don't Succeed

Americans would show less skepticism toward presidential promises if it weren't for the long history of escalation and sacrifice in Vietnam. Starting from the original commitment of economic aid and military equipment to the French in 1950 in their colonialist war against the Viet Minh, the U.S. proceeded to fill France's shoes and extend economic and technical support to the Diem regime after 1954. A major military step-up occurred in 1961 under the Kennedy administration, consisting of an infusion of civilian and military technicians at every level, more U.S. Special Forces teams, and new American-manned air support for South Vietnamese forces. From 1961 through 1964, yearly U.S. troop figures went from 3,000 to 11,000 to 16,000 to 21,000. Despite this, from the American point of view, the situation in South Vietnam went from bad to worse.

Rapid escalation began in 1965 with the initiation of the bombing of North Vietnam and the massive introduction of American troops. But even Johnson in 1965 sought to preserve the appearance of the "moderate" escalation of the past. Therefore he adopted a technique of piecemeal escalation using the actions of the other side as pretexts for his own escalation. As Townsend Hoopes, former undersecretary of the air force, describes it, through this strategy President Johnson started "a process that would lead in a series of acceptable steps to the required enlargement of the U.S. military effort."[1] The process of escalation and troop increases became regularized through Robert McNamara's "strong instinct for managed decision-making." The former secretary of defense, traveling to Vietnam every six months or so to bargain directly with the generals, would insist that they scale down their requests to make them bureaucratically and politically palatable at home, in return for which "he gave his public endorsement to the amended build-up."[2] By this means the U.S. troop commitment to Vietnam increased twenty-five-fold—from 21,000 to 510,000 over a three-year period! It is clear that the U.S. escalation was not in reaction to an enemy buildup but was an autonomous process having an inner logic of its own.

The Escalation Machine

What is this inner logic of the process of escalation? Who or what is to blame? The answer lies less in individuals than in a bureaucratic point of view which dissolves the distinctions between ends and means, and is obsessed with military solutions to basically political problems. As early as 1961, Dean Rusk is said to have regarded Vietnam as "essentially a military problem." According to Richard J. Barnet, a former State Department official, the fearsome momentum of escalation can be explained by the failure of the national security bureaucracy to offer anything but military, instrumental alternatives. Negotiation or compromise is simply not plugged into the team computer. Military victory is the unquestioned goal.

Each part of the bureaucracy has its own pet solutions: the air force its bombing raids; the army its search-and-destroy missions; the CIA its covert counterinsurrection; the Chemical Corps its defoliation; ad infinitum. At each point of escalation, a new combination of methods and emphases is possible. Barnet explains:

> Unlike a major war where the United States is endangered, the consequences of failure of any particular military operation against a distant underdeveloped country appear limited. The bureaucracy falls prey to the illusion that they are able to control events

because they are free of the fear of retaliation. They feel they have all the options and they try them one by one.[3]

Because of the low risks and seemingly inexhaustible resources of the United States, there has been little to stop the established momentum toward escalation.

The Human Factor

But within a bureaucracy there are human beings, and certainly some should have awakened to what was happening. Some did, and left. But most, for various reasons, did not until late in the game. For one thing, the role of the war-involved bureaucrat is a detached one, to say the least. The huge emphasis upon devising new methods, tactics, and gimmicks (the most renowned perhaps being McNamara's electric anti-infiltration barrier) draws attention away from the ends that these means are serving. A coverlet of euphemistic vocabulary (e.g., surgical strikes, pacification, protective reaction) separates the functionary from the cruelty of a war thousands of miles away.

For those higher up in the bureaucracy, "human ego investment" becomes an important factor. Men intent on proving their original decisions correct and saving their reputations are hardly those best able to admit a mistake and turn a policy around.

The Politics of Escalation

How and in what context were escalations put into effect? Were they, as some U.S. policy spokesmen have claimed, merely reactions to the other side? Dean Rusk asserted that escalation should not be viewed as having depended "upon decisions made by the United States" but rather upon aggression by the North Vietnamese (February 18, 1966). Such an assertion is unsupported by the facts.

Far from being simple reactions to enemy incursions, American escalations have been geared to sustaining the momentum of the American war effort in Vietnam. In this connection the political fluctuations of the Saigon regime have been of critical importance. In the past whenever political events in Saigon threatened the war regime there, or whenever the other side indicated a willingness to negotiate a settlement, the U.S. responded by a show of strength or a qualitative step-up of its military involvement. According to a citizens' white paper of 1966 (*The Politics of Escalation*), such escalations have frequently occurred just as a break in the war clouds indicated a possible accommodation with the NLF. Almost always they were timed to give the lagging war effort a good shot in the arm. Let us cite one or two examples.

The famous Tonkin Gulf reprisals of August 1964—the first aerial attacks against North Vietnam—were supposedly a response to "aggression" by two North Vietnamese PT boats against a U.S. destroyer. The blame for the provocation is ambiguous at best, since the U.S. vessels were within North Vietnam's twelve-mile limit or what it considered to be its territorial waters at the very moment South Vietnamese ships were attacking another part of North Vietnam's coast. Moreover, it seems extremely doubtful that the alleged attack which served as the pretext for the reprisals even took place![4] Of special significance, however, was the fact that the Saigon regime of General Khanh was having no success on the battlefield at this time, was nervously hearing appeals for negotiations from de Gaulle, the USSR, and U Thant in July 1964, and was itself desperately suggesting the use of force against the North (July 29). Within a week of the latter suggestion, the U.S. was launching a massive bombing raid on North Vietnamese coastal bases. One has to be more than a little gullible to believe that such a step-up was due simply to two North Vietnamese PT boats.

The even more serious bombing of North Vietnam on

February 7, 1965, which began the regularization of bombing raids, was said to be a response to a guerrilla raid on an American base at Pleiku which killed eight Americans. However, since the bombing was carried out a mere eight hours after the beginning of the raid, it seems obvious that the bombing mission had been prepared in advance. A more probable set of reasons for the bombing was the unprecedented number of strikes and demonstrations going on in Vietnam throughout the month of January, the growing rumors of a possible negotiated settlement, and a coup bringing in a new government on January 27 "whose commitment to continue the war appeared increasingly dubious."[5] The war against "communism" needed yet another quick shot in the arm, and it soon got it.

If one looks at President Nixon's recent incursion into Cambodia it seems obvious that, as in the preceding instances of escalation, Communist aggression there was not the causal factor. Confidence had been waning in the effectiveness of "Vietnamization." The NLF and the North Vietnamese in Cambodia, pressed on the west by Lon Nol's hostile regime and on the east by the U.S. B-52s and unannounced attacks across the Cambodian border, were beginning to move away from their border "sanctuaries."

Far from posing a threat to American lives, they were maneuvering to avoid being flanked on two sides. At the same time, the Thieu–Ky regime was eager to take advantage of the momentary change and to "test" its forces in another land. The picture forms of a U.S. tempted to expand a war rather than one valiantly forced to defend its men against threatened attack.

The Prospects for Further Escalation

America has been escalating in Indochina for twenty years now, and the momentum for further escalation is immense. For years the military and intelligence bureaucracy has chafed at the restrictions of a limited war—restrictions which can be maintained only by determined civilian leaders in government. Neither President Johnson nor President Nixon has shown such determination.

In a few short years the "limited war" in South Vietnam has expanded both in scope and intensity into an open-ended conflict in which few restraints remain. In the Cambodian venture the president apparently bypassed or ignored his civilian advisers and hearkened to the voice of the Joint Chiefs of Staff. He shares their belief in the necessity of attaining that military victory which has been so elusive in Indochina. In his news conference on May 8, 1970, the president plainly hinted at the nature of further escalation. In response to any further enemy actions, the president said, "We will move decisively and not step by step." The precise meaning of this threat is, of course, unclear, but the remaining options are not many. Will the withdrawal of U.S. ground forces from Cambodia be followed by a Laotian-type massive bombing, and a resumption of the bombing of North Vietnam with no holds barred? Is a U.S. invasion of Laos and/or North Vietnam a likely prospect? Will the U.S. encourage the Thais and other client governments to take a larger part in the war? Will a president who needs little convincing from the military be tempted to employ tactical nuclear weapons in Indochina, perhaps finally to confront even China? In the light of the history of escalation it does not seem possible to foreclose even the last of these possibilities. Unless American leaders abandon pursuit of the phantom of a military victory in Indochina, further escalation of the war seems not a likelihood but a certainty.

CHAPTER 28

Intelligence and Decision Making

"We have to trust the president and his advisors. They have the facts and we don't" is an honestly felt sentiment based upon nearly two centuries of public confidence in America's leaders. But the words portray the tragic narrowness of outlook which has come to mark U.S. foreign policy in recent times. They reveal an assumption that America's most vital decisions on war and peace, on invasion and neutrality and wholesale destruction of populations are no longer the concern of the people, but must be determined by secret intelligence reports which are the province of a specially authorized elite. Yet the U.S. record in Indochina proves that both the intelligence system and the policy-making process which it nourishes have become a travesty of responsible government and a contemptuous affront to the American people.

Intelligence and Unintelligence

How could it happen that in 1954 Washington thought forty B-26 bombers and a handful of "technicians" would save Dienbienphu? How could McNamara say in 1962,

"Every quantitative measurement we have shows we are winning the war," and declare that the U.S. military task in Vietnam would be completed in 1965? How could General Westmoreland in 1967 declare that the Vietnamese Communists were no longer capable of fighting anywhere "except at the edge of [their] sanctuaries"—and a few weeks later the enemy's Tet offensive carried the war into downtown Saigon and a hundred other cities as far from the sanctuaries as it is possible to get and still be in Vietnam? And how could President Nixon tell the nation on April 30, 1970, that "tonight, American and South Vietnam units will attack the headquarters of the entire Communist military operation in South Vietnam," yet weeks later administration press officers still were admonishing reporters for not having realized that our invasion of course could not be expected to uncover the "headquarters," which now was portrayed as a kind of floating crap game with no fixed abode.

The Politics of Military Intelligence

What lies behind this catalog of absurd miscalculations and predictions which has misled the public for so many years? For one thing, the American military has been blighted by the same cultural and racial blindness which affected the French colonial rulers of Vietnam—the inability to believe that immense applications of modern weapons technology can be withstood by "funny little men who six months ago were rickshaw coolies."[1] Equally important has been the compulsion to make military reporting from the field support established policy and give an impression of continuing progress. Military men are charged with the task of winning. If they don't, their generals replace them with those who can or who can *show* they can. The persistent and patent fallacy that "the essence of the problem in Vietnam is military" (General Wheeler) accounts for the invasion of Cambodia, the latest of the series of intelligence failures.

The ambitious or cowed army officer in the field must show results or suffer damage to his career. The result has been a procession of "intelligence estimates" proclaiming "the light at the end of the tunnel," a phrase now regarded as an unfunny joke even in Washington and Saigon. The Cambodian adventure has produced the latest evidence that attitudes and fears productive of false information are as prevalent as ever. One such example was the visit of Brigadier General Robert Shoemaker to the "Fishhook" during which he made clear his active dislike for even the mildest hint of bad news.[2] His attitude became understandable when it was revealed that Defense Secretary Laird had cabled General Abrams, the commander of all U.S. forces in Vietnam, a list of military successes by which "the American public would be impressed." Significantly, the first combined statistics for body counts and captured weapons were released shortly thereafter with suspiciously inflated totals.

Militarization of the Civilian Bureaucracy

Ultimately, however, the responsibility lies not with the military, but with the civilians in government who, by abdicating from the decision-making process, have failed to provide the counterweight to military aggrandizement which our governmental system requires. This atrophy of the civilian side now extends from the embassy in Saigon to the highest levels of policy making in Washington.

The increasing dominance of the military in foreign policy can be traced back to the Second World War when FDR began to place greater reliance upon his generals for political counsel than on his civilian political advisers. After the war, the establishment of the Defense Department and the National Security Council placed military men in positions of nominal parity but real advantage in intragovernmental policy discussions. As a result, we have come to witness the realization of the fear expressed by General George Marshall years ago when he warned against the danger of discussing any foreign policy issue in military terms. To do so, said Marshall, "might make it a military problem."

The Tame Task Force Technique

A landmark of this process was the invention of the "task force," a concept which prettifies bureaucratic rigidity with an aura of dynamism. The State Department, the National Security Council, the White House, and the CIA have all established not only their own little foreign ministries, but their own Vietnam "desk" as well. Some have two or three. The most favored of these have been those staffed with officials chosen for their conformity to established, that is, military-oriented, policies. It now appears that this "tame task force" technique was used in the decision to invade Cambodia. The color of administration-wide approval was provided by a so-called "special action committee," a task force composed of those predisposed to a military solution, notably Deputy Defense Secretary Packard and the defense industry millionaire and Undersecretary of State Alexis Johnson, considered to be "the Pentagon's man in the State Department."[3]

Civilian Abdication and Military Aggrandizement Overseas

Overseas, the dual phenomena of civilian abdication and military aggrandizement have been under way for years, as civilian officials in East and Southeast Asia have either avoided the situation out of a sense of protest or hopelessness, or have simply chosen to go along with the trend. In 1969 alone, 150 Foreign Service employees refused to serve in Vietnam (and the number must be increasing, for State has now ordered officers to accept such assignments or resign). The result has been a Saigon embassy staffed largely by those who accept the established policy of U.S. military involvement. (And, as is well known, CIA officials have long been noted for their acquiescence to this point of view.)

The Foreign Service, whose diplomatic professionalism should provide a bulwark against such fawning behavior, has been progressively eroded in recent years. As former U.S. Ambassador Reischauer has pointed out, the State Department's failure to function adequately as the chief formulator and executor of policy has been due to inadequate authority and funds. In the field as well as in Washington, State has had neither the money nor the manpower to prepare position papers for the contest of wills with the military at policy sessions. It is noteworthy that President Nixon's call for a 10 percent cut in the number of U.S. officials serving overseas has been carried out in the Foreign Service, but has specifically exempted the military-CIA-FBI overseas intelligence phalanx. The government's Chinese language school in Formosa, created to train diplomats, is now 90 percent composed of army intelligence and CIA trainees. And to ensure that the remnants of the Foreign Service got the message, the administration on May 21 reprimanded for "disloyalty to the President" the fifty Foreign Service officers who expressed their concern over the invasion of Cambodia to Secretary of State Rogers.

These efforts to induce timidity bring results. When the State Department's long and arduous effort to reopen diplomatic contacts with China at Warsaw was threatened by the sudden resumption, after a one-and-a-half-year pause, of U.S. reconnaissance overflights of the Chinese mainland in late 1969, one State official concerned explained his failure to protest by pointing out that the intrusions were so drastic a step that "the White House must have had a good reason." In fact, one wonders whether the White House knew at all. Mr. Nixon boasted on April 30, 1970, for example, that he "had stopped the bombing of North Vietnam," yet raids resumed the next day. Subsequent probing by the press indicated that the Secretary of State and the Secretary of Defense were informed *after* the decision to resume bombing was taken. Pieced together, facts indicated that either the Joint Chief's of Staff circumvented their civilian superiors and were in direct touch with the White House, or that the president himself never authorized the raids.[4]

Circumventing Congress

The Cambodian adventure was most remarkable, however, for having breached the last civilian bulwark against the military—Congress. In the tragic recent tradition of joint Pentagon-White House efforts to confound Congress and the public on foreign policy (such as the Tonkin Gulf hoax, the cover-up of U.S. involvement in Laos, and the Mylai massacre), the president failed to inform Congress. His own party's leader in the Senate was publicly denying the resumption of the bombing of the North as raids were taking place. This unconstitutional act was raised to the status of U.S. policy by White House explanations that such sudden adventures were part of a U.S. strategy of "unpredictability." One ruefully recalls Mr. Nixon's campaign pledge to end just such practices in foreign policy making.

CHAPTER 29

Careerism and Ego Investment

The Indochina war is in large part a product of sheer institutional momentum. Never in history has such a vast, expensive, and technologically sophisticated governmental apparatus been focused for so long on "success" in one small region abroad. And never in America have the careers of so many public servants been at stake in such an undertaking.

Conformity in the Civilian Bureaucracy

On the civilian side of the ledger, Vietnam has represented an ongoing "ego investment" in terms of both men and agencies. The State Department, AID, CIA, and other units compete in the field against each other, and also against the military, to produce a non-Communist outcome.

Within the ranks of these agencies, two forms of pressure upon people have long been identifiable. First, there hangs over the heads of Foreign Service officers and others the dark shadow of the "loss of China." From the mid-1950s onward, FSOs were keenly aware of the terrible harm done to their colleagues of the old China service through the investigations and purges of McCarthy, Mc-Carran, and Dulles's security chief, Scott McLeod. One root cause of the China witch-hunt lay in the written and even oral expressions of doubts by officers as to the wisdom of trying to save the Chinese Nationalist government; such doubters later saw their careers ruined or blighted by charges of treason, procommunism, or "softness" on communism. For Vietnam personnel, the bureaucratic lesson of China has been clear and compelling: Keep your doubts to yourself. Such caution was compounded by the excesses of ambassadors in Saigon, Bangkok, and elsewhere who refused to forward reports from those few bold enough to register their doubts. It was also compounded by the "curator mentality" within a service whose promotion system placed a premium on simply staying out of trouble.

A second type of pressure has been the relentless demand for good news from increasingly beleaguered administrators in Washington. Silence about doubts was not enough; what was required from the field, first to Embassy Saigon, then to Washington, was affirmation—positive indicators of success: the strength and numbers of the "strategic hamlet" program (exploded as a myth with the death of Diem), statistics on "pacified" and "secure" villages (exploded as a myth with the Tet offensive), and today optimistic data on the Cambodian adventure and on "Vietnamization."

Such pressures are further intensified by government agencies' demand for Vietnam tours of duty from those who hope to rise within the career ranks. Indochina experience has become a major ingredient in Washington's career development system, a process termed by some "the discipline of disappointment." One significant byproduct, of course, is the flight of able men from the career services—and the inability of the services to replenish such lost talent from the younger generation emerging from the colleges.

Personal Ego Investment

In the field, then, the war has produced severe constraints and muted, distorted reporting among the careerists. But more dangerous is the war's impact back in Washington. Here the phenomenon of ego investment is striking.

At the heart of the matter is the continuity in office of men in the upper echelons who participated in or enlarged upon early Vietnam decisions and who therefore have deep personal stakes in those decisions and the outcome. Such continuity was striking in the 1960s. Among the war's chief civilian architects were Dean Rusk, Walt Rostow, Robert McNamara, McGeorge Bundy, William Bundy, and Alexis Johnson. Of this group, Rusk, Rostow, and William Bundy persisted in one office or another for eight years; and Alexis Johnson, a former ambassador to Thailand, Saigon, and Japan, stays on today as an undersecretary of state and a chief planner of the Cambodian invasion. Such men, during their tenure, rejected innumerable opportunities for an exit from Vietnam. They did so because at moments of decision they simply could not accept the risk of an outcome that was less than "success." Beneath this visible tier of decision makers is also a less visible layer of Indochina careerists in all the agencies, men similarly tied to the mistakes of the past.

As one former White House aide has written:

> Men who have participated in a decision develop a stake in that decision. As they participate in further, related decisions, their stake increases. It might have been possible to dissuade a man of strong self-confidence at an early stage of the ladder of decision; but it is infinitely harder at later stages since a change of mind there usually involves implicit or explicit repudiation of a chain of previous decisions. To put it bluntly: at the heart of the Vietnam calamity is a group of able, dedicated men who have been regularly

and repeatedly wrong—and whose standing with their contemporaries, and more important, with history, depends, as they see it, on being proven right. These are not men who can be asked to extricate themselves from error.[1]

Little wonder, then, that so many of Vietnam's planners who have left the constraints of government service remain silent even today—Rusk, the two Bundys, McNamara, to name a few; for a repudiation of the enterprise, even now, is an admission of personal failure in the past. Nixon's "silent majority" includes within it a small cheering section of those who still seek personal vindication in the outcome.

Military Momentum

If careerism and ego investment are at work in the civilian end of the Indochina disaster, they are doubly at work and even more significant in the military aspects of our involvement.

From the early 1960s onward, and particularly since the dramatic escalations of 1965, the Vietnam war has served a number of functions for the government's largest and best-financed subdivision, the armed forces. It has provided a unique laboratory and testing ground for an infinite variety of weaponry and tactics; it has provided an arena for interservice competition and therefore growth and development through escalating demands on the federal budget; it has provided that rare and much-desired boon to the peacetime military, a real war and hence a route to rapid rise within the services; and it has kept our military in the national limelight—as "heroic" field commanders (Westmoreland and Abrams), as an entrenched elite with a Washington veto power (the Joint Chiefs), and as soldiers turned policy makers (General Wheeler, at times, and General Maxwell Taylor throughout).

It is no secret that the salesmen of "counterinsurgency" persuaded both Kennedys to press for "covert" ground involvement in Indochina; nor that the salesmen of air power persuaded Lyndon Johnson to bomb North Vietnam; nor even that Nixon's Cambodian lunge, in various forms, has been regularly pressed upon administrations by the Pentagon since the early 1960s. What has been involved in these and other moves is a doctrine or formula in search of proof; and what has happened in each case is a search for further and more elaborate testing once each doctrine or formula fails to achieve its aim. (Once "counterinsurgency" begins to fail, bombing is introduced to force "negotiations"; and as bombing begins to fail, ground forces are brought in massively. What stands waiting offstage, unused but itching for use, is "tactical nukes" and also perhaps not so tactical ones—complete with a full-fledged doctrine to be tested.)

Military Careerism

As the war's folly has become more widely understood and accepted, many in the lower ranks of the military have begun to speak out—and, in some cases, to suffer the consequences. But few at the top have lifted the veil on the military ingredient of the Indochina disaster as fully and courageously as the former Marine Corps commandant, General David M. Shoup.[2]

From General Shoup comes a sobering comment on the military's career investment in the Indochina war: "Civilians can scarcely understand or even believe that many ambitious military professionals truly yearn for wars and the opportunities for glory and distinction afforded only in combat. A career of peacetime duty is a dull and frustrating prospect for the normal regular officer to contemplate." Hence the personal as well as institutional involvement of the services in Indochina. And as General Shoup further reports, the institutional aspect is compounded by interservice rivalry: ". . . in Vietnam during 1965 the four services were racing to build up combat strength in that hapless country. This effort was ostensibly to save South Vietnam from Viet Cong and North Vietnamese aggression. It should also be noted that it was motivated in part by the same old interservice rivalry to demonstrate respective importance and combat effectiveness." As for the bombing of North Vietnam that 1965 produced, Shoup describes it as "one of the most wasteful and expensive hoaxes ever to be put over on the American people. . . . air power use in general has to a large degree been a contest for the operations planners, 'fine experience' for young pilots, and opportunity for career officers."

The war's "career opportunity" aspect is further spelled out by Lieutenant Colonel Edward L. King, a retired army officer: "Another instrument for enforcing conformity—and getting men to 'voluntarily' serve in Vietnam—is the Army's 'career incentives' policy. Promotion is not possible without a Vietnam tour . . . There has therefore been hot competition for combat commands."[3]

Military Deception

On the analysis or reporting of the results of actions undertaken by the various services, General Shoup has some news for the public:

> Each of the services and all of the major commands practice techniques of controlling the news and the release of self-serving propaganda: in "the interests of national defense," to make the service look good, to cover up mistakes, to build up and publicize a distinguished military personality, or to win a round in the continuous gamesmanship of the interservice contest.

Why is the United States fighting in Indochina? In part because several thousand Americans, and especially a large handful in both Washington and Southeast Asia, have their own reasons—their own personal stakes as careerists on the promotion ladder or as upper-echelon leaders answerable to "history"—for supporting the enterprise through thick and thin, however misconceived it may have been, whatever disasters it may produce, until success and vindication are attained. Given such a weight of collective ego investments within the civilian and military bureaucracy, it is hardly surprising that nothing much changes despite new leadership at the top.

CHAPTER 30

Pax Americana: The Military Dimension

One useful framework for understanding American policy in Asia lies in simply identifying the formal military components of American global power: defense treaties, bases and overseas troops, client armies, and various types of military aid. These are described in the sections which follow, and at the same time some suggestion is given as to the relationship between the American military presence in various Asian countries and the social, political, and economic problems of those same countries.

Treaties

Over forty nations have a treaty right to call upon the United States to come to their defense. These range from the capitalist democracies of Western Europe and the fascist regime in Greece, covered by NATO, to a score of dictatorships in Latin America, covered by the Rio Pact. Within Asia, the list is equally long. Here, America's least important multilateral alliance, ANZUS, is with the white regimes of Australia and New Zealand, both of which would be natural allies even without formal alli-

ances. This is not true of the U.S.-Japan Security Treaty
—the most important bilateral alliance which the U.S.
has with an Asian nation. First signed in September 1951,
it has since evolved into an alliance of an increasingly
offensive nature. A brief review of its history illustrates
how this has come about.

The first Security Treaty, negotiated while Japan was
still under American occupation, allowed the U.S. to use
Japan as a military arsenal and base sanctuary from
which to wage war in the Korean peninsula. In late 1951
and early 1952, before the U.S. Senate ratified this and
the separate peace treaty, the U.S. brought pressure upon
Japan not to restore normal diplomatic and economic relations with China. In effect, it made Japan take sides in
the "cold war." Following this, the U.S. began a pervasive, long-term effort to underwrite and spur on Japanese
rearmament. On March 8, 1954, the two countries signed a
Mutual Defense Assistance Agreement, on the basis of
which Japan reorganized its armed forces and moved to
restore diplomatic and economic ties with the nations of
Southeast Asia. Japanese defense production grew steadily
thereafter, aided by the continuation from the Korean War
of U.S. "special procurements," which averaged $600 mil-
lion annually between 1951 and 1960. By the late 1960s,
long after the original treaty had been renewed on a more
equitable basis, the clear outlines of a Japanese military-
industrial complex with strong ties to American defense
industry had emerged. Fed by industrial licensing agreements and joint arms production programs with American
defense contractors, the Japanese complex also benefited
from little-noticed military technical agreements and memoranda such as the November 1962 Military Data Exchange Agreement, the June 1968 Memorandum on
Military Research and Development, and the July 1969
Aerospace Cooperation Agreement.[1]

Rising nationalism and a fast growing military-industrial complex today generates strong pressures within Japan for an autonomous foreign policy. For the 1970s,
however, Japan seems likely to remain politically within

the American imperial system, while gradually assuming a subordinate police-keeping role limited geographically to East Asia. It was this development which the Nixon-Sato joint communiqué of November 1969 reflected when it linked the defense of Japan to the defense of the military dictatorships in Taiwan and South Korea.

South Korea is another country which has a lien on American military power. The U.S. commitment to propping up successive anti-Communist, antidemocratic dictatorships predates the Korean War and has been legally enshrined in another bilateral military alliance. The U.S.-South Korean Mutual Defense Treaty of July 23, 1953, was made originally to win Syngman Rhee's support for an armistice to end the Korean War; it can be activated only "in the event of an armed attack against South Korea."[2]

In countries where, unlike Korea, the U.S. has not had its fingers burned by war, there was a tendency to gradually eliminate constitutional restrictions on the activation of military alliances. This can be seen in the U.S.-Philippines Mutual Defense Treaty. Concluded in 1951—four years after an earlier agreement giving the U.S. rights to twenty-three bases in the Philippines—it rationalized a colonial relationship dating back to the turn of the century when the U.S. crushed the Philippine revolution and began the process of entrenching the power of the present ruling class. Over the course of the next decade, however, executive statements and formal memoranda rendered meaningless this treaty's original constitutional clause requiring the participation of Congress before repelling an armed attack. In 1959, the Bohlen-Serrano Memorandum made the original defense commitment "immediate and automatic" by referring to U.S. forces stationed in the islands. This was later reaffirmed in a joint communiqué between Presidents Johnson and Macapagal (October 6, 1964) and in an exchange of notes between Secretary of State Rusk and Philippine Foreign Secretary Ramos (1966).[3]

Hardly less open-ended is a fourth military alliance,

made in December 1954, which commits the U.S. to the defense of the historically moribund Nationalist dictatorship on Taiwan (Formosa), as well as to continued interference in the Chinese civil war. Shortly after it was signed, President Eisenhower obtained from Congress the famous "Formosa Straits Resolution" authorizing the president to use American forces "as he deems necessary" to protect Taiwan and the Pescadores Islands against armed attack from the People's Republic of China. This was again underscored by President Kennedy's statement of June 27, 1962, that the U.S. would take "the action necessary to assure the defense of Formosa and the Pescadores," and would defend Quemoy and Matsu islands if "there were an attack which was part of an attack on Formosa and the Pescadores."[4]

As the epicenter of conflict moved from East to Southeast Asia, it came to be reflected in yet another collective "defense" treaty. In 1954 Secretary of State John Foster Dulles, reacting angrily to the Geneva accords, succeeded in persuading six countries, only two of which were in Southeast Asia—the Philippines and Thailand—to sign the treaty creating SEATO (Southeast Asia Treaty Organization). Designed to counter the Geneva accords and provide a legal justification for future U.S. activities in Indochina, it postulated an ill-defined American defense commitment against both external and internal "aggression." Successive administrations cited it during the early 1960s as imposing an obligation to defend the nonmember government of South Vietnam; by the end of the decade it was most commonly invoked as justification for U.S. air bases in Thailand, where, in 1962, its application had been bilateralized by the Rusk-Thanat Joint Communiqué.

The defense treaties just reviewed—with Japan, South Korea, Taiwan, the Philippines, and SEATO—are the pivotal American military alliances in Asia. Individually, each was negotiated with certain particular considerations in mind, but collectively they have come to function primarily as an alliance directed against the People's Republic of China. Countries which have signed them have all yielded up bases to the U.S. for the land and sea encirclement of China. In treaties such as these, all negotiated, signed, and ratified in the years from 1947 to 1955, it is not difficult to see "the assumptions and objectives of American policy makers at the height of the Cold War." At the same time, one should not ignore the element of ideological continuity which links prewar and postwar American imperialism, as seen, for example, in John Foster Dulles's passionate words, inscribed at the Dulles Library in Princeton:

> This nation of ours is not merely a self-serving society but was founded with a mission to help build a world where liberty and justice would prevail.
>
> Love of peace by itself has never been sufficient to deter war. There can never in the long run be real peace unless there is justice and law and the will and the capacity to use force to punish an aggressor. The task of winning peace and its necessary component, justice, is one which demands our finest effort.[5]

Dulles was led to construct an Asian alliance network because, among other things, he was a victim of the hereditary American belief that the United States is not like other nations but has a unique responsibility to define the sort of international order the world will have and then use righteous force to achieve it. The same belief is embodied in the Monroe Doctrine, which announced to the world a century and a half ago that only the U.S. could direct the affairs of North and South America. Taken all together, the American defense treaties discussed here represent a Monroe Doctrine for large areas of Asia.

Lastly, over and above their positive effects or initial purposes, the treaties lend structure to the global American imperial system. Characterized by an absence of formal territorial controls and a professed ideology of "anti-imperialism," that system in actuality uses treaties as one of several means to keep its member states firmly integrated into a world capitalist market system dominated by the United States.

Bases

Defense treaties embody the objectives of foreign policy and reflect its underlying spirit. But they must be interpreted and are often ambiguous. Such is not the case with bases. Globe-encircling systems of military bases are the hardest, least ambiguous symbols of an American propensity for world domination. In 1969 the Defense Department reported having 340 major bases overseas (not including Vietnam) and another 2,270 minor installations, denoting anything from navigational aids to "small administrative buildings supporting incidental activities."[6] Altogether, these occupied 4,000 square miles of land in thirty-three foreign countries.[7] The number of major U.S. bases in Vietnam was fifty-nine in September 1969.

Historically, base expansion in Asia occurred in two waves, separated by over four decades. The first wave saw Hawaii and the Philippines annexed at the end of the nineteenth century for essentially economic reasons: both were "necessary stepping stones to the penetration of China." Thereafter, Japan's growing naval strength thwarted further American base acquisition closer to East Asia, which, after the Russo-Japanese War, had emerged as an independent focal point of international relations. Not until World War II provided the opportunity was U.S. base expansion renewed. When the second wave formed, it involved a two-stage process. Having spent the first half of the 1940s conquering Japan, while, at the same time, working to build up China as a counterweight to her, the U.S. in the aftermath of the war viewed retention of its Pacific bases mainly in terms of preventing a resurgence of Japanese militarism. Base construction, with but few exceptions, was allowed to lapse, and was not renewed until after it had become clear that American efforts could not prevent a revolutionary regime from coming to power in China.

In the early 1950s base construction for the purpose of isolating and containing China centered on East Asia, particularly Okinawa; after 1954 it shifted to Southeast Asia in an attempt to ring in China from its southern flank. The key U.S. bases in Asia today follow the line of treaty commitments. Apart from bases in South Vietnam and on Guam (Anderson Air Base), these are located in Japan, Okinawa, South Korea, Taiwan, the Philippines, and Thailand.

Japan, which in 1952 had 2,500 U.S. installations, today has 126 of which 48 are designated major.[8] These include the air bases at Misawa, Yokoda, Itazuke, Fuchu, Atsugi, and Iwakuni and the naval bases at Yokosuka and Sasebo. Japan's alienated possession, Okinawa, an island three-eighths the area of Rhode Island, has a $2 billion complex consisting of 120 bases occupying 25 percent of its total land area. Okinawa is "the only Asian base in which the U.S. has a totally free hand" . . . to bomb Indochina with B-52s from Kadena, to store nuclear weapons or poison gas, to beam Voice of America broadcasts to mainland China, to train Special Forces for operations in Vietnam.[9] This total freedom of use will be ended when the U.S. returns Okinawa to formal Japanese control after the end of the Vietnam slaughter.

South Korea has fifty-five major American bases of which the air bases at Kunsan, Suwon, Taegu, Yongsan, and Osau are the largest.[10] Following the January 1968 seizure of the *Pueblo* by North Korea, the U.S. began a major buildup of air and naval power in the Korean peninsula. The U.S. Eighth Army Command was turned into a field command; the Third and Seventy-first squadrons, formerly attached to the U.S. Seventh Fleet, were permanently deployed to Korean waters; the advanced headquarters of the U.S. Fifth Air Force was moved from Fuchu, Japan, to Tosan, increasing the number of American warplanes in South Korea by over two hundred; lastly, construction was started on thirty-four HAWK missile sites around Seoul, and on fifty to sixty new air force facilities. Included in the last was the construction of facilities for storing nuclear weapons on Cheju Island.[11]

Taipei, Tainan, and Ching Chuang-kang are large U.S. air bases in Taiwan from which B-52 attacks or missiles could be launched against China. In the Philippines—which was obliged to lease twenty-three bases to the U.S. for ninety-nine years by a March 1947 agreement—Clark, Sangley Point, and Macatan remain key air bases, while the naval facilities at Subic Bay rank with Sasebo, Yokosuka, and Guam as one of the U.S. Navy's four major Pacific ports. Of far more utility than any of these at the moment, however, are the U.S. base sanctuaries in Thailand. The death and maiming of tens of thousands of Vietnamese, Laotians, and Cambodians can be traced to planes flying from bases such as Korat, Nakhon Phanom, Takhli, Ubon, U-tapao, and Don Muang (Bangkok). In addition, the Sattahip naval complex in Thailand has emerged as one of America's major bases for naval operations in South and Southeast Asia.

The American Military Presence and Its Effects on Asian Countries

Depth can be added to a structural sketch of the American imperial system by introducing American troops and their foreign allies. In 1969 the number of people encased in U.S. overseas bases, including dependents and foreign personnel as well as servicemen, was 1.75 million. Including Vietnam and the Seventh Fleet, the U.S. now has close to 1 million men on duty in Asia. As of September 1969, U.S. combat forces stationed on Asian territory were distributed as follows:[12]

Japan	40,000
South Korea	56,000
Okinawa	45,000
Taiwan	10,000
Philippines	30,000
South Vietnam	508,000

Thailand	47,000
Guam	14,000
Pacific Fleet	250,000

In accordance with the withdrawal of U.S. troops from Vietnam plus the "Nixon Doctrine" policy of replacing American garrisons with Asians, these figures are declining—and new strategies and technologies emerging to take their place.

In Japan, the physical inconspicuousness of the U.S. garrison goes hand in hand with its military redundancy. For Japan already has the third most powerful navy and air force in the Pacific after the U.S. and the Soviet Union, while its small but highly mechanized army "has a high percentage of officers and non-coms and could easily be expanded to millions if the Japanese Constitution were revised and a conscription law enacted."[13] That possibility is enhanced by the Nixon Doctrine of Asians fighting Asians, which, vis-à-vis Japan, takes the form of pressuring the conservative Sato government to keep on increasing defense expenditures. Japan's defense allocation for fiscal 1970 registered an almost 18 percent increase over its 1969 defense allocation.[14]

Unlike Japan, the governments of client states such as South Korea, Thailand, and the Philippines value U.S. bases, troops, and military assistance from the point of view of their own internal as well as external security. For example, the Park Chung Hee dictatorship, which came to power in a military coup in May 1961, still feels insecure despite a 620,000-man army and its annual military subsidy from Washington of $140 million. Even the promise of a further $1 billion in military aid spread over the next five years has not dampened its resistance to planned American troop withdrawals. Not surprisingly, Park welcomes anything American from nuclear bombs to Las Vegas technical advisers for his country's gambling casinos.[15] Yet economic and social complications stemming from the U.S. presence do exist and will eventually have to be dealt with.

North of Seoul, in the town of Munsan, for example,

more than half the population of 34,000 "depend for their livelihood on spending by members of the U.S. Second Division." "Many townspeople work on American installations. Others, like tailors, bar and nightclub owners, shopkeepers and a swarm of plump, pretty and aggressive prostitutes make their living from the money spent in town by off-duty soldiers."[16] South Korea is full of Munsans—as indeed are all the countries in Asia in which the American military presence is conspicuous.

More serious, however, is the structural economic deformity wrought by the American commitment to an oppressive military elite and, by extension, the political and economic status quo in the divided peninsula. This is manifested in the widened gap between city and countryside. "Rural income is only 60 percent of urban income. . . ." One sixty-eight-year-old farmer, interviewed by an American correspondent in June 1970, reported that "he was as badly off now as at any time in his life and that he saw no difference between the Government of President Park and the dictatorial Government of President Syngman Rhee, which was overthrown in 1960."[17]

One finds similar kinds of problems in the Philippines. In fact, because American bases have been here longer, the parasitism and corruption associated with them more often take violent forms. For example:

> In the town of Angeles, rathole honky-tonk of vice adjoining the Clark gate, there was a serious row between the local authorities and the Air Force last fall. It followed a wave of muggings, unruly demonstrations, and other abuses of Americans, including an incident in which an American was bludgeoned to death after he got into a dispute with a bus driver.[18]

While on the one hand American bases bring honkytonk ratholes to Asia, on the other they play an undeniably important role in underdeveloped countries. The U.S. military presence contributes $300–$450 million annually to a chronically ill Filipino economy. Indices of illness: in the Philippines the population is 37 million and growing rapidly but the GNP is only $7 billion; annual per capita income is $193 but median per capita income is only about $50; 25 percent of the labor force is either unemployed or underemployed; 70 percent of all agricultural workers do not own their land; and the entire amount of the most important crop, sugar, is exported, as in colonial days, to a protected American market. Financially, the Philippine government hovers on the brink of bankruptcy: only American dollar assistance saves the peso from drastic devaluation and local industry from stagnation.[19]

In these circumstances, growing numbers of Filipinos, spurred by students who have broken free from myths about both the U.S. and their own national history, have correctly summarized their problem as the bases, the unequal treaties, and the American business and embassy establishments, all of which function as crucial props for the tiny, corrupt ruling class which the U.S. has mothered for the better part of a century. Today, that class is experiencing its most serious crisis since the early 1950s, when it had to call on American aid to crush a serious decolonization movement. Through its representative, President Marcos, it has issued a call for a "revolution at the top."[20] At the same time, it seeks a way out in minimizing the visibility of the American presence, though not American control. The government, accordingly, has "formally requested that Sangley be given up entirely; that unused portions of the 130,000 acres at Clark be returned, and that Filipinos share in command of the bases."[21]

Japan, South Korea, and the Philippines—more countries could be mentioned as examples—were chosen because they exhibit a range of characteristic effects from the pervasive postwar American military presence. Japan now has its own problem of an expanding military-industrial complex. In the Philippines and South Korea, the most striking facet of the American presence is its inherent tendency to support and exacerbate indigenous social, economic, and political contradictions. Viewed from the outside the American imperial tiger looks sleek and powerful. But only its paws are strong, not the ground it stands on.

Aid, Patronage, Training

Between fiscal 1946 and fiscal 1968 foreign aid amounted to $133.5 billion, of which $94.7 billion was classified as economic and $36 billion as military aid. Although countries to which the U.S. was bound by defense treaties received large amounts in this period (NATO received $46.8 billion, SEATO $26.7 billion), many nontreaty countries were also major recipients. India, for example, received $7.8 billion in economic aid and an undisclosed amount of military aid.[22]

Other parts of foreign aid are the Military Assistance Program (MAP) and the Foreign Military Sales Program (FMS), both administered by the Pentagon. The man in charge of them, Lieutenant General Robert H. Warren, described MAP and FMS as

> . . . means by which the United States supports, strengthens and participates in free world collective security. . . . The armed forces we thus support represent an extension of our own defensive posture and a major deterrent to Communist aggression.[23]

While total MAP expenditures between fiscal 1950 and 1969 were nearly $35 billion, the grand total for Foreign Military Sales (FMS) in a six-year period, fiscal 1962 to 1968, was as much as $11.5 billion.[24]

Quite apart from the fact that such sales nurture an arms race in the underdeveloped world, the two programs in question reveal another parasitic feature of the American imperial system. MAP and FMS programs are administered by 7,100 personnel attached to U.S. military assistance groups, military missions, and embassies in fifty foreign countries. Together with their counterparts in the U.S., each year they train about ten thousand foreign soldiers.[25] Here one sees American foreign policy striving to achieve the utopian goal of disposing of its system-sustaining wars without fighting a single battle. And in the official justifications for training programs for mercenaries and "friendly" powers, one sees the high regard that policy places on friendships in a hostile world. As one Pentagon official put it:

> While military equipment and hardware may deteriorate in time, an understanding of American technology and management techniques, and most importantly, of American culture, carries over long after the foreign national returns to his own country. . . . Such an understanding and appreciation of the United States may be worth far more in the long run than outright grants or sales of military equipment.[26]

An outline of the formal components of American power can end right here with the way in which the system digs its own grave by arming, educating, training, and indoctrinating "indigenous military men."

CHAPTER 31

Pax Americana: The Economic Dimension

He who holds or has influence in Vietnam can affect the future of the Philippines and Formosa to the east, Thailand and Burma with their huge rice surpluses to the west, and Malaysia and Indonesia with their rubber, ore and tin to the south. Vietnam thus does not exist in a geographical vacuum—from it large storehouses of wealth and population can be influenced and undermined.
—Henry Cabot Lodge. *Boston Globe,*
February 28. 1965

That empire in Southeast Asia is the last major resource area outside the control of any one of the major powers on the globe . . . I believe that the condition of the Vietnamese people, and the direction in which their future may be going, are at this stage secondary, not primary.
—Senator McGee (D.-Wyo.), in the Senate,
February 17, 1965

One of Japan's greatest opportunities for increased trade lies in a free and developing Southeast Asia . . . The great need in one country is for raw materials, in the other for manufactured goods. The two regions complement each other markedly. By strengthening of Vietnam and helping insure the

safety of the South Pacific and Southeast Asia, we gradually develop the great trade potential between this region . . . and highly developed Japan to the benefit of both. In this way freedom in the Western Pacific will be greatly strengthened.
—President Eisenhower, April 4, 1959[1]

There must be a reason for the war in Indochina. Year after year, president after president, the U.S. keeps on fighting, keeps on ignoring chances to withdraw. Blunders, stupidity, inertia, and even saving face can scarcely explain such a costly and consistent policy. Rhetoric to the contrary, important wars are fought for important reasons.

Three government figures, quoted above, suggest a reason for the war. Bluntly, they suggest the U.S. is fighting to defend an economic empire—fighting to control the markets and the resources of a wealthy corner of the globe. In this view, the U.S. is, indeed, fighting to defend freedom: freedom for U.S. economic penetration of Asia.

Claims that U.S. imperialism is involved in Indochina provoke heated controversy. The most common, and most serious, counterargument simply points to the lack of current U.S. economic involvement in the region. U.S. direct private investments in the Far East (excluding India, Japan, and the Philippines) are valued at less than $1 billion, or just over 1 percent of all U.S. direct private foreign investment. All of Southeast Asia, including Indonesia and the Philippines, absorbs about 3 percent of U.S. exports. And many of the "vital" raw materials found in Southeast Asia can be found elsewhere as well. Would sensible imperialists spend over $100 billion and 40,000 soldiers' lives to defend such a small economic stake?

There are two flaws in this demonstration of the economic irrationality of the war. First, it looks only at the current value of Southeast Asia, while the above quotes emphasize the potential future value of the region. Second, and more significant, it assumes too simple a connection between economic interests and military intervention. But this point can be more easily explained after a look at the workings of America's overseas economic involvements.

Foreign Profits

In 1966 U.S. profits on direct foreign investment totaled $5.1 billion, or 10.4 percent of total corporate profits of $49.3 billion. Of the foreign profits, slightly under half came from Canada, Europe, and Japan; slightly more than half came from the third world.[2] However, most U.S. businesses are too small to invest in other countries; the foreign profits are concentrated in the hands of a few giant corporations. Of the 1966 foreign profits which were returned to the U.S. (70 percent of total foreign profits was returned to the U.S.; the remainder was kept in foreign countries), half was received by seventeen companies, all among the forty largest U.S. industrial corporations.[3]

For these companies, which include many of the country's most powerful corporations, foreign profits were very important. For the seventeen companies foreign profits returned to the U.S. were 27.6 percent of total profits, compared to 8.1 percent for the economy as a whole. And some of the seventeen were even more dependent on foreign earnings. Three large oil companies, Standard of New Jersey, Standard of California, and Mobil, reported foreign profits returned to the U.S. were over half of total domestic profits. Although the giant oil companies are notorious for juggling their books, and the exact reported profit figures may be misleading, few people would question that foreign investments are crucial to the oil industry. And the oil companies are not alone. International Telephone and Telegraph and International Business Machines, with half and a third respectively of domestic profits received from abroad, both live up to their names.

Foreign Investment and
Underdevelopment

Giant corporations profit in several ways from their foreign investments. Entering a new country, either with exports or with a local subsidiary, means new and growing markets, and sometimes a chance at gaining a local monopoly. Natural resources are exploited, in mines, oil wells, and plantations, often at amazingly low prices. And foreign labor is available at low wages, with the nuisance of unions eliminated by obliging governments in many countries.

But the existence of profits does not prove that foreign investment hurts the country in which it occurs. In fact, foreign investment is often defended as a positive contribution to the development of poor countries. It is said that foreign investment and foreign aid are the only channels through which poor countries can obtain the capital they require for development. This theory of economic development has a grim but allegedly realistic corollary: if political stability is necessary to attract foreign aid and investment, and if military force, perhaps even U.S. military force, is necessary to maintain stability, then . . . maybe U.S. interventions and military dictatorships are sometimes needed for development.

The defense of foreign investment and aid is false on two grounds. First, very little capital has been transferred from the U.S. to poor countries, either by investment or by aid. Second, even if capital is transferred to poor countries, it is not used to encourage development.

From 1950 to 1965 the flow of direct investment from the U.S. to Europe and Canada totaled $14.9 billion, and income on this capital returned to the U.S. was $11.4 billion, leaving a net outflow from the U.S. of $3.5 billion. For the rest of the world, the corresponding figures were $9.0 billion direct investment outflow, and $25.6 billion income returned to the U.S., a net inflow to the U.S. of $16.6 billion, about a billion dollars a year.[4] U.S. foreign investment, on balance, supplied capital to developed countries, and took capital from underdeveloped countries.

Foreign aid amounts to surprisingly little transfer of capital to poor countries. Nonmilitary aid expenditures by AID and its predecessors, from July 1949 to June 1966, totaled only $11.3 billion, or around two-thirds of the investment inflow of $16.6 billion described above.[5] In the same period, the same agencies spent $12.1 billion on military aid to countries outside Europe. But not nearly all of the $11.3 billion of nonmilitary aid represents net transfer to poor countries. At least $4.8 billion of the total was loaned, not given, to the recipients. Most aid, whether loans or grants, must be spent on purchases from U.S. suppliers, who often sell well above world market prices. Aid purchases must also be shipped on U.S. ships, whose freight charges are far above—sometime double—charges on other countries' ships.[6] President Kennedy described the purposes of these restrictions, if not of the whole non-military aid program, in 1963:

> Too little attention has been paid to the part which an early exposure to American goods, skills, and American ways of doing things can play in forming the tastes and desires of newly emerging countries—or to the fact that, even when our aid ends, the desire and need for our products continue, and trade relations last far beyond the termination of our assistance.[7]

However, the problem would not be solved by more capital flowing through the existing channels. The channels themselves are a part of the problem. Over half of U.S. investment in Latin America, Asia, and Africa is in mining and petroleum.[8] These industries simply exploit the natural resources of the country, creating few jobs and adding little to the country's development. Even in the growing foreign investments in manufacturing in the third world, capital flows primarily into production for useless luxury consumption, rather than for national development. In Karachi, the capital of Pakistan, for example, in 1967 there were only three sources of bottled milk for a city of several million people, while eleven different soft drinks made with imported concentrates could be bought.[9] Other cases may be subtler, but are fundamentally similar. Consider Brazil, one of the supposed success stories of capitalist development in Latin America. Here the major accomplishment of foreign manufacturers has been the creation of an automobile industry, producing 300,000 poorly built cars annually, at prices higher than U.S. car prices. Meanwhile, the vast majority of Brazilians, who cannot afford cars—the farm workers, badly in need of modern equipment; the people of the northeast, dying in 1970 from one of Brazil's periodic droughts; the urban slum dwellers, living in shantytowns—are all untouched by the progress of industry.

Foreign investors did not create all the inequalities of Brazil or Pakistan. But in these countries, as in others, foreign manufacturers reinforce an unequal society, and profit from it in the only way they can, through producing useless luxury consumption items. Any capital invested in this kind of manufacturing simply creates another vested interest in the status quo, without contributing anything to development.

In summary, it is hard to believe foreign aid and investment help poor countries. Taking out more capital than it puts in, going into extractive industries and luxury production, foreign investments are profitable almost exclusively for the foreign investor. More than half of foreign aid is military aid; the small amounts of nonmilitary aid are encumbered with restrictions that benefit American exporters rather than the aid recipients.

Profits and Foreign Policy

American military intervention abroad is nothing new. It has occurred almost continuously since World War II, and its origins can be traced back much further.[10] In

Greece in 1947–48, Iran in 1953, Guatemala in 1954, the Dominican Republic in 1965, and many other cases, American troops, "advisers," or the CIA have helped to overthrow governments suspected of communism. On countless other occasions, local armed forces trained and equipped by the U.S. have done the same job.[11] The war in Indochina is not unusual because the U.S. is intervening; it is merely unusual because the U.S. is losing.

From the point of view of most Americans, U.S. military interventions abroad seem like unfortunate, irrational blunders. But multinational corporations with large foreign investments have sound financial reasons for wanting the free world kept "free." From their point of view, U.S. interventions are quite rational. American interventions are almost always against governments which threaten to curtail foreign business operations; the regimes created by interventions, whatever else they do, are careful to preserve freedom for business.

This is not to imply that foreign policy decisions are made in corporate boardrooms. Obviously the world is more complex than that. The anti-Communist ideology which shapes U.S. foreign policy has deep roots in American history. Still, whatever its origins, whatever its supposed virtues in the minds of its supporters, American anti-Communist foreign policy brings only the draft and high taxes to most American families, military dictatorship and economic exploitation to the third world, and huge profits to a few large corporations. It is the effects of American foreign policy that matter, and in its effects, if not in its motivations, it is a foreign policy well suited to the interests of major corporations.

An interventionist, anti-Communist foreign policy requires a large military machine. U.S. military spending is currently about $80 billion a year, enough to absorb almost all personal income tax payments (which totaled $90.5 billion in 1969). About half of military spending, or $36.9 billion in fiscal 1969, goes to defense contractors. Like foreign profits, defense contracts are concentrated in the hands of a few large corporations: two-thirds of all

Pentagon contracts go to the hundred largest contractors.[12] To a great extent, these are the same companies that benefit from foreign investment. In 1968, twenty of the twenty-five largest industrial corporations were among the hundred largest defense contractors.[13] Cost overruns and padded profits on defense work are well known, but there are no figures for total profits on military contracts.

So, from the corporate point of view, defense of the free world and foreign profits is itself a profitable activity. The two sources of profit—foreign investment and military contracts—combine to create a powerful corporate interest in maintaining an interventionist, anti-Communist foreign policy.

The Threat of Revolution

Revolutions have always been a threat to America's "free world" empire. Since World War II, three successful revolutions (in China, Cuba, and Vietnam) have closed their doors to foreign capital, and reoriented their economies toward the needs of the masses. In Cuba, illiteracy has been virtually eliminated, and each year Cuban medical schools graduate three times as many doctors per capita as do medical schools in the United States. In China, the threat of starvation has been overcome for the first time in history, and impressive beginnings of industrialization have been forged. In Vietnam, before the escalation of the war, land reform was carried out by the NLF in the South, and schools and hospitals were built in every province of the North.

These revolutions and their accomplishments inspire revolutionaries elsewhere, creating an ever-present threat to free world stability. Preventing the spread of revolution has therefore become a major goal of U.S. foreign policy. Throughout the 1950s Latin American countries were forgotten neighbors—until the Cuban revolution prompted the Alliance for Progress, a hastily-constructed "alternative" to further revolutions. In addition to its more dramatic military interventions, the U.S. has aid programs, CIA agents, and military advisers at work throughout Latin America, making sure it doesn't happen again.[14]

A revolution anywhere is seen as a setback to U.S. foreign policy, even in an area with no major U.S. economic interests—even in Indochina. Successful revolution in Indochina not only deprives the U.S. of any potential profits in the area, but also in the corporate view, sets a "bad example" for more immediately valuable countries. If a peasant revolution can drive out the U.S. in Southeast Asia, what will stop the guerrillas in the Middle East, Brazil, Guatemala . . . ?

Imperialism and the War

By now the relevance of economic imperialism to the war in Indochina should be clear. It is true that the current value of Indochina to U.S. business interests is virtually nil. But, as mentioned above, there are two reasons why this does not prove the war is irrational from the corporate point of view. First, the potential value of the region is believed to be great; second, defense of the "free world" empire requires the suppression of revolution everywhere, not just in the more valuable regions. Both of these reasons can be illustrated in the recent history of Southeast Asia.

In the early days of the war, before the Tet offensive of 1968, many U.S. businessmen thought the war would soon be over, and began planning postwar investments in Vietnam. As Henry M. Sperry, vice-president of the First National City Bank of New York, saw it in 1965:

> We believe that we're going to win this war. Afterwards you'll have a major job of reconstruction on your hands. That will take financing and financing means banks . . . It would be illogical to permit the English and French to monopolize the banking business because South Vietnam's economy is becoming more and more United States oriented.[15]

Thoughts about possible postwar reconstruction in Vietnam, however, were just a part of the broader consequences of the war. For as a Chase Manhattan Bank vice-president explained in 1965:

In the past, foreign investors have been somewhat wary of the over-all political prospect for the [Southeast Asia] region. I must say, though, that the U.S. actions in Vietnam this year—which have demonstrated that the U.S. will continue to give effective protection to the free nations of the region—have considerably reassured both Asian and Western investors. In fact, I see some reason for hope that the same sort of economic growth may take place in the free economies of Asia that took place in Europe after the Truman Doctrine and after NATO provided a protective shield. The same thing also took place in Japan after the U.S. intervention in Korea removed investor doubts.[16]

American business, however, was by no means united on its long-range interests in Southeast Asia, or on its relation to the conflict in Vietnam. But until the Tet offensive, opposition was relatively muted. Thereafter enthusiasm for America's military involvement was confined predominantly to defense contractors, while the increasingly obvious costs of failure and impact of the war on the overall economy made the search for "disengagement" more pronounced among business leaders. Nevertheless, the economic reasons that formed the backdrop to political miscalculation remain.

PART IV

What Can the
Future Hold
for Indochina?

CHAPTER 32

Asia and the Nixon Doctrine:
Ten Points of Note

Since the summer of 1969, the U.S. government has placed increasing emphasis upon its alleged adoption of a new policy toward Asia. First suggested by the president in July at an informal press conference on Guam, the so-called "Nixon Doctrine" is generally and correctly associated with the projected partial "disengagement" of American combat forces from Asia. This includes not only proposed troop withdrawals from Vietnam, but also from American bases elsewhere in Asia. Thus a reduction of the substantial American garrison which has been maintained in Korea since the Korean War has already been announced; the November 1969 Sato-Nixon communiqué calling for return of Okinawa to Japanese rule by 1972 is generally described as part of the Nixon Doctrine, and it is anticipated that during the 1970s the Japanese military will gradually take over many functions now carried out by U.S. servicemen in both Okinawa and Japan proper. The Thai government has announced that it expects the number of American soldiers stationed in Thailand to be reduced "after" the present Indochina conflict; and so on. The essential ingredient in the new "low posture" or "low profile," in short, is that the most

281

visible American presence in Asia—its combat troops there (now close to 1 million in number)—will be partly reduced.

The other side of the Nixon Doctrine, which the administration also stresses, is Asian self-help. In the president's phrase, "Asian hands must shape the Asian future." More specifically, pro-American Asian regimes are to be strengthened militarily so that in the suppression of future "insurgencies" they can shoulder a major part of the burden borne up to now by the U.S. At the same time, the United States will stand by with its nuclear arsenal and tactical support, honoring its commitments and vigilant against external aggression. In the president's words:

> First, the United States will keep all of its treaty commitments.
>
> Second, we shall provide a shield if a nuclear power threatens the freedom of a nation allied with us, or of a nation whose survival we consider vital to our security.
>
> Third, in cases involving other types of aggression we shall furnish military and economic assistance when requested in accordance with our treaty commitments. But we shall look to the nation directly threatened to assume the primary responsibility of providing the manpower for its defense.[1]

While the primary thrust of the doctrine is military, the economic side is not ignored. Here the president stresses interregional cooperation—"Asian initiatives in an Asian framework"—abetted by "multinational" corporations and organizations. At the same time, however, it is acknowledged that in both military and economic matters, "Japan's partnership with us will be a key to the success of the Nixon Doctrine in Asia."

Since the present situation is tragic, the future uncertain, and some of the sentiments of the Nixon Doctrine rather admirable on the surface, it is generally regarded as uncharitable to speak harshly of the president's vision of the future relationship between the United States and Asia.

Still, it might be of some help in looking to that future to keep the following considerations in mind:

1. *The Nixon Doctrine is not new:* Rather, like many of the president's basic views, it can be traced back to the early years of the cold war and particularly the Dulles policy of "letting Asians fight Asians." Also, nothing in the president's various formulations of the doctrine (notably on July 25 and November 3, 1969, and January 22 and February 18, 1970) would have been rejected by the policy makers (including Mr. Nixon himself in the early 1950s) who encouraged and planned the American intervention in Indochina over the past decades. Following the "State of the World" message of February 18, 1970, for example, Max Frankel noted that "Mr. Nixon's aides concede . . . that there is nothing in his new doctrine that excludes a Dominican-style intervention in defense of vital interests. They say that the document is a call to the nation and Government to define those interests more precisely and prudently than in the past, but they have only begun that job and it is never really finished until the moment of crisis."[2]

2. *The basic analysis of the situation in Asia and of America's proper relation to it has not changed:* On the one hand, "We remain involved in Asia. We are a Pacific power." (In his 1967 *Foreign Affairs* article, Nixon argues that "both our interests and our ideals propel us westward across the Pacific"—a sentiment which can be traced back to the American expansionists of 1898 and the vision of Asia as the "new Far West.") On the other hand, the goals of containing China, checking "communism," suppressing "insurgencies," and continuing to support pro-American Asian regimes, however corrupt, remain.

In the State of the World message, the president did acknowledge that nationalism had proven itself destructive of "international Communist unity," and he also called for "improved practical relations with Peking." In the same breath, however, he reaffirmed America's military commitment to the Nationalist regime in Taiwan, and reiterated the familiar condescending and hypocritical hope that "sooner or later Communist China will be ready to re-enter the international community." There is no indication that, despite the ongoing American bloodbath in Indochina and the restraint China has demonstrated in the face of this, the president has revised his view that China poses the greatest threat in Asia today. Both the military and State Department have faithfully reiterated this same point; as recently as July 9, 1970, for example, scarcely two months after the U.S. invasion of Cambodia, Secretary of State William P. Rogers appeared on a television interview in Tokyo and blandly urged China to abandon its "belligerent attitude" toward the world and play "a sensible role in the international community."

In a similar manner, the new official version of polycentric communism has not prevented the president from reviving and reemphasizing the domino theory (most notably in his television interview of July 2, 1970), or the Pentagon from viewing the objective in Asia as "the development of good land forces capable of offering a credible deterrent to a Communist aggression."[3] Perhaps of even greater significance, neither the political and social, as well as military, viability of the NLF and Pathet Lao— nor the sharply contrasting corruption and inefficiency of the regimes the U.S. supports against them—has caused the government to reconsider its attitude of total opposition to popular revolutionary movements in Asia. This, in fact, remains a bedrock of the Nixon Doctrine. In Secretary of Defense Melvin Laird's words:

> The principal threat to the independent nations in Asia is internal insurgency, supported by external assistance. This is an important aspect of the threat to which our General Purpose Force planning for Asia should be oriented.[4]

In the future as in the past (as seen in the case of China as well as Indochina) it can be anticipated that American officials will continue to place unwarranted emphasis on the role of "external assistance" while minimizing more relevant and determining indigenous developments. But the fundamental American objective in Asia remains— as has been the case since before the Second World War— containment and counterrevolution.

3. *The Nixon Doctrine is fundamentally a cost-conscious policy, aimed at maintaining a major U.S. role in Asia at less cost in both dollars and American lives:* This emerges vividly in Ambassador Bunker's statement that Vietnamization simply means changing the color of the corpses. In a similar manner, former Defense Secretary Clark Clifford informed Congress in January 1969 that "an Asian soldier costs about 1/15 as much as his American counterpart,"[5] and the present secretary of defense, Mr. Laird, argued for an expanded Military Assistance Program (MAP), mostly for Asia, on the grounds that "a MAP dollar is of far greater value than a dollar spent directly on U.S. forces."[6] One key benefit of a substantial withdrawal of manpower from Asia will be that this could permit reduction of the defense budget and provide a substantial check on the "dollar drain." As suggested below, the consequences of attempting to maintain the old objectives asd commitments on the cheap may well be to increase the likelihood of a resort to tactical nuclear weapons.

4. *The plan to withdraw American troops is itself a qualified one:* In the first place, the emphasis is on ground combat troops, while support forces, particularly the aviation units whose destructiveness has been described in part II, are being retained to a large extent. In addition, as indicated in the Introduction, there is no reason to believe that anything other than a "Korean solution" is being considered for Vietnam—that is, that withdrawals will continue after a certain level, probably in the 100,000 to 200,000 range. Furthermore, the U.S. government has given no clear indication of which if any of its several hundred major bases in Asia it intends to relinquish. While some may indeed be phased out as obsolete or uneconomical, there is no intention of abandoning the "ring of steel" around China.

5. *Client armies are to assume some of the functions now carried out by the U.S. military:* "Vietnamization"— the corrupt, brutalizing policy by which the South Vietnamese army is now supposedly assuming increased military responsibility—is cited as a model of the Nixon Doctrine in action. So also is the deployment of South Vietnamese (ARVN) and Thai troops in an essentially mercenary capacity in Cambodia—to prop up a regime which is acknowledged to lack popular support. Despite the fact that the 1-million-man ARVN has been in the making for over a decade and still cannot hold its own without decisive American air and combat support against numerically and technologically inferior NLF and North Vietnamese forces, this appears to be the path of the future for America's Asian allies: more U.S. military aid (note the accelerating commitment to the Lon Nol regime in Cambodia); more U.S. military advisers (as witness the new John F. Kennedy Center for Military Assistance at Fort Bragg);[7] more military training for Asian nationals (Thai soldiers, for example, are already receiving CBW training in the U.S. in preparation for the day when they too can participate in the defoliation of their land);[8] a larger policy-making role for the Pentagon and CIA (witness the recent proposal to turn AID functions over to the Pentagon);[9] emphasis upon police functions and control mechanisms within the society (close to 50 percent of the "civilian" aid budget to Thailand is now being spent on police stations and specially trained Special Police);[10] and so on. In effect, the U.S. seeks to defend its ambitions in Asia through proxy armies and client regimes.

6. *American military planners also anticipate that much of the slack of disengagement will be taken up by major technological advances in warfare:* These include the transportation revolution represented by the C-5A super-transport—an innovation which to a considerable extent makes the need for an intricate network of overseas forward bases obsolete. In the words of its manufacturer, Lockheed:

The C-5A Galaxy is more than the world's largest airplane. It's a new kind of defense system. It's like having a military base in nearly every strategic spot on the globe.

To the new concept of rapid deployment must be added the Westmoreland dream of the electronic battlefield [described in chapter 7]. This too, it is anticipated, will greatly lessen the manpower requirements of future "counterinsurgency" situations—if it works. As Westmoreland describes it, "With surveillance devices that can continually track the enemy, the need for large forces to fix the opposition physically will be less important."[11] Even without a "Nixon Doctrine," the logic of military technology would have dictated a gradual "disengagement" of manpower from Asia.

7. *The combination of old objectives, cost-consciousness, and reluctance to become mired in another land war in Asia increases the possibility of resort to nuclear weapons in the future:* As vice-president, Nixon himself publicly declared in 1955 that:

It is foolish to talk about the possibility that the weapons which might be used in the event war breaks out in the Pacific would be limited to the conventional Korean and World War II types of explosives. Our forces could not fight an effective war in the Pacific with those types of explosives if they wanted to. Tactical atomic explosives are now conventional and will be used against the military targets of any aggressive force.[12]

A policy of defending one's "commitments" by withdrawing and relying upon disreputable client armies and unperfected battlefield electronics is a shaky one at best, and very likely to find itself challenged. Neither the president's past attitude toward nuclear weapons, his recent pledges to take "decisive" action in Indochina if challenged (for example, May 8, 1970), his reliance upon advisers known to be especially tolerant of using tactical nuclear weapons in certain situations, nor his personal propensity for equating virility with destruction dispel this concern.

8. *In the economic realm, the Nixon Doctrine offers no real alternative to policies already discredited:* The rubric of "multinationalism" cannot cover the fact that the future economic development projected by the doctrine is to take place within a capitalist system dominated by the United States and Japan, with a high probability that the underdeveloped countries of Asia—as has been the case in Latin America—will be locked into a state of permanent dependence. The problems of foreign investment and foreign aid [discussed in chapter 31] are not faced squarely by the Nixon Doctrine, and it remains an unquestioned assumption that capitalism alone can offer hope for a better future to the third world. In fact, the record suggests otherwise. The consequences of American involvement can be seen quite clearly in Latin America, where—in the words of a Brazilian political economist— "the countries have lost their individual viability" under U.S. dominance.[13] A classic Asian example is the Philippines, conquered by the United States from its own population at the turn of the century and still today a "colonial economy of the classical type." For the Philippine peasantry, three-fourths of the population, living standards have not risen since the Spanish occupation.[14]

The United States is capable of creating an artificial consumer economy for the rich in the midst of rural stagnation and urban decay, or—at best—an economy such as that of South Korea, dominated by Japanese and American corporations, with enormous foreign debts and hopeless corruption. In the typical American dependency, economic policies favor consumer goods for the privileged while a pool of cheap labor provides services for the middle and upper classes; and "political democracy" offers the people a choice between representatives of the elite. In Bangkok, for example, there are no sanitation facilities for the majority of the population, while color television is available in the country.[15] In Saigon, a liter of rice is more expensive than a liter of gasoline and the import-export ratio is currently about 50 to 1.[16] Two Yale economists recently surveyed the results of postwar economic development in the "private enterprise economies" of Southeast Asia and concluded that "in human terms, the result of the last twenty-five years has meant abysmally low levels of consumption, education, health and welfare for about two-thirds of the people."[17]

It should be kept in mind also that as "multinational" stakes in the country increase, the pressure for outside intervention to suppress popular protest and threats to the status quo will also increase.

9. *In the political and social realms, the Nixon Doctrine promises support of the same type of generally corrupt, inefficient, exploitative regimes which the United States has favored in the past:* The focus remains upon attempting to bring about change through a military or urban elite which—as case after case has shown—can never carry out thoroughgoing and meaningful reforms without undermining its own privileged position. The absurdity of the American claim to be "defending the rights of the people of Southeast Asia" by defending pro-American regimes against forces within their own societies is evident in the most obvious American contribution to Indochina today: a moonscape of craters and defoliated forests and devastated rice fields, with millions of refugees rotting in urban slums and refugee camps. It is evident in the venal puppet regimes in Saigon and Vientiane. It is evident outside the theater of war—in the Philippines, for example, where seven decades of intimate American involvement have produced the "democracy" of the 1969 Philippine elections:

> Filipinos view elections as a confirmation of the power of the wealthy business and landed interests who back both parties but usually pick the winners before Election Day and quietly give them the most support. In this case they picked President Marcos.[18]

Yet once again, the model offered in the Nixon Doctrine ignores the record and ignores as well the dynamic of social and political change which has thus far proven itself most viable in underdeveloped, largely peasant societies: change initiated in the countryside and calling upon the energies of the people themselves.

10. *In the realm of international affairs, the Nixon Doctrine enforces bipolarization:* Whatever verbal allegations the administration may make to the contrary, the record clearly indicates that American support invariably goes to those elements in a country who in external affairs support the United States and in internal affairs endorse private enterprise and are tolerant of considerable foreign involvement. The result is to polarize forces within the society on the one hand (as seen in South Vietnam), and on the other hand to make adherence to an independent role in diplomacy extremely difficult for nations caught in the path of the American juggernaut (as witness the effect of American actions on Cambodia, Laos, and both North and South Vietnam). The attitude that neutrality is inherently immoral has its roots in the moral globalism of the Dulles period, but whatever its origins, the fact remains that [as indicated in chapter 25] there is a greater degree of national sovereignty and greater independence in foreign affairs within the so-called "Communist camp" in Asia than exists among the nations of what Mr. Nixon chooses to call "free Asia." The latter remains an alliance heavily reliant upon American aid; greatly indebted to America's postwar military spending and wars in Asia for much of its economic growth; increasingly dependent upon a market system dominated by the United States and Japan; and predominantly judged not by its contribution to the well-being of its peoples, but rather by its anti-Communist credentials and its contribution, real or potential, to American military objectives in Asia.

CHAPTER 33

The Case for Total, Immediate,
Unilateral American
Withdrawal

I

There is not now nor has there ever been an American policy for ending the war in Indochina.

Ever since American troops first became heavily involved in Indochina, successive presidents have paid lip service to an eventual withdrawal of American troops. President Johnson was forced to abandon hope of reelection because he could not do it; President Nixon was elected because he said that he would. But a rapid withdrawal has always been taboo. Even today, nearly two years after Nixon took office, over 400,000 troops remain in Vietnam and the war has spilled over the border into Cambodia.

Logistically an immediate and total withdrawal has always been possible. The president himself said so in his television interview of July 2, 1970. He had cited earlier, in his November 1969 speech, the reasons for delaying withdrawal. "Three American presidents," he announced, have recognized the great stakes involved in Vietnam and understood what had to be done. . . . We believe strongly in that. We are not going to withdraw from that effort. In my opinion for us to withdraw from that effort would mean a collapse not only of South Vietnam but of Southeast Asia. So we're going to stay.

Nixon's intentions are clear. His goals remain essentially unchanged from those of his predecessors, and he is "going to stay" in Indochina until those goals have been achieved. The hollow, fictional nature of the goals themselves has already been discussed in part III. Several points need to be made about Nixon's plan for attaining them.

1. *Present U.S. "withdrawal" policy does not aim at ending the war, but rather at continuing it under a different guise, notably "Vietnamization."* "Vietnamization" is an old policy disguised by a new name. Its aim is to establish a stable regime in Saigon that can carry on the war without massive outside assistance. As such the term "Vietnamization" is equally applicable to American policy toward Diem in the 1950s as well as to the French attempt to consolidate their colonial position. It was President Johnson's goal as well. His intent, he said in March 1968, was—

> . . . to accelerate the reequipment of South Vietnam's armed forces in order to meet the enemy's increased firepower. This will enable them progressively to undertake a larger share of combat operations against the Communist invaders.

This is an excellent definition of Vietnamization, but not a way out of the war in Indochina. It never has been and it never will be. In fact Nixon does not intend it to be. Support for the Saigon dictatorship remains the mainstay of his strategy. It is a "heads I win, tails you lose" formula in which "phased withdrawal" has become merely a euphemism for victory.

2. *Even successful Vietnamization will leave a large force of American troops in Indochina.* Politically, Vietnamization is a means of tempering the discontent of an American public increasingly dissatisfied with the war without abandoning the goal of military victory in Vietnam. American casualties can be reduced to a level "acceptable" to public opinion, while the business of winning the war will depend more on air power, increasingly effective technological weapons, and client armies. Present projected levels of troop withdrawal involve primarily the removal of those ground combat forces not needed to protect base camp areas. This will leave a "residual" force of approximately 225,000 military personnel in Vietnam. This would be an occupation army larger than that used by the Japanese for all of Indochina, larger than the German occupation army in France, larger than the Soviet occupation forces now remaining in Czechoslovakia.

3. *The Nixon strategy has alarming potential for future reescalation of the conflict.* The presence of the residual force would provide a constant incentive for military planners to "go in and get the job over with." At the very least, the need to "protect" the residual force against the inevitable NLF-DRV attempts to drive it out of the country will provide a ready pretext for the reintroduction of American power. Faced with a deteriorating situation, the United States will, as in the past, have to choose between liquidating its position or taking more powerful measures to save it. The history of the last decade reveals that a "commitment" always leads to escalation, never withdrawal. The only question would be over the nature of the escalation. Would it consist of the reintroduction of ground combat forces, reliance on still more intensive air operations, the bombing of new targets such as the Red River dikes, or perhaps even the use of tactical nuclear weapons?

4. *The other side correctly recognizes that the Nixon formula is a policy of continued war rather than of com-*

promise and accommodation. Pham Van Dong, prime minister of North Vietnam, has described Vietnamization as America's "grand design" for victory. President Nixon, in his view, is saying only this: "I will reduce U.S. forces in Vietnam to a level which the American people will accept, and these forces will be used to keep the present South Vietnamese government in power for years to come."[1] Given this reasonable assessment of American policy, it is inevitable that the other side will continue to maintain a high level of military operations. The war will go on because the issues for which the other side has been fighting for twenty-five years will remain unresolved.

II

Clearly, the Nixon plan, while admitting the desirability of scaled-down fighting, abandons none of the original American objectives of the war. Nixon, like Johnson before him, assumes that there is something to be gained from fighting on a little longer, something to be lost by ending the conflict now.

An immediate and total withdrawal is based on the opposite assumption. The preceding sections of this volume have shown that the objectives of American policy are themselves undesirable. There is nothing to be gained in protecting from their own people a coterie of landlords and generals in Saigon who have profiteered from the war and who comprise a government that would fall by the weight of its own incompetence were American support to be withdrawn from it. By the same token, there is no honor or gain in defeating an "enemy" that happens to be the most progressive, popular, and effective political force in Vietnam. Except for the Thieu–Ky government, there are few if any Vietnamese, whether Buddhists, intellectuals, workers, farmers, or students, who want the Americans to stay another day in Vietnam. Vietnamization, real Vietnamization, can take place only after the Americans have departed from the country. Only then can the Vietnamese erect native political structures and get on with the job of rebuilding their devastated land.

One need not know all the statistics, all the facts and figures, all the theories of political development, to be able to make the most important argument for immediate withdrawal from Indochina that can be made: this is an immoral war. There is clearly no evil greater than the war itself. There is no good that can result from the war capable of vindicating the death and destruction that the war has caused. No top-secret files can justify the destruction of a society, as indeed the people of Indochina themselves have been saying for many years. Here is one of them—not a Communist but a Catholic teacher in Saigon named Ly Chanh Trung:

> Because I am Vietnamese I can no longer bear the spectacle of foreigners rudely destroying my country with the most up-to-date and most horrible methods, nor can I tolerate this talk of "protecting the freedom" of the people of the South. . . . Tragically the people of the South have never enjoyed freedom and have never been masters of their own destiny, principally because of the Americans who have the slogan of protecting freedom but who really are protecting the systems which trample down freedom.[2]

There is nothing accidental about this. The immorality of the war arises from the nature of the war itself. When all the arguments for war are made, when all the good intentions have been uttered and all the plans for pacification and Vietnamization put into practice, one elementary but inescapable fact remains: for American goals to be achieved, Indochina itself must be laid to waste. In Vietnam, for example, as long as the social fabric survives, the National Liberation Front will survive with it. Because guerrillas cannot be separated from the population, the tactics of the United States and its mercenary armies must be directed against the population; there can be no distinction between an atrocity and an ordinary act of war. "To kill the enemy it . . . appears that one must kill the entire population."[3] Under these conditions, there can be but one result: the logic of American policy in Indochina is genocide.

Only total, immediate, and unilateral withdrawal recognizes the bankruptcy of America's objectives in Indochina. Only that can save Vietnam and the rest of Indochina from the horrors of a war that Americans should not want to win. Withdrawal alone can turn the fate of Indochina over to the Indochinese peoples themselves. The withdrawal must be total to insure against the inevitable tendency to expand the conflict. It must be immediate because delay will only enable the decision makers to play politics with death. It must be unilateral for it is the Americans who are the foreigners in Indochina. Only a complete disengagement cuts through all the twists and turns of official rhetoric, the lies and distortions, the stream of optimistic predictions from men who have amply demonstrated their ignorance, delusion, and moral indifference.

III

The demand for total, immediate, unilateral withdrawal should be put forward as a part of an effort to build a new America. It should be a call for a changed political consciousness, one that appreciates the revolutionary changes developed by such groups as the Viet Minh, the National Liberation Front, and the Pathet Lao. It should be a demand that America end its role as "leader of a world-wide anti-revolutionary movement in defense of vested interests."[4] Acceptance of this demand will be a step toward an America more humane and just in its relations with the world.

This book has given some indication of the attempts of revolutionary groups in Indochina to introduce educational, health, agricultural, and political changes in their traditionally exploited countries. And it has analyzed the American response—opposition to these revolutionary movements. The contradiction in American policy is a striking one: Why do the regimes capable of carrying out most of the reforms that America professes to advocate generally oppose the United States?

Today it is fashionable to blame Diem, once the "democratic" alternative to Ho Chi Minh, for his failings. Yet why did so many expect that an aristocrat, absent from his country during its war against the French, then propped up by American dollars and guns, could provide a substitute for the men and women who had devoted their lifetimes to the struggle for Vietnamese independence? Why did they hope he would defeat a movement whose ties with the peasants were already cemented by a bitter struggle for social justice? Why, as even Vice-President Ky lamented, does "the whole world respect Ho Chi Minh and Defense Minister Giap. Why? Who are they? . . . Why can't we find a man in the South and make him respected by the whole world?"[5]

Why, indeed, has the American government wanted men like Diem to succeed? His program, as described in part I, was a policy of indiscriminate terror, persecution of all political opposition, and the prevention of any basic changes in Vietnamese society. And this remains the program of his successors. What has America itself offered? A counterrevolutionary ideology to compete with a revolutionary one; "strategic hamlets" and "refugee" camps instead of popular base areas; psychological warfare instead of revolutionary transformation; "pacification" teams instead of revolutionary cadres.

Over the past twenty years in Indochina, it is those whom the U.S. has taken as its enemies, not its friends, who have offered the peasantry a more dignified, fulfilling life. The outrage expressed by American officials over the revolutionary alternatives arising from China to Vietnam to Cuba fails to touch on the main point. The central motivation and attraction of these alternatives is the destruction of all those structures—feudalistic social bonds, private inertia and exploitation, foreign-supported elites benefiting from such conditions—which have kept the people "in their place."

Without a doubt, such revolutionary changes in the world do constitute a threat to the way America is organized today. They do portend an end of an American-dominated global military system. They do challenge the viability of a capitalist economy so heavily involved in exploitative extensions around the world. They require a recognition by the U.S. that it no longer constitutes the model on which the future may be based.

In part, America's hostility to revolutionary movements reflects years of intensive cold-war indoctrination and a fear that the U.S will lose its place in the sun. There is also a lurking fear of "violence," of the blunt rejection of American values by these revolutionary groups. Certainly revolutionary movements do bring a ruthless will to their desire to change everything. But nonrevolutionary regimes —like those in Thailand, Laos, and South Vietnam— seem unable to make any basic improvements in the life of the common people. In fact, to rule, they require continuing peasant poverty and subordination and the legitimizing myth of a blissful, passive village life. Even to survive, they must depend on the continuous infusion of foreign "aid," urban-centered foreign industrial development, and external support for their internal security forces. Who would not welcome the best of both worlds —the dedication, enthusiasm, and the ability to change of the revolutionary, and the tolerance of the gradualist? But that is not the choice.

The question is: Will the United States continue to use its power to control, contain, or destroy through exploitative elites throughout the world, or can another American role be defined? Even today, numerous critics of the American war effort are discouraged only by its prohibitive costs. These costs, it is argued, require withdrawal. Opposition might well have never risen beyond a whisper had America in the 1950s successfully created a modern police state through its attempts to strengthen Saigon's police and army. Certainly America's past "successes" in setting up or supporting the right-wing dictatorships which dot the Asian map—from South Korea, Taiwan, Thailand, to Pakistan—were not widely protested.

Only now is this being seriously questioned. For America's failure in Vietnam has made the process clearer. But if it becomes clear that America has neither the right to impose "order" within other countries, nor to ensure their "development" through a capitalist system, nor even to seek victory against insurgency movements, then there is nothing to negotiate in Vietnam. America's total, immediate withdrawal would not only allow what is left of Vietnam—and the rest of Indochina—to be saved from destruction. It would also be a step toward building a different America.

But it would be only a step. Can this nation go further and accept a massive scaling-down of its position in Asia and Latin America? It would entail profound changes in its outlook and institutions. It would mean the recognition that revolutionary regimes in the third world represent perhaps the only chance these areas have of escaping their poverty. It would mean a recognition that "our side" must substantially change its political goals, ideology, and economic system so that they no longer impel the U.S. in the direction of opposing revolutionary change wherever it occurs. This will undoubtedly require a reasonable policy and a clear understanding of the limits of American power and its frequently destructive impact. In short, it means an America willing to allow other societies to undergo revolutionary change under revolutionary—generally Communist—leadership, without American interference, either direct or through sponsored mercenaries.

It is probable that the chances for these changes are small. It may be that vested interests, anti-Communist dogma, the power of the military-industrial complex, and the demands of the American economic system will maintain the U.S. on its present course. Perhaps the bleak future in store for Asia in the Nixon Doctrine will be realized. But there is some hope that Americans can draw upon the undercurrent of humanism in their tradition to say "no" to the world system which prefers the absence of meaningful development to revolutionary transformation, "no" to the growing split between the rich and the poor, and "no" to the massive array of American military might and the economy of death that seeks to destroy or contain those who manifest their hostility toward American dominion.

An immediate, unilateral, total American withdrawal, therefore, is the only moral, the only plausible tactical demand, and the minimal first step toward creating a new political consciousness in America. It is the beginning from which to build.

Notes

Introduction

1. *New York Times,* November 26, 1969.
2. *Hearings Before the Subcommittee on U.S. Security Agreements and Commitments Abroad* of the Committee on Foreign Relations, U.S. Senate, 91st Congress, First Session. Spring 1970, p. 821.
3. Robert Scigliano, *South Vietnam: Nation Under Stress* (Boston: Houghton Mifflin, 1964), pp. 80, 142, 145.
4. Douglas Pike, *War, Peace and the Viet Cong* (Cambridge: MIT Press, 1969), p. 6. He also claims that by 1968, the percentage supporting the Viet Cong was down to 10 to 15 percent.
5. June 2, 1969, cited in E. Herman and R. Du Boff, *How to Coo Like a Dove While Fighting to Win,* 2d ed. (Philadelphia: SANE, September 1969).
6. *Christian Science Monitor,* June 17, 1970.
7. Joseph Kraft, *Boston Globe,* June 18, 1970.
8. Such a man might also have pointed to those who "voted with their feet" by going to Canada. And he might have noted that with about 300,000 able-bodied men in the thirteen colonies, Washington's army rarely exceeded 8,000 men, and was, furthermore, backed by almost 32,000 French ground troops and 12,600 sailors and marines manning sixty-one major vessels. See B. Fall, *Last Reflections on a War* (New York: Doubleday, 1967), p. 276.
9. Ibid., pp. 33, 47.
10. Hoopes, *The Limits of Intervention* (New York: McKay, 1969), p. 129. We stop short, he says, because of our Christian values and our realization "that genocide is a terrible burden to bear."
11. Thompson, *No Exit from Vietnam* (London: Chatto and Windus, 1969), p. 125.
12. E. Herman, *"Atrocities" in Vietnam: Myths and Realities* (Pilgrim Press, 1970).
13. See Gabriel Kolko, "The Vietnam War and Diplomacy," *London Bulletin,* August 1969.
14. Testimony before the House Appropriations Committee,

301

released December 2. Quoted in *I. F. Stone's Weekly,* December 15, 1969.
15. Ibid., p. 187.
16. All quotes from Hoopes, op. cit., chap. 1.
17. November 2, 1966.
18. *New York Times,* May 9, 1970.
19. Eugene Rostow, *Law, Power, and the Pursuit of Peace* (Lincoln: University of Nebraska, 1968), preface, pp. 14f., 48.
20. Fall, *Vietnam Witness* (New York: Praeger, 1966), p. 203.

Chapter 1

1. Ellen Hammer, *The Struggle for Indo-China* (Stanford, Calif., 1954), p. 62.
2. Robert Scigliano, *South Vietnam: Nation Under Stress* (Boston, 1963), p. 7.
3. Hammer, op. cit., pp. 62–63.
4. Joseph Buttinger, *Vietnam: A Political History* (New York, 1968), chap. 7.
5. John McAlister and Paul Mus, *The Vietnamese and Their Revolution* (New York, 1970), p. 81.
6. Hammer, op. cit., p. 69. Also see Buttinger, op. cit., chap. 9.
7. Cited by Douglas Pike, *Viet Cong* (Cambridge, Mass., 1966), p. 41.
8. Ibid., p. 41.
9. John T. McAlister, Jr., *Vietnam: The Origins of Revolution* (New York, 1969), pp. 69–70.
10. Buttinger, op. cit., p. 163.
11. Ibid., p. 120.
12. Harold Issacs, *No Peace for Asia* (Cambridge, Mass., 1967), p. 144.
13. Ibid., p. 144.
14. Ibid., p. 147.
15. Quoted, ibid.
16. Ibid., p. 136.
17. Ibid., p. 143–44.
18. Ibid., p. 18.
19. For good background information on the Vietnamese Communists, see Buttinger, op. cit., chap. 9; Jean Lacouture's biography of *Ho Chi Minh* (New York, 1968).
20. Issacs, op. cit., p. 143.
21. Buttinger, op. cit., p. 188.
22. For information on the formation of Viet Minh base areas, see McAlister, *Vietnam,* chap. 12.
23. Buttinger, op. cit., p. 233.
24. George Kahin and John Lewis, *The United States in Vietnam* (New York, 1967), p. 24.
25. Ibid., p. 24.

26. General MacArthur, quoted in Harry Ashmore and William Baggs, *Mission to Hanoi* (New York: Putnam's, 1968), pp. 205–6.

27. Ho Chi Minh, quoted in Lacouture, op. cit., p. 182.

28. For a lengthy analysis of the Haiphong massacre, see Paul Mus, *Sociologie d'une guerre* (Paris, 1952).

29. Lacouture, op. cit., p. 277.

30. Pike, op. cit., p. 54.

31. Joseph Starobin, *Eyewitness in Indo-China* (New York, 1954), pp. 100–102.

32. Jean Chesneaux, *Contribution à l'histoire de la nation vietnamienne* (Paris, 1955), p. 279.

33. Jacques Doyon, *Les viet cong* (Paris, 1968), p. 233.

34. Joseph Alsop, "A Man in a Mirror," *The Reporter,* June 25, 1955, pp. 35–36.

35. Bernard Fall, *Two Viet-nams: A Political and Military Analysis* (New York, 1967), p. 107.

36. Ibid., pp. 106–7.

37. Ibid., p. 111.

38. Ibid., p. 110.

39. One of the best critiques of U.S. policy toward Vietnam, and an insightful analysis of the strategy of John Foster Dulles before and during the Geneva conference, is by Victor Bator, *Viet-Nam: A Diplomatic Tragedy* (New York, 1965).

40. Quoted by Ashmore and Baggs, op. cit., p. 211.

41. Roscoe Drummond and Gaston Coblentz, *Duel at the Brink* (New York, 1960), p. 26.

42. Quoted by Richard Barnet, *Intervention and Revolution: The United States in the Third World* (New York, 1968), p. 192.

43. Bernard Fall, "Dienbienphu: A Battle to Remember," in *Vietnam,* ed. Marvin Gettleman (New York, 1965), p. 107.

44. Ibid., p. 113.

45. Pike, op. cit., p. 52.

46. Kahin and Lewis, op. cit., chap. 3.

47. Quoted by Ashmore and Baggs, op. cit., p. 220.

48. James Gavin, *Crisis Now* (New York, 1968), p. 48.

49. Ibid., pp. 47–48.

50. Quoted in Joseph Buttinger, *Vietnam: A Dragon Embattled* (New York, 1967), II, 808.

51. Kahin and Lewis, op. cit., p. 32.

52. Gavin, op. cit., p. 49.

53. Sulzberger quoting Dulles, cited by Bator, op. cit., p. 220.

54. Quoted by Ashmore and Baggs, op. cit., p. 231.

55. Ibid., p. 230.

56. Edward Herman and Richard Du Boff, *America's Vietnam Policy: The Strategy of Deception* (Washington, D.C., 1968), pp. 82–88.

57. State Department White Paper, 1961, quoted by ibid., p. 84.

58. Buttinger, *Vietnam: A Political History,* p. 457.

59. Diem, quoted by Kahin and Lewis, op. cit., p. 81.

60. Quoted by Kahin and Lewis, op. cit., p. 86.

61. Dwight D. Eisenhower, *Mandate for Change* (New York, 1963), p. 372.

62. *Life* magazine, May 13, 1957; Bernard Fall, "Vietnam's Twelve Elections," *New Republic,* May 14, 1966.

63. Anthony Eden quoting Dulles, cited by Kahin and Lewis, op. cit., p. 60.

64. Robert Scheer and Warren Hinckle, "The Viet-Nam Lobby," in *The Viet-Nam Reader,* eds. Marcus Raskin and Bernard Fall (New York, 1965), p. 67.

65. For an examination of the individuals who supported Diem, see Robert Scheer, "The Genesis of United States Support for Ngo Dinh Diem," in *Vietnam,* ed. Gettleman, pp. 235–53.

66. Kahin and Lewis, op. cit., p. 70.

67. Mark Selden, "People's War and the Transformation of Peasant Society," *Bulletin of Concerned Asian Scholars,* October 1969.

68. Bernard Fall, *Le Viet-Minh* (Paris, 1960), p. 167.

69. Kahin and Lewis, op. cit., p. 75.

70. Philip Devillers and Jean Lacouture, *End of a War: Indochina 1954* (New York, 1969).

71. Bernard Fall, *Le Viet-Minh,* pp. 153–54.

72. Kahin and Lewis, op. cit., p. 75.

73. Philip Devillers, quoted by Peggy Duff, "The Truth Is Great, and Will Prevail," *Our Generation,* VII, 71.

74. Buttinger, *Vietnam: A Political History,* pp. 447–48.

75. Bernard Fall, *Last Reflections on a War* (New York, 1967), pp. 198–99.

76. *New York Times,* international ed., December 3, 1969. Also *Thoi Bao Ga,* November 1969 and April 1970.

77. Kahn and Lewis, op. cit., pp. 69–70.

78. Ibid., p. 81.

79. Philippe Devillers, "The Struggle for the Unification of Vietnam," in *North Vietnam Today,* ed. P. J. Honey (New York, 1962), p. 36.

80. Richard Morrock, "Revolution and Intervention in Vietnam," in *Containment and Revolution,* ed. David Horowitz (Boston, 1967), p. 233.

81. Quoted by Kahin and Lewis, op. cit., p. 101.

82. Ibid., pp. 108–9.

83. Jean Lacouture, *Vietnam: Between Two Truces* (New York, 1966), pp. 53–54.

84. Kahin and Lewis, op. cit., pp. 111–16.

85. Ellen Hammer, *The Struggle for Indochina Continues* (Stanford, Calif., 1955), p. 36.

86. Walt Rostow, "Guerrilla Warfare in Underdeveloped Areas," in *Viet-Nam Reader,* ed. Raskin and Fall, p. 113.

87. Secretary Dean Rusk, *Department of State Bulletin,* May 10, 1965.

88. Doyon, op. cit., p. 68.

89. Ibid., pp. 205–6.
90. Robert Scigliano, "Vietnam: A Country at War," *Asian Survey,* January 1963.
91. Wilfred Burchett, *Vietnam: Inside Story of a Guerilla War* (New York, 1965), p. 38.
92. Pike, op. cit., p. 277.
93. Doyon, op. cit., p. 236.
94. NLF document quoted by Selden, op. cit., pp. 39–40.
95. Pike, op. cit., p. 273.
96. Quoted, ibid, pp. 173, 174.
97. Ibid., pp. 172–73.
98. Katsuichi Honda, *The National Liberation Front* (Tokyo, 1968), p. 22.
99. Roger Pic, *Au cœur de Vietnam* (Paris, 1968), pp. 119–21.
100. Doyon, op. cit., pp. 269–70.
101. Quoted by Barnet, op. cit., p. 212.
102. Ibid., pp. 212–14.
103. Pike, op. cit.

Chapter 2

1. Jacques Decornoy, "Laos: The Forgotten War," *Bulletin of Concerned Asian Scholars,* July-August 1970, p. 27.
2. Ibid., pp. 23–24.
3. Ibid., p. 27.
4. Joel Halpern, *Government, Politics, and Social Structure in Laos* (New Haven, 1964), pp. 5–8.
5. Hugh Toye, *Laos: Buffer State or Battleground* (New York, 1968).
6. Arthur Dommen, *Conflict in Laos* (New York, 1968), p. 78.
7. Halpern, op. cit., pp. 5–8.
8. *The Observer,* February 7, 1965.
9. *New York Times,* May 4, 1964, p. 10.
10. Bernard Fall, *Anatomy of a Crisis* (New York, 1969), pp. 164–66.
11. Banning Garrett, "The Vietnamization of Laos," *Ramparts,* June 1970.
12. Ibid.
13. New York Times, October 26, 1969. Also Peter Dale Scott, "Air America: Flying into Laos," *Ramparts,* February 1970.
14. Peter Dale Scott, "Cambodia: Why the Generals Won," *New York Review of Books,* June 18, 1970, p. 31.
15. Decornoy, op. cit., p. 22.
16. *New York Times,* October 1, 1967.
17. Jean Lacouture, "From the Vietnam War to the Indochina War," *Foreign Affairs,* July 1970, p. 623.
18. Fall, op. cit., pp. 23–25.
19. Decornoy, op. cit., p. 26.
20. Dommen, op. cit., p. 45.

21. Ibid., p. 88.
22. Fall, op. cit., p. 86.
23. Ibid., p. 118.
24. Decornoy, op. cit., p. 26.

Chapter 3

1. *Le Monde,* Weekly Selection, June 3, 1970, p. 4.
2. Richard Dudman, *New York Times,* June 24, 1970, p. 4.
3. Cynthia Fredrick, "Cambodia: Operation Total Victory No. 43," *Bulletin of Concerned Asian Scholars,* April-July 1970.
4. *Le Monde,* Weekly Selection, May 6, 1970.
5. Ibid.
6. Roger Smith, *Cambodia's Foreign Policy* (Ithaca, N.Y., 1965), p. 117.
7. Quoted by Fredrick, op. cit., p. 10.
8. Quoted by Wilfred Burchett, *Mekong Upstream* (Hanoi, 1957), p. 157. Similar quotes in Smith, op. cit., p. 95.
9. Quoted in *I. F. Stone's Weekly,* May 18, 1970. Also by Daniel Roy in *Le Monde Diplomatique,* April 1970.
10. Michael Leifer, *Cambodia: The Search for Security* (New York, 1967), p. 16.
11. Ibid., p. 24.
12. *Le Monde,* Weekly Selection, April 18, 1970.
13. Michael Morrow, *Boston Globe,* June 25, 1970.
14. Richard Dudman, *New York Times,* June 25, 1970, p. 2.

Chapter 4

1. *United States Security Agreements and Commitments Abroad: Kingdom of Thailand.* Hearings before the Subcommittee on U.S. Security Agreements and Commitments Abroad of the Committee of Foreign Relations, U.S. Senate, 91st Congress, 1st Session (Washington, D.C.: Government Printing Office, 1969), November 10, 1969, p. 610.
2. David A. Wilson, quoted in Gunnar Myrdal, *Asian Drama* (New York, 1967), p. 392.
3. Myrdal, ibid., p. 394.
4. Frank Darling, *Thailand and the United States* (Washington, D. C., 1965), pp. 66, 69.
5. Richard Butwell, "Thailand after Vietnam," *Current History,* December 1969, p. 339.
6. *I. F. Stone's Bi-Weekly,* May 18, 1970, p. 2.
7. Richard Halloran, *New York Times,* December 1, 1969.
8. *Washington Post,* Augsut 25, 1969.
9. Hearings, op. cit., p. 754.
10. "Thailand in the Eye of the Storm," *Le Monde,* Weekly Selection, March 25, 1970.

11. *Washington Post,* August 25, 1969.
12. *New York Times,* October 2, 1968.
13. Sakamoto Toshio, "Prosperity and Poverty in Southeast Asia—Record of a Journey to Thailand, India, and Indonesia," *Zenei,* May 1970, p. 115.
14. Hearings, op. cit., p. 638.
15. Michael Klare, "The Great South Asian War," *The Nation,* March 9, 1970, p. 269.
16. Hearings, op. cit., pp. 613, 614, 621.
17. Toshio, op. cit., p. 117.

Chapter 5

1. *New York Times,* series of editorials on "Wars of Liberation," June 30–July 3, 1965.
2. W. W. Rostow, speech at the University of Leeds.
3. E. G. Lansdale, "Vietnam: Do We Understand Revolution," *Foreign Affairs,* October 1964.
4. I. F. Stone, *In Time of Torment,* pp. 173–74.
5. Don Luce and John Sommer, *Vietnam: The Unheard Voices* (Ithaca, N.Y.: Cornell University, 1969), p. 6.

Chapter 6

1. Devillers, "The Struggle for the Unification of Vietnam," in *North Vietnam Today,* ed. P. J. Honey (New York, 1962), p. 36.
2. Senate Foreign Relations Committee hearings (transcript), November 18–19, 1969 (Washington: U. S. Government Publications), pp. 7–8.
3. W. A. Nighswonger, *Rural Pacification in Vietnam* (New York: Praeger, 1966), p. 46.
4. Nguyen Khac Nhan, "Policy of Key Rural Agrovilles, *Asian Culture* (July-December 1961), III, 32.
5. Don Luce and John Sommer, *Vietnam: The Unheard Voices* (Ithaca, N.Y.: Cornell University Press), p. 164.
6. *Thoi-Bao Ga* (Cambridge, Mass.), No. 9, April 1970, p. 4.
7. Luce and Sommer, op. cit., p. 147.
8. Ibid., p. 148.
9. Ibid., pp. 153, 164.
10. Ibid., pp. 156–59.
11. Jonathan Schell, *The Village of Ben Suc* (New York: Vintage, 1967).
12. *Song Moi* (Saigon), December 13, 1967.
13. Luce and Sommer, op. cit., p. 149.
14. *New York Times Index* for January 16–31, 1970.
15. Ralph Blumenthal, *New York Times,* May 26, 1970.

16. Henry Kamm, *New York Times,* February 5, 1970, p. 4; also *Washington Post,* March 2, 1970.

17. Tad Szulc, *New York Times,* June 7, 1970.

Chapter 7

1. Address by General Westmoreland, October 14, 1969. Reprinted in *Congressional Record,* October 16, 1969.

2. Testimony of Jean Pierre Vigier, research director for scientific research and former officer-in-charge of armaments inspection of the French army. Quoted in NARMIC (National Action/Research on the Military-Industrial Complex), *Weapons for Counterinsurgency* (American Friends Service Committee), p. 46.

3. *Aviation Week,* March 21, 1966.

4. American Friends Service Committee, *Vietnam 1969* (May 5, 1969).

5. NARMIC, op. cit., p. 41.

6. Eric Prokosch, " 'Conventional' Killers: The Latest in Antipersonnel Weapons," *New Republic,* November 1, 1969.

7. See Richard D. (Max) McCarthy, *The Ultimate Folly* (New York: Knopf, 1969) for a general treatment.

8. Quoted in NARMIC, op. cit., pp. 14–15.

9. *Congressional Record,* October 16, 1969.

10. *New York Times,* May 28, 1967.

11. A general treatment is available in DMS (Defense Market Service) Market Intelligence Report, "Electronic Battlefield" (New York: McGraw-Hill, November 1969).

Chapter 8

1. Noam Chomsky, citing Gabriel Kolko, in the *London Bulletin,* August 1969.

2. *The Nation,* April 21, 1969.

3. *New Republic,* May 30, 1970.

4. Jonathan Schell, *The Military Half* (New York: Vintage, 1968), pp. 114–15.

5. Frank Harvey, *Air War: Vietnam* (New York: Bantam, 1967), p. 2.

6. Schell, op. cit., p. 18.

Chapter 9

1. Commission for Investigation on the American Imperialists' War Crimes in Vietnam (Hanoi: Democratic Republic of Vietnam, October 1966), pp. 16–17. See also Jonathan Schell, *The Village of Ben Suc* (New York: Vintage, 1967).

2. Don Luce and John Sommer, *Vietnam: The Unheard Voices* (Ithaca, N.Y.: Cornell University, 1969) pp. 195–96.

3. See for instance Schell, op. cit., pp. 33–37; or Luce and Sommer, op. cit., pp. 196–97.

4. Reuters, February 11, 1966.

5. Commission . . . , op. cit., pp. 23–24 and illustration 3.

6. *Pacific Stars and Stripes,* November 23, 1967.

7. James P. Sterba, *New York Times Magazine,* February 8, 1970, p. 31.

8. Luce and Sommer, op. cit., pp. 188–89.

9. Senator Cooper (Ky.) in transcript of Hearings before the Committee on Foreign Relations, November 18–19, 1969 (Washington, D.C.: U.S. Government Publications), p. 102.

10. Sterba, op. cit., pp. 31, 91.

11. Luce and Sommer, op. cit., p. 193.

12. *Look,* June 16, 1970.

Chapter 10

1. Samuel Huntington, *Foreign Affairs,* July 1968.

2. Seymour M. Hersch, "Our Chemical War," *The New York Review of Books,* April 25, 1968.

3. Lt. Colonel Arthur F. McConnell, Jr., "Mission Ranch Hand," *Air University Review,* XXI(2), 89–94.

4. Ngo Vinh Long, *Thoi-Bao Ga,* November 5, 1969.

5. G. H. Orians and W. Pfeiffer, "Ecological Effects of the War in Vietnam," *Science* (1970), CLXVIII, 544.

General References

Thomas Whiteside, *Defoliation,* (New York: Ballantine Books, 1970).

"Chemical-Biological Warfare: U.S. Policies and International Effects." Hearing Before the Subcommittee on National Security Policy and Scientific Developments of the Committee on Foreign Affairs. House of Representatives, November 18–December 19, 1969.

Seymour Hersch, *Chemical and Biological Warfare* (Indianapolis: Bobbs-Merrill, 1968).

Richard D. (Max) McCarthy, *The Ultimate Folly* (New York: Knopf, 1969).

Chapter 11

1. *Congressional Record,* CXIV(11), 13692–93.

2. Corson, *The Betrayal* (New York: Norton); cited in the *New Republic,* October 26, 1968, p. 29.

3. François Sully, "South Vietnam's Urban Revolution," *Newsweek,* January 20, 1969, p. 32.

4. Ibid.
5. *New York Times,* July 6, 1968, pp. 1, 6.
6. *New York Times,* June 23, 1968, p. 6.
7. *Against the Crime of Silence,* p. 479.
8. Ibid., p. 407.
9. Jonathan Schell, *The Military Half,* p. 62.
10. *New York Times,* June 23, 1968, p. 6.
11. Schell, op. cit., p. 61.
12. Ibid., p. 69.
13. *New York Times,* June 23, 1968, p. 6.
14. T. D. Allman, "The Price of Neutrality," *Far Eastern Economic Review,* February 26, 1970.
15. One account appears in UN Document s/7820 15/ 3/6 and is quoted in *Is Cambodia Next?* (Washington, D.C.: Russell Press, 1967).
16. *New York Times,* May 26, 1970, p. 3.
17. Compare *New York Times,* Oct. 1, 1969, p. 9.
18. "The Refugees of Laos," *The Nation,* January 26, 1970, p. 76. See also *Washington Post,* March 2, 1970, pp. 1, 6.
19. Ibid., p. 77.
20. Ibid.

Chapter 12

1. Nuremberg Principle VI, clause b. The full text can be found in *The Nation,* January 26, 1970, p. 78.
2. *Against the Crime of Silence,* proceedings of the Russell International War Crimes Tribunal, O'Hare, 1968, p. 409.
3. Ibid., pp. 408–9.
4. Ibid., p. 433.
5. Ibid., p. 411.
6. Ibid., pp. 312f, 312i.
7. Ibid., p. 189.
8. *New York Times,* November 30, 1969.
9. Nuremberg Principles IV and V.
10. From a letter to the *New York Times,* November 26, 1969, by Orville and Jonathan Schell.

Chapter 13

1. Harvey Meyerson, *Vinh Long* (Boston: Houghton Mifflin, 1970), p. 138.
2. *New York Herald Tribune,* March 3, 1964.

Chapter 14

1. Bernard Fall, *Street Without Joy,* p. 263.
2. Roger Hilsman, *To Move a Nation.*

3. Arnold Abrams, *FEER*, January 1, 1970.

4. *FEER*, November 13, 1969.

5. Ralph Blumenthal, *New York Times*, May 27, 1970.

6. *FEER*, October 9, 1969; Chalmers Roberts, *Washington Post*, June 10, 1970.

7. *New York Times*, January 15, 1970.

8. *FEER*, May 2, 1968, p. 248.

9. Chalmers Roberts, *Washington Post*, June 4, 1970.

Chapter 15

1. Dwight D. Eisenhower, *Mandate for Change*, p. 372.

2. Bernard Fall, *Two Vietnams*, p. 257.

3. George Kahin and John Lewis, *The United States in Vietnam* (New York, 1967).

4. Alfred Hassler, *Saigon, U.S.A.*, pp. 29–30.

5. Ibid., p. 32.

6. Ibid., p. 34.

7. Douglas Pike, *Viet Cong* (Cambridge, Mass., 1966), p. 110.

8. Hassler, op. cit., p. 139.

9. Hugh Toye, *Laos: Buffer State or Battleground*, pp. 110–11.

10. Ibid., p. 118.

11. Arthur Schlesinger, Jr., *A Thousand Days*. Quoted in Peter Dale Scott, "Laos: The Story Nixon Won't Tell," *New York Review of Books*, April 9, 1970, p. 35.

12. Roger M. Smith, "Laos in Perspective," *Asian Survey*, January 1963, p. 63. Quoted in Toye, op. cit., p. 119.

13. Toye, op. cit., p. 132, n. 76.

14. Ibid., pp. 133–35.

15. Ibid., p. 135.

Chapter 16

1. *Newsweek*, May 18, 1970.

2. *Saturday Review*, June 6, 1970.

3. *Boston Globe*, May 25, 1970.

4. *Newsweek*, February 26, 1968.

5. Department of Defense, Office of Command Information, Vietnam *Scrapbook*, ed. 13.

6. *Time*, February 9, 1970.

7. *Pacific Stars and Stripes*, October 12, 1967; *Saigon Post*, October 10, 1967.

8. *Boston Globe*, January 7, 1970; *Newsweek*, January 12, 1970.

9. *Tropic Lightning News*, 25th Infantry Division, Vietnam, September 11, 1967.

Chapter 19

1. Peter Dale Scott, "Laos: The Story Nixon Won't Tell," *New York Review of Books,* April 9, 1970, pp. 35–41.
2. David Kraslow and Stuart H. Loory, *The Secret Search for Peace in Vietnam* (New York: Vintage, 1968), p. 65.
3. *New York Times,* June 11, 1970, p. 14.
4. For a detailed discussion of the missed possibilities for peace in 1963–66, see Franz Schurmann, Peter Dale Scott, and Reginald Zelnick, *The Politics of Escalation in Vietnam* (Boston: Beacon Press, 1966).
5. Kraslow and Loory, op. cit., p. 53.
6. Schurmann, Scott, and Zelnick, op. cit., pp. 110–19; Kraslow and Loory, op. cit., p. 147.
7. George McTurnan Kahin and John Wilson Lewis, *The United States in Vietnam,* rev. ed. (New York: Dial Press, 1969), pp. 381–85.
8. *Three Documents of the National Liberation Front,* introduction by Gabriel Kolko (Boston: Beacon Press, 1970), pp. 15–23.
9. *New York Times,* July 1 and 3, 1970.
10. Kahin and Lewis, op. cit., pp. 394–405.
11. *New York Times,* July 31, 1970.
12. On the 1967 elections, see Don Luce and John Sommer, *Vietnam: The Unheard Voices* (Ithaca, N.Y.: Cornell University, 1969), pp. 61–64.

Chapter 21

1. Harold Hinton, *Communist China in World Politics.*
2. Perkins and Halperin, *Communist China and Arms Control.*

Chapter 22

1. Marvin Gettleman, ed., *Vietnam* (New York, 1965).
2. Marcus Raskin and Bernard Fall, *The Viet-Nam Reader* (New York, 1965), p. 97.
3. Cited in Draper, *Abuse of Power,* p. 92.
4. Ibid., p. 93.
5. Interview, *U.S. News and World Report,* September 28, 1964, p. 60.; cited ibid.
6. Draper, op. cit., p. 81.
7. See Bernard Fall in *The Communist Revolution in Asia,* ed. R. Scalapino, pp. 173–97.
8. See Peter Dale Scott "Laos: The Story Nixon Won't Tell," *New York Review of Books,* April 9, 1970.

9. *Far Eastern Economic Review*, April 9, 1970. p. 21.
10. Ibid., Feb. 26, 1970.
11. Thomas Whiteside, *Defoliation*, 1970.
12. Daniel Roy. *Le Monde Diplomatique*, April 1970.

Chapter 24

1. See report of the Senate Foreign Relations Committee, cited in *New York Times,* June 7, 1970.

Chapter 25

1. *New York Times,* November 2, 1963.
2. *Congressional Record,* 1969, H4985.

Chapter 26

1. John W. Dower, "Occupied Japan and the American Lake, 1945–1950," in *America's Asia,* ed. Mark Selden and Edward Friedman (New York: Pantheon, 1970).
2. Dean Acheson, *Present at the Creation* (New York: Norton, 1969), p. 375.
3. Walter LaFeber, *America, Russia, and the Cold War, 1945–1966* (New York: Wiley, 1967), p. 90.
4. Harry Truman, *Memoirs,* II, chap. 25.
5. *Department of State Bulletin,* July 3, 1950; cited in Harry S. Ashmore and William C. Baggs, *Mission to Hanoi* (New York: Putnam's, 1968), p. 208.
6. *Defense Industry Bulletin,* April 1970, p. 12.
7. *New York Times,* April 8, 1954; cited in Ashmore and Baggs, op. cit., pp. 224–25.
8. *New York Times,* July 5, 1970.

Chapter 27

1. Hoopes, *The Limits of Intervention,* p. 30.
2. Ibid., p. 163.
3. Richard Pfeffer, ed., *No More Vietnams?,* p. 53.
4. Joseph Goulden, *Truth Is the First Casualty.*
5. *Politics of Escalation,* p. 44.

Chapter 28

1. Jean Larteguy, *The Centurions* (London: Hutchinson, 1961).
2. *New York Times,* May 8, 1970.

3. Joseph Kraft, *Washington Post,* May 6, 1970.
4. *Washington Post,* May 20, 1970.

Chapter 29

1. James C. Thomson, Jr., "How Could Vietnam Happen?" *Atlantic Monthly,* April 1968.
2. *Atlantic Monthly,* April 1969.
3. *New Republic,* May 30, 1970.

Chapter 30

1. Herbert P. Bix, "The Security Treaty System and the Japanese Military-Industrial Complex," *Bulletin of Concerned Asian Scholars.*
2. *Global Defense—U.S. Military Commitments Abroad.* A Publication of the Congressional Quarterly Service, 1735 K Street, N.W., Washington, D.C., September 1969, p. 13.
3. *The Republic of the Philippines.* Hearings Before the Subcommittee on U.S. Security Agreements and Commitments Abroad of the Committee on Foreign Relations, U.S. Senate, 91st Congress, 1st session, part I, September 30–October 3, 1969 (Washington, D.C.: Government Printing Office, 1969), pp. 6–7.
4. *Global Defense,* op. cit., p. 27.
5. Ibid., p. 26.
6. Ibid., pp. 37–38.
7. *New York Times,* April 27, 1969.
8. *Global Defense,* op. cit., p. 34; Colonel James A. Donovan, *Militarism, U.S.A.* (New York: Scribner, 1970), p. 53.
9. *Global Defense,* op. cit., p. 34.
10. Ibid., p. 38.
11. Takahashi Hajime, "The Essence of the Crisis in the Korean Peninsula," *Ajia* (March 1970), pp. 32–33. In Japanese.
12. *Global Defense,* op. cit., p. 38; *Business Week,* June 7, 1969.
13. Bix, op. cit., p. 30.
14. *New York Times,* January 25, 1970.
15. Philip Shabecoff, *New York Times,* June 24, 1970; William Beecher, *New York Times,* June 12, 1970.
16. *New York Times,* June 20, 1970.
17. *New York Times,* June 25, 1970.
18. John Mecklin in *Fortune* magazine, as quoted in Hearings, op. cit., p. 207.
19. Bernadino Ronquillo, "Philippines," *Far Eastern Economic Review,* March 1970, p. 34; Philip Shabecoff, *New York Times,* March 8, 1970; March 12, 1970.
20. *Far Eastern Economic Review,* March 12, 1970, p. 4.
21. Hearings, op. cit., p. 207.
22. *Global Defense,* op. cit., pp. 39, 42.

23. Ibid., p. 43.
24. Ibid., pp. 42, 43.
25. Ibid., p. 43.
26. Ibid.

Chapter 31

1. As cited in Harry Magdoff, *The Age of Imperialism* (New York: Monthly Review Press, 1969), p. 53. This section on economic imperialism is indebted to Magdoff's analysis.

2. Total profits are from *Economic Report of the President,* 1968, table B–69. Foreign profits are from Walter Lederer and Frederick Cutler, "International Investments of the U.S. in 1966," *Survey of Current Business,* September 1967. Both foreign and total profit figures are after tax. Under foreign tax credit provisions of U.S. tax laws, most of foreign profits are not taxed by the U.S. For the most recent years for which data are available, 1960–62, foreign tax credits reduce the taxes due on foreign profits by 80 percent (calculated from IRS, *Statistics of Income 1962. Supplemental Report on Foreign Income and Taxes Reported on Corporation Income Tax Returns,* Table 10). Thus on $1000 of profits, the U.S. tax rate was about 50 percent or $500. On foreign profits, foreign tax credits reduced the tax rate by 80 percent or $400 of the $500. Thus the actual U.S. tax paid was around $100 per $1,000 of foreign profits. In calculating foreign profits after tax for 1966, the same 80 percent reduction in taxes on foreign profits was assumed to hold.

3. All data on the seventeen corporations, including data on individual companies in the next paragraph of text, are obtained from 10K forms (Annual Reports Pursuant to Section 13 or 15(d) of the Securities Exchange Act of 1934). The seventeen corporations, in order of foreign profits returned to the U.S., are: Standard Oil of New Jersey; Texaco; Standard Oil of California; Mobil Oil; IBM; Gulf Oil; General Motors; Ford Motors; Eastman Kodak; IT&T; Goodyear; Union Carbide; Procter & Gamble; Continental Oil; National Dairy Products; International Harvester; and RCA. Other corporations among the top forty industrials, known to have significant foreign operations, were not included because foreign profit data are not available. For example, General Electric, Chrysler, and Du Pont each reported foreign sales over 15 percent of total sales, but did not report foreign profits.

4. Magdoff, op. cit., p. 198.

5. *Operations Report, Data as of June 30, 1966* (Agency for International Development), p. 5.

6. Magdoff, op. cit., pp. 129–36. Magdoff's chap. 4 is an excellent source on the shortcomings of U.S. aid.

7. Cited in Magdoff, op. cit., p. 133.

8. Lederer and Cutler, op. cit.

9. Magdoff, op. cit., p. 126.

10. For example see William A. Williams, *The Tragedy of American Diplomacy* (New York: Delta, 1962).

11. In addition to Magdoff, op. cit., and Williams, op. cit., see Carl Oglesby and Richard Shaull, *Containment and Change* (New York: Macmillan, 1967); and David Horowitz, ed., *Containment and Revolution* (Boston: Beacon, 1967).

12. Calculated from Defense Department figures in *Congressional Record,* May 1, 1970.

13. R. F. Kaufman, "We Must Guard Against Unwarranted Influence by the Military-Industrial Complex," *New York Times Magazine,* June 22, 1969.

14. See, for instance, John Gerassi, *The Great Fear in Latin America* (New York: Collier Books, 1963).

15. Cited in Peter Wiley, "Vietnam and the Pacific Rim Strategy," *Leviathan,* June 1969; also in Magdoff, op. cit., p. 68. Original source is *New York Times,* December 9, 1965.

16. Magdoff, op. cit., p. 176.

Chapter 32

1. *New York Times,* November 4, 1969. A slightly revised version of this passage was included in the president's "State of the World" address of February 18, 1970.

2. *New York Times,* February 19, 1970.

3. From the Pentagon's budget message to Congress for fiscal year 1970, cited in Michael T. Klare, "The Sun Never Sets on America's Empire: U.S. Bases in Asia," *Commonweal,* May 22, 1970. The identification of all military threats to the status quo as "Communist aggression" continues to pervade the Pentagon's treatment of the situation faced by America's allies in Asia.

4. *Defense Industry Bulletin,* April 1970, pp. 22, 27.

5. Cited in Michael Klare, "The Great South Asian War," *The Nation,* March 9, 1970. Klare, who is associated with the North American Congress on Latin America (NACLA), has written a number of excellent articles on U.S. imperialism in Asia.

6. *Defense Industry Bulletin,* April 1970, p. 23.

7. *New York Times,* June 10 and 11, 1970.

8. *Congressional Record,* November 29, 1969.

9. *New York Times,* June 10, 1970.

10. Klare, *The Nation,* March 9, 1970.

11. *Congressional Record,* October 16, 1969.

12. Speech to the Executive Club of Chicago, March 17, 1955. Cited by Richard Barnet in *Hard Times,* May 25–June 1, 1970. See the fuller quote in chap. 33 of this book.

13. Helio Jaguaribe, "A Brazilian View," in *How Latin America Views the American Investor,* ed. R. Vernon (1966).

14. Philippine UN Ambassador Salvador Lopez, "The Colonial Relationship," in *The United States and the Philippines,* ed. F. H. Golay (Englewood Cliffs, N.J.: Prentice-Hall, 1966). See also

George Taylor, *The Philippines and the United States* (New York: Praeger, 1964).

15. Peter Bell and Stephen A. Resnick, *Journal of Contemporary Asia* (London, vol. 1, no. 1), June 1970.

16. *Newsweek*, June 15, 1970.

17. Bell and Resnick, op. cit.

18. Tillman Durdin, *New York Times,* November 16, 1969.

Chapter 33

1. Richard J. Barnet, "How Hanoi Sees Nixon," *New York Review of Books,* January 29, 1970, pp. 20–21.

2. Cited in fact sheets issued by Committee of Concerned Asian Scholars, Harvard Chapter, summer 1970.

3. Don Luce and John Sommer, *Vietnam: The Unheard Voices* (Ithaca, N.Y.: Cornell University, 1969), p. 306.

4. Arnold Toynbee, quoted by Noam Chomsky, *American Power and the New Mandarins* (New York: Pantheon, 1969), p. 313.

5. Luce and Sommer, op. cit., p. 57.

Chronology

VIETNAM

1800–1945	REUNIFICATION, COLONIALISM, RE-SISTANCE, AND WAR.
1802	Gialong (Nguyen-Anh), emperor, reunites imperial domain after a period of dynastic struggle and civil war (1772–1802).
1858	Joint French-Spanish expedition bombards coast and occupies Saigon.
1862, June 5	Treaty of Saigon. French acquire three eastern provinces of Cochin China (Mekong Delta area), receive indemnity. Free exercise of Catholicism permitted and three ports opened to French trade.
1867	France occupies three western provinces of Cochin China.
1874	Tu Duc, emperor, forced to recognize French possession of Cochin China.
1883, Aug. 25	Treaty of Hue. French protectorate extended to include Tonkin (northern Vietnam) and Annam (central Vietnam).
1883–85	War between China and France over French penetration in Vietnam. China defeated.
1885–95	French pacification of Tonkin and Indochina in general. Many revolts in interior, those in Tonkin led by De Tham.
1887	Cochin China, Cambodia, Annam, and Tonkin administratively united as the Indochinese Union.
1930–31	Serious outbreaks against French rule follow founding of Indochina Communist party in 1930. Agitation vigorously put down.
1941	Japan invades French Indochina. World War II in the Pacific. American OSS officers

318

and NLF areas in South. U.S. Marines land in South.

1965–66	HANOI PEACE PLAN REJECTED—U.S. INSTITUTES BOMBING PAUSE.
1965, Apr.–May	Hanoi four-point proposal: withdrawal of U.S. military; cessation of hostilities against North; honor Geneva accords; Vietnamese to solve own problems. U.S. orders bombing halt conditional on reduction in hostilities by other side. Bombing resumed after five days.
June	New regime in Saigon under Brigadier General (Air Vice-Marshal) Nguyen Cao Ky.
July–Dec.	Johnson offers "unconditional discussions" with "any government." Saigon refuses to negotiate with NLF. Repeated peace feelers from Hanoi bring U.S. request for "clarification" while U.S. carries out first air strike on Hanoi-Haiphong complex. U.S. forces reach 154,000 (Nov. 4).
1965–66, Dec.–Jan.	U.S. begins (Dec. 24) a bombing pause over the North which finally is to last thirty-seven days. North Vietnamese forces cease various military actions in South. Administration ignores Senate appeal for continuation of bombing pause. Hanoi calls for implementation of Geneva accords.
1966–68	ELECTIONS HELD IN SOUTH—TET OFFENSIVE SHAKES U.S. CONFIDENCE.
1966, Feb. 6	Johnson, Ky, and South Vietnamese Chief of State General Nguyen Van Thieu meet at Honolulu. Ky refuses to join in promises to negotiate with Hanoi or the NLF.
Mar.–June	Buddhist demonstrations in Hue and Danang put down with American military support and Saigon promise of election of a constituent assembly. Buddhist rebels refuse cooperation with Viet Cong. Buddhist military and religious leaders detained and brought to Saigon after Hue occupied by Ky forces (June 10).
July 25	Premier Ky calls for armed confrontation with Communist China now rather than later. He urges allied forces to invade North Vietnam even at risk of bringing China into

war. Ky adamant against possibility of talks with the NLF.

July 30

Forty-four Democratic and three Republican representatives (after a similar statement by some senators led by Mike Mansfield on July 26) urge the administration to disassociate itself from the "spirit of escalation" advocated by Ky and urge new initiatives to reach negotiated peace.

Sept. 11

One hundred and seventeen deputies elected to Constituent Assembly in South Vietnam. Only candidates acceptable to the government (no Communists or neutralists) allowed to run.

Oct. 24–25

Manila Summit (Australia, South Korea, New Zealand, Philippines, Thailand, U.S., South Vietnam). Agreement that allied forces shall be withdrawn as the other side withdraws its forces to North.

Dec. 8

U.S. troop levels reach 362,000 in South Vietnam.

1967, Feb.

Johnson (on first day of Tet truce in letter to Ho Chi Minh) refuses to stop bombing until North stops all infiltration of South. Bombing resumed before reply received.

Sept.

Vietnamese presidential elections result in Thieu (Pres.)–Ky (Vice-Pres.) victory with 35 percent plurality. All known advocates of peaceful settlement or negotiations with NLF banned. Civilian candidate who finished second to Thieu later (1968) sentenced by military court to five years at hard labor because he advocated talks with NLF and a peaceful solution to the war.

1967–68

"Free-fire" zones established, resulting in estimated 4 million refugees (25 percent of population).

1968, Jan.–Feb.

Tet offensive. Vietcong and North Vietnamese troops attack thirty-six of South Vietnam's forty-four provincial capitals, holding major portions of Saigon and Hue. Heavy fighting in Hue.

1968–69

JOHNSON ANNOUNCES BOMBING HALT—PEACE CONFERENCE BOGS DOWN.

1968, Apr.–June

Peace moves in U.S. escalate after Tet offensive shakes U.S. Johnson announces bombing halt north of twentieth parallel as first step to "de-escalate the conflict" and "move immediately to peace through negotiations." Total halt to follow signs of restraint from other side. Hanoi agrees to meet U.S. representatives in Paris; talks begin in May. Subsequent decline in North Vietnamese offensive operations.

Oct.   Johnson announces total bombing halt. NLF and Saigon governments to join peace talks.

1969, Jan.   Four-party talks begin in Paris.

Apr.–May   Peace talks stalemate over issues of troop withdrawals and interim government. Hanoi/NLF demand U.S. commitment to total withdrawal and call for provisional coalition government representing all who favor peace, independence, and neutrality.

May   President Nixon announces start of gradual troop withdrawals (U.S. troop strength in South Vietnam at 540,000).

Nov.–Dec.   U.S. and world opinion shocked by news of U.S. troops killing Vietnamese civilians in massacre at Mylai.

1969–70   STALEMATE IN PARIS AND VIETNAM —ESCALATION IN LAOS AND CAMBODIA.

1969–70, Dec.–Mar. Senate Foreign Relations Committee increasingly critical of U.S. involvement in Southeast Asia. Senate-House Conference Committee proposes legislation barring use of U.S. combat troops in Laos.

Dec.   U.S. chief delegate to Paris talks (Henry Cabot Lodge) resigns; neither he nor deputy replaced. Thieu government closes two Saigon newspapers, seizes fifteen student leaders, purges and imprisons three critics in House of Representatives. Vice-President Spiro Agnew, on Asian tour, deems it inappropriate for U.S. to press Thieu to broaden his popular support.

1970, Jan.–Feb. Administration states that infiltration from North Vietnam decreases. U.S. carries out retaliatory bombings on North for attacks on U.S. reconnaissance planes.

Jan.–Mar.   Increased fighting in Laos, with U.S. bombing wide areas in support of Laotian government troops. Numerous civilian casualties and large numbers of refugees. Deep U.S. involvement in training, arming, financing, and directing clandestine army of Meo tribesmen (non-Lao hill peoples) revealed. Laotian government requests reconvening of Geneva conference. Pathet Lao seek to open direct negotiations with Laotian government and demand U.S. end bombing.

Mar.–Apr.

Coup in Cambodia deposes neutralist Sihanouk and calls for military actions against Viet Cong and North Vietnamese bases in Cambodian border areas. South Vietnamese forces begin attacks on suspected Viet Cong base camps in Cambodia with U.S. helicopter support. Many of Cambodia's Vietnamese minority killed as result of anti-Vietnamese campaign on part of new Cambodian military government. Viet Cong offensive moves westward.

Apr. 20

Nixon pledges to withdraw an additional 150,000 troops from Vietnam during 1970 because progress in "Vietnamization" exceeding expectations.

Apr. 30

Nixon announces the invasion of Cambodia by U.S. and South Vietnamese troops.

May

Nationwide uproar in U.S. (including first national student strike in U.S. history) over Cambodian invasion. Nixon promises all U.S. troops will be out of Cambodia by June 30. South Vietnamese set no time limits on their operations in Cambodia. U.S. officials refuse to rule out continued bombing of Cambodia after June 30 troop withdrawal deadline. Various moves in the Senate to end the Cambodian venture, the war in Indochina itself, and to reassert the constitutional role of the Congress in matters of war.

June–July

Senate votes 81 to 10 to repeal Gulf of Tonkin resolution (June 24), and after thirty-four days of debate adopts the Church-Cooper amendment (58 to 37) intended to limit presidential action in Cambodia (June 30). Last U.S. troops leave Cambodia June 29, although American bombing continues and South Vietnamese troops remain. Nixon appoints David K. E. Bruce Ambassador to the Paris peace talks.

LAOS

Early 18th century	Laos divided into three kingdoms.
1945–54	**INDOCHINA WAR.**
1945	French begin effort to reimpose empire in Laos. Lao leaders under royal prince organize anti-French Lao Issara.
1946	French military forces take control of Laos and crown Lao king. Anti-French Lao Issara abandons Laos and establishes exile group in Bangkok, Thailand.
1949	Because some Lao leaders in Lao Issara decide to accommodate French, provisional government of Lao in Bangkok is dissolved.
1950	Souphanouvong, refusing to agree to accommodations with French, establishes resistance government in northeast Laos, under the control of his organization the Pathet Lao (PL).
1951	U.S. signs an economic and military assistance agreement with France and the pro-French Royal Laotian Government. Anti-French PL persist in armed resistance in northeast Laos.
1954	**GENEVA AGREEMENTS AND SOUTHEAST ASIA TREATY ORGANIZATION.**
1954, July	U.S. does not join other participants at Geneva conference in adhering to Final Declaration. U.S. does agree *not* to use force to subvert the agreements which provide for an independent, unified Laos which is to be removed, as far as possible, from the cold war.
1954, Sept.	U.S. establishes SEATO, an anti-Communist coalition, and extends security guarantees to Laos, thereby involving Laos in the cold war, a step directly contrary to the intent of the Geneva accords.
1955–70	**U.S. OPPOSES NATIONAL RECONCILIATION.**

1955	U.S. undertakes to expand the size of the Royal Lao army and expands aid program to finance it.
1957	Pursuant to the intent of Geneva accords and in order to unify Lao administration, pro-French Prime Minister Souvanna Phouma succeeds in negotiating Vientiane agreements which provide for government of national union, including two PL ministers.
1958, May	The only free elections ever held in Laos reveal strong PL and neutralist political base. Right-wing groups with U.S. backing oust Prime Minister Souvanna Phouma, replacing him with the government of Phoui Sananikone, which is militantly anti-Communist. Phoui government removes PL ministers including Souphanouvong, and allies itself closely to U.S. and SEATO allies.
1959, Dec. 16	Phoui fires American-backed right-wing ministers from cabinet and threatens to return to a "policy of effective neutrality."
Dec. 25	With American support, right-wing military elements bring down Phoui government.
1960, Jan. 7	Right-wing caretaker government formed to preside over elections.
Apr.	Blatantly rigged elections result in victory for right-wing groups.
May 23	PL leader Souphanouvong, one of two PL ministers removed and arrested, escapes from prison in Vientiane, Laotian capital.
Fall	Political chaos and polarization. U.S.-backed General Phoumi Nosavan building army in south after "neutralist" Kong Le forces stage coup and make Souvanna Phouma prime minister. PL in eastern Laos. U.S. withdraws support from legal government under "neutralist" Souvanna Phouma/Kong Le and supports Phoumi Nosavan. American SEATO ally Thailand blockades Vientiane to help Phoumi. "Neutralist" Souvanna Phouma therefore accepts Soviet airlift of economic aid. Phoumi Nosavan seizes Vientiane. "Neutralist" Kong Le/Souvanna Phouma join PL who are based in Plaine des Jarres. U.S.-backed Phoumi Nosavan government installed in Vientiane, capital of Laos.

1961, Jan.–Mar. "Neutralist" Kong Le/Souvanna Phouma in alliance with PL seize the offensive and threaten Phoumi Nosavan government.

Apr. 20 American military mission, formerly covered in hidden AID mission, becomes MAAG, Military Assistance Advisory Group.

Apr. 24 "Neutralist" Kong Le/Souvanna Phouma in alliance with PL forces captures U.S. Special Forces personnel.

Apr. U.S. accepts reconvening of Geneva conference, after opposing it for months, as a means of avoiding total collapse of Phoumi Nosavan government.

1962, July Geneva accords are signed, by which Laos is to be neutralized. A tripartite coalition government (leftist-neutralist-rightist) with "neutralist" Souvanna Phouma as prime minister is to be established. Foreign forces are to be withdrawn. Pending integration of the army and police, a de facto partition is to be in effect in Laos.

1962 Anti-Communists retain control of government, army, police, and finances. "Neutralist" Souvanna Phouma decides to cooperate with Americans and right wing while the Vang Pao's Meo "irregulars" behind the de facto partition line receive American support in direct violation of the Geneva accords of 1962. U.S. charges that North Vietnamese have not withdrawn cadres supporting PL.

1963, Feb. Outbreak of conflict between pro-Souvanna Phouma/Kong Le "neutralists" and dissident "neutralists" who disagree with Souvanna Phouma's cooperation with the Americans. Conflict is located on the Plaine des Jarres in northeast Laos.

Apr. Foreign Minister Quinim Pholsena, dissident "neutralist," is assassinated in Vientiane. Dissident "neutralists" opposed to Souvanna Phouma's cooperation with right wing and U.S. fight with Kong Le neutralists. PL takes Xieng Khouang, a major town in Plaine des Jarres. PL ministers leave Vientiane because of assassination and coalition government dissolves.

1964, Apr. Right-wing coup attempt against Souvanna Phouma fails due to American opposition.

May	U.S. begins air raids against PL forces on the Plaine des Jarres. The PL takes control of the Plaine des Jarres.
1965	Conflict among right-wing factions in Vientiane for control of government.
1966, Jan.	Thai infantry and artillery, backed by U.S., engaged in Laos against PL and dissident "neutralists."
Nov.	Kong Le, leader of pro-Souvanna Phouma "neutralists," resigns and leaves Laos in protest against integration of "neutralists" and right-wing forces.
1968, Jan.	PL takes town north of Luang Prabang.
Mar.	Fighting in southern Laos between PL and right-wing elements.
Fall	American air raids increase tenfold in PL-populated areas.
1969, June	Lao government loses Muong Soui on outskirts of Plaine des Jarres to PL.
Aug.	CIA-backed Meo tribesmen take Plaine des Jarres from PL.
1970, Jan.	Fighting begins again on Plaine des Jarres and Souvanna Phouma proposes to Hanoi that the Plaine des Jarres be neutralized. Hanoi refuses, arguing that the Plaine des Jarres is PL territory according to cease-fire in 1962.
Feb.	PL takes back Plaine des Jarres. Effectiveness of the Meo army is virtually destroyed.
Feb.	Americans evacuate 20,000 pro-government civilians and Meo "irregulars" and begin to bomb systematically Plaine des Jarres and PL territory resulting in about 600,000 refugees, a high percentage of all people who live in PL zone.
Feb.	PL forces defeat Meo special forces who are supported and led by Americans and Thai, and PL consolidate their hold on Plaine des Jarres.
May	Capture of Attopeu in southern Laos by PL evacuation of Saravane in response to American escalation in Cambodia.
June	Pathet Lao announces the capture of the last government fortified town, Mong-Bua, in the crucial Saravane area of Laos.

CAMBODIA

	TRADITIONAL CAMBODIA — THE SPLENDOR OF THE KHMERS AND THE STRUGGLE AGAINST STRONGER NEIGHBORS.
10th to 13th centuries	Apogee of the Khmer empire, centered on Angkor, stretching from the South China Sea to the Indian Ocean, covering much of what is now South Vietnam, Laos, large parts of Thailand, and the northern part of the Malay Peninsula.
1431	Thais sack Angkor and claim suzerainty over Cambodia.
1603	Thais annex several of Cambodia's western provinces (including Siemreap and Battambang). Cambodian kings forced to seek investiture by the Thais, to pay regular tribute to the Thai king, and to send military contingents to assist Thailand against Burma.
17th to 18th centuries	To counter Thai power, Cambodians offer special privileges to the Vietnamese who were then beginning to settle in the lower Mekong Delta around Saigon, then still Cambodian territory. Vietnamese wrest control of southern Vietnam area from Cambodia.
From 1800	Vietnamese claim suzerainty over Cambodia.
1800–63	War and crisis. Thai and Vietnamese armies march and countermarch across Cambodian territory. Commerce at a standstill; peasants flee fields; epidemics decimate population. Finally King Norodom accepts French protectorate to rid himself of both enemies.
1863	France declares Cambodia a protectorate. Thais continue to occupy northwestern provinces of Battambang and Siemreap.
1887	Cambodia becomes part of French Indochinese Union.

1907	Under French pressure, Thais give back Battambang and Siemreap.

1941   Thais declare war on Allies and reoccupy northwestern Cambodia provinces (returned to Indochina in 1946 upon UN verdict).

1945–50   POSTWAR SETTLEMENT—A FRENCH-CONTROLLED CAMBODIA.

1945   Authority over Cambodia returned to France. Collaborationist Premier Son Ngoc Thanh wins national referendum in independence move. Thanh arrested. Supporters flee to Thailand and form dissident nationalist movement (Khmer Issarak).

1946   Cambodia becomes "autonomous state within French Union"; French retain veto power and control of army, police, finances, and judiciary. An anti-French party wins elections but King Sihanouk favors gradual achievement of negotiated independence.

1949   French sign treaty stating they will transfer de jure independence to kingdom of Cambodia providing control over its own army and police except in time of war; but French officially stipulate a continuing state of war.

1950   U.S. establishes diplomatic relations. Nationalist activity increases as total independence proves hollow reality. "Liberation government" named by Viet Minh for Cambodia.

1950–56   CAMBODIA BECOMES INDEPENDENT —SIHANOUK ANNOUNCES NEUTRAL FOREIGN POLICY.

1950   Sihanouk takes stronger nationalist stance in face of increased Viet Minh activity in Cambodia.

1952   Increasing antigovernment activity from both Communists and non-Communists. Sihanouk takes emergency powers.

1953   Sihanouk's "royal crusade for independence" seeks U.S. aid to pressure French. U.S. refuses. Continued French presence causes many non-Communist elements to join insurgents. Sihanouk enters voluntary exile and declares intent to lead "holy war for independence."

1953, Oct.–Dec.	French finally agree to independence in effort to prevent two-front war in Indochina. Sihanouk begins efforts to oust Viet Minh forces; U.S. offers aid.
1954, Dec.	Sihanouk announces Cambodia will remain unaligned and will conduct a neutral foreign policy.
1955	Sihanouk abdicates throne; competes in national election. His party wins overwhelming victory. Bandung Conference understanding between Sihanouk and Communist China for peaceful coexistence and no foreign bases in Cambodia. Sihanouk renounces SEATO protection.
1956	Thailand and South Vietnam impose economic blockade of Cambodia in retaliation for Sihanouk signature of aid agreement with China. U.S. suspends aid. Subsequent negotiations result in lifting of blockade.
1957–60	U.S. OPPOSES SIHANOUK CHINA POLICY—FOREIGN ELEMENTS WORK AGAINST SIHANOUK.
1958	South Vietnamese army units invade Cambodia border areas. Cambodia appeals to U.S. to restrain Saigon; U.S. refuses. Cambodia proposes diplomatic relations with China. U.S. considers cutting off aid as anti-Sihanouk move. Khmer Serai (Free Cambodia) movement organized reportedly with CIA, Thai, and Vietnamese aid. Thai begins anti-Cambodian campaign; Cambodia suspends diplomatic relations with Thailand.
1959	Bangkok plot exposed. Plot called for anti-Sihanouk invasion from Thailand by foreign-supported Khmer Serai forces and creation of new opposition political party. U.S., Thailand, and South Vietnam implicated in plot. Eisenhower denies U.S. involvement; Thailand and South Vietnam cease provocative actions. Diplomatic relations with Thailand restored.
1960	National referendum gives near-unanimous support to Sihanouk policies. (Non-Communist opposition elements compromised by implication in Bangkok plot.) Sihanouk made chief of state for life.

1960–64   SIHANOUK SEEKS GUARANTEE OF NEUTRAL CAMBODIA—OUTSIDE INTERFERENCE CONTINUES.

1960   Sihanouk calls for international conference on Laos.

1961   At Geneva conference on Laos, Sihanouk proposes that neutralization of Laos be extended to Cambodia. Saigon persecution of Cambodian minority in Vietnam results in refugees fleeing to Cambodia. Thai accuse Cambodia of giving sanctuary to Communist elements which seek to subvert rest of Southeast Asia; Cambodia breaks diplomatic relations with Thailand.

1962   Sihanouk calls for new conference in Geneva, this time to extend "international protection" to Cambodia; U.S. noncommittal. Sihanouk offers to accept international control in return for recognition of existing borders. South Vietnamese oppose, carry out continued border violations.

1963   Cambodian protest at continued Saigon repression of Vietnamese Buddhists and discrimination against Cambodian minority in Vietnam; diplomatic relations broken. Anti-Sihanouk activity by Khmer Serai resumes at new intensity; includes virulent propaganda from CIA-furnished transmitters in Thailand and South Vietnam. Sihanouk cancels U.S. aid agreements; Pentagon reacts by calling for intervention in Cambodia.

1964   Continuing border violations from South Vietnam (including at least one attack in mid-March by South Vietnamese unit with American adviser). USSR and France ask U.S. support for declaration of Cambodian neutrality. U.S. refuses unless Cambodia first resolves its differences with its neighbors.

1964, Apr.   Cambodia recalls its diplomatic mission from Washington. U.S. delegate in UN denies Cambodian charges about continuing U.S. involvement in border violations and states that U.S. is convinced "Vietnam has no aggressive designs toward Cambodia."

Fall   North Vietnam infiltrates first large force of regular troops through Cambodia into Mekong Delta. U.S. requests negotiations with Cambodia.

1964–67	U.S. AND CAMBODIA RENEW DISCUSSIONS—BORDER VIOLATIONS CONTINUE.
1964, Dec.	U.S. and Cambodia open talks in Cambodia; disagree over question of border determinations. Cambodia wants recognition of boundaries before international conference takes place. Talks broken off.
1965, Apr.	Rusk indicates U.S. would participate in international conference on Cambodian neutrality.
May–Oct.	Cambodia severs diplomatic relations with U.S. Border violations continue; U.S. planes attack two Cambodian border villages in May and napalm a third in October.
Nov.	Sihanouk conditions for renewed U.S. relations: recognition of Cambodian territorial integrity; cessation of military incursion; indemnity for losses to life and property.
1966, Jan.	U.S. fourteen-point peace plan for Southeast Asia includes possibility of neutralization. Armed border incursions continue. Rusk announces continued U.S. support for Cambodian neutrality, adds that Hanoi and Viet Cong have abused it. UN mediation of Thai-Cambodian border conflict fails; border attacks continue.
1967	U.S. hires members of Khmer Serai for covert missions in Cambodia (revealed at 1968 trial of Green Beret captain). U.S. informs Cambodia as to Communist use of its territory.
1967–69	LEFTIST AS WELL AS RIGHTIST ELEMENTS PRESSURE SIHANOUK—BORDER INCURSIONS CONTINUE.
1967, Apr.–May	Sihanouk sends army against Communist rebels and continues his military action to counter Khmer Serai attacks still being mounted from South Vietnam and Thailand. Sihanouk given full powers by national assembly. Lon Nol dropped as premier after leftist pressures. Sihanouk refuses U.S. request for talks on use of Cambodia by North Vietnamese troops.
June	Cambodia establishes diplomatic relations with North Vietnam; offers to renew relations with Thailand if borders recognized.

July–Aug.
: U.S. sponsored Khmer Serai attacks continue into Cambodia and penetrate up to twelve miles.

Sept.–Oct.
: Sihanouk accuses China of imperialism and internal interference in Cambodia and threatens to seek aid from U.S.

Nov.
: Reconciliation between Cambodia and Peking.

Nov.–Dec.
: U.S. continues refusal to recognize existing borders; it considers this is a matter for negotiations between Cambodia and its neighbors. U.S. upholds border incursions by U.S. army in "hot pursuit."

1968, Jan.
: Bowles mission to Cambodia; inconclusive in matter of reestablishing diplomatic relations. USSR condemns violation of Cambodian territorial integrity but opposes strengthening of International Control Commission. Sihanouk accuses Communist elements of fomenting civil war in northwestern Cambodia.

Mar.–July
: Sihanouk charges Communists support rebel activity in northeastern Cambodia. Sihanouk complains to U.S. on continuing U.S. and South Vietnamese border violations in south.

Sept.
: U.S. charges use of Cambodia for bases by Viet Cong and North Vietnamese forces in northeast Cambodia and Svayrieng provinces has tripled.

Nov.–Dec.
: Cambodia charges that U.S. air attacks killed three hundred Cambodians in border villages. Four captured American flyers released.

1969–70
: SIHANOUK RAPPROCHEMENT WITH U.S.—MILITARY COUP OUSTS SIHANOUK.

1969, Apr.
: Cambodia offers to reestablish diplomatic relations with U.S. in exchange for recognition of her territorial integrity. U.S. states that it "recognizes and respects sovereignty, independence, neutrality and territorial integrity" of Cambodia. U.S. planes bomb border regions.

May
: Two U.S. helicopters downed in Cambodia; NLF mission in Cambodia raised to embassy status.

Aug.	American embassy reopened in Pnompenh. Sihanouk says new cabinet formed under General Lon Nol will reexamine issue of U.S. aid.
Aug.	Sihanouk alleges 40,000 Communist troops in Cambodia.
Oct.	Sihanouk protests U.S. bombing of border provinces.
1970, Jan.	U.S. pays compensation for Cambodian losses resulting from continuing border clashes.
Mar. 11-13	While Sihanouk in Europe, Premier Lon Nol and Cambodian army sanction the sacking of North Vietnamese and NLF embassies by Cambodian youths in Pnompenh; action termed a protest against Communist infiltration. Lon Nol's government orders Viet Cong and North Vietnamese troops out of Cambodia. Cambodian military reportedly backs continuing demonstrations against NLF and Hanoi.
Mar. 18	Sihanouk ousted in coup led by Lon Nol. New regime begins campaign to destroy Sihanouk's prestige. Sihanouk plans government in exile. (U.S. says recognition of Cambodia unaffected by overthrow of Sihanouk.)
Mar. 20–26	Cambodian army moves against pro-Sihanouk demonstration. New leaders reaffirm Cambodian neutrality but pledge to root out Communist troops in border sanctuaries. U.S. planes attack inside Cambodia. North Vietnam and NLF recall diplomats from Pnompenh.
1970, Mar.–July	LON NOL GOVERNMENT BATTLES COMMUNISTS—U.S. LAUNCHES FULL-SCALE INVASION OF CAMBODIA.
1970, Mar. 27	South Vietnamese troops launch first major attack against Cambodian sanctuaries with U.S. helicopters.
Mar. 28	White House announces American troops may cross border in response to enemy threats.
Mar. 29–30	Pro-Sihanouk demonstrations in eastern provinces. North Vietnamese and Viet Cong troops move against government forces.

Vietnamese residents in Cambodia flee to South Vietnam as a result of widespread persecution in eastern provinces.

Mar. 30   Cambodia appeals for UN observers, asks for return of ICC.

Apr. 1   Cambodia says would accept U.S. military aid but not ground troops. France calls for general conference on Indochina.

Apr. 3   *New York Times* reports that authoritative Nixon administration sources say Viet Cong headquarters was moved in late March from Cambodia to South Vietnam. (This is the "headquarters" for the Communist operations in South Vietnam, or COSVN.)

Apr. 9   Cambodian troops withdraw from Parrot's Beak area on border abandoning it to virtual Viet Cong control. Continuing reports of Vietnamese civilians in Cambodia being massacred.

Apr. 15   All diplomatic missions in Pnompenh receive official request for arms and equipment for use against Communist forces.

Apr. 21   Reports say that Vietnamese Communists are in complete control of three Cambodian provinces (with partial control of three others) and are within fifteen to twenty miles of Pnompenh.

Apr. 22   U.S. agrees to send captured arms from Vietnam to Cambodia. U.S. calls situation in Cambodia a "foreign invasion of a neutral country." South Vietnam sends delegation to Pnompenh to discuss repatriation of Vietnamese civilians.

Apr. 27   U.S. Senate Foreign Relations Committee states opposition to extension of military aid to Cambodia.

Apr. 30   Nixon authorizes joint U.S.-South Vietnamese attacks into Cambodia to clean out the Communist bases. He states that enemy actions in Cambodia "clearly endanger the lives of Americans who are in Vietnam." Merely to send arms, he says, would be ineffective. He rejects calls for peace at any price, claiming that the situation is a test of American will and character (particularly COSVN).

May 2   Military planners say it was feared the Viet Cong were planning to take over Cambodia and turn it into a massive supply base/staging area; this would have "outflanked" the U.S. in South Vietnam and "our strategy of Vietnamization would have had very little chance."

May 3
Elaborate underground facilities believed to house COSVN not yet found, although there are indications many enemy troops fled recently from Fishhook area. "VC" houses in area burned by South Vietnamese troops.

May 4
Supply cache found in Fishhook area, but few enemy troops and no headquarters. Reconnaissance area extended thirty miles inside Fishhook; U.S. bombing area sixty miles inside Fishhook. U.S. secretly sends 2,000-man Cambodian mercenary unit (which had been part of border mobile strike force led and paid by Green Berets) to Pnompenh in response to April 20 request of Lon Nol; not accompanied by U.S. or South Vietnamese advisers.

May 5
Large enemy base area, two miles long and one mile wide, called "the City," found in the Fishhook area, includes storage sheds, bunkers, etc.; at same time U.S. officials in Saigon scale down definition of success in Cambodian operation to measure of supplies captured and facilities destroyed. Few now say they expect to find elaborate installations which could definitely be identified as the headquarters for the entire Communist military operation in South Vietnam. Other forays into eastern Cambodia are believed inevitable as is postponement of substantial withdrawals of U.S. troops from South Vietnam.

May 6
Nixon states to congressional committees that U.S. troops will leave Cambodia within three to seven weeks and will not penetrate more than twenty-one miles without prior congressional approval. Third major allied assault into Cambodia begins. More Khmer mercenaries flown into Pnompenh; Vietnamese Communist troops continue advance on Cambodian capital.

May 7
Total of 50,000 allied troops now committed to Cambodian operation. U.S. launches two new assaults.

May 8
White House announces discovery of "most

sophisticated base complex" yet found; no verification that it is part of COSVN. White House spokesman says, "COSVN is probably a group of men who move around." Saigon announces planned South Vietnamese gunboat flotilla up Mekong to rescue Vietnamese refugees in Pnompenh.

May 9

Intelligence officers say they are fairly certain "the City" is only a large supply depot and does not contain COSVN; removing the supplies could take weeks or months. Lon Nol government welcomes South Vietnamese flotilla plans. Twenty thousand Vietnamese reportedly under arrest in Pnompenh.

May 10

White House terms the Cambodian drive a success as the destruction of enemy bases will prevent widened enemy activity inside South Vietnam; admits COSVN not found. Nixon at press conference says U.S. will begin withdrawal next week. Flotilla of sixty South Vietnamese and thirty U.S. gunboats start up Mekong; two new ground assaults across Cambodian border.

May 11

U.S. field commanders say Nixon time limit too short to allow thorough search of seized densely jungled sanctuaries.

May 13

South Vietnamese leaders reiterate plan to continue military operations in Cambodia after U.S. withdrawal of June 30. Joint U.S.-South Vietnamese naval blockade of Cambodia begins.

May

U.S. officials refuse to rule out bombing in Cambodia (either to interdict Communist supply lines or in support of Cambodian government) after June 30 withdrawal.

June–July

Prince Sihanouk condemned to death by Lon Nol regime on June 1. Economy continues to collapse as 90 percent of all rubber plantations cease to function and tourist trade halts. Lon Nol regime issues decree of "General Mobilization" requiring everyone from eighteen to sixty to perform military duty or some "service of national interest" and making all property subject to government requisition (June 25). Pnompenh regime abandons entire northeast quadrant of the country to Communist forces. Lon Nol urges Americans to stay, but last U.S. troops in Cambodia return June 29 to the Central

Highlands in South Vietnam. Forty thousand South Vietnamese troops remain in Cambodia to defend the major towns. American saturation bombing and B-52 raids increase. Air support for South Vietnamese military operations continues. U.S. gives $7.9 million in last-minute military aid to Lon Nol and Pentagon announces plans for another $50 million in military aid for fiscal year beginning July 1, 1970.

THAILAND

EARLY SIAM AT AYUTHIA.

1350	Thai kingdom of Siam founded at Ayuthia by Rama Tiboti.
1350–1460	Siamese invasions of Cambodia finally lead to abandonment of Angkor and collapse of Khmer empire.
1371	A Siamese embassy at Nanking inaugurates tributary relations with the newly founded Ming dynasty of China.
1765	Destruction of Ayuthia by the Burmese marks the end of the old Siamese kingdom. After long years of war the Burmese are driven out of the country and a new dynasty (the Chakri) is founded, beginning in 1782.
1756–1932	A NEW DYNASTY, SIAM'S UNEQUAL TREATIES, AND THE BEGINNINGS OF MODERN SIAM.
1782	Rama I (Phra Buddha Yod Fa Chulalok) begins new line.
1855, Apr. 18	Unequal Treaty with Great Britain, modeled on the unequal Anglo-Chinese treaty. Opening of Siam: consuls to be established; extraterritorial system introduced; right to trade for foreigners throughout the kingdom. Similar treaties concluded with U.S. (1856, May 29) and France (1856, August 15), and thereafter with many other powers.
1868–1910	Rama V (Phra Maha Chulalonkorn), the real founder of modern Siam. After attaining his majority (1873) he devoted himself

almost entirely to the reform of his government and the improvement of his country: feudal system abolished; slavery reduced and stamped out; administrative reform (central bureaucracy); taxation and financial reform; postal service; modernization of the army; introduction of the telegraph (1883); opening of first railway (1893).

1893, Oct. 3   Siamese forced to accept treaty with French by which they abandoned all claim to territory east of the Mekong.

1917, July 22   Siam declares war on Germany and Austria-Hungary.

1920, Jan. 10   Siam becomes an original member of the League of Nations.

1920–26   In a series of agreements with the various powers, Siam recovers full jurisdiction and tariff autonomy, thus ending unequal treaties.

Post–1932   **THE END OF ABSOLUTISM, THE COUPS D'ETAT, AND INCREASING U.S. INVOLVEMENT.**

1932, June 24   Coup d'etat puts end to absolute government of king. A group of young radicals, educated in Europe or influenced by European ideas, forms a People's party and gets king to agree to a form of constitutional monarchy.

Dec. 10   Constitution adopted.

1941   Siam declares war on U.S. and Allies after Japanese invasion of Dec. 8.

1947, Nov. 8   Coup by army group under Marshal Luang Pibul Songgram.

1949, May 11   Siam henceforth to be known again as Thailand.

1950   Thailand recognizes South Korea and sends a contingent to participate in the Korean War on the UN side. Military aid program with U.S. agreed upon.

1951, Nov. 29   Army "silent" coup. Also called "radio" coup because the change of constitution took place by a mere announcement over the radio.

1954   Shortly after signing of Geneva accords, Thailand joins U.S. and six other countries in SEATO.

1957, Sept. 16	Coup by military group under leadership of Field Marshal Sarit Thanarat.
Dec.	General Thanom Kittikachorn, Sarik's immediate deputy in the army, takes over office of prime minister. Sarit, in precarious state of health, leaves for extended medical treatment in U.S.
1958, Oct.	Sarit returns to Thailand and, in another coup, overthrows entire system and establishes himself as dictator.
1962, Mar.	Communiqué issued by Secretary of State Rusk and Thai Foreign Minister Thanat Khoman stating that the U.S. does not interpret its treaty obligation to Thailand as depending on the approval of all SEATO members since "this treaty obligation is individual as well as collective."
1963, Dec.	Field Marshal Sarit dies in Bangkok hospital. King Phumiphon appoints General Thanom Kittikachorn as the new premier.
1964	The U.S. and Thailand begin drafting a bilateral military contingency plan. U.S. begins construction of air bases in Thailand.
1965	U.S. bombing of North Vietnam and northern Laos from Thai bases.
1966	Bilateral military contingency plan signed by U.S. and Thailand.
1967	B-52 bombers stationed in Thailand. Secret agreement entered into by U.S. and Thailand by which Thailand will send the 11,000-man Thai Black Panther Division to South Vietnam. The cost of this division to the U.S. (not revealed to the U.S. public until June 1970) is to be $50 million a year, to cover equipment, training, logistic support, and extra pay and allowances (mustering-out and death benefits as well as entertainment funds for Thai troops in Vietnam, etc.). To encourage the Thais to send this force and to allay Thai fears that such action would weaken security at home, the U.S. also agrees to accelerate the modernization of the Thai forces by increasing military assistance programs in fiscal 1968 and 1969 by $30 million. The U.S. further agrees, due to Thai apprehension that the growing number of U.S. warplanes in Thailand will en-

courage Communist retaliation, to provide Thailand with a battery of HAWK antiaircraft missiles.

1969, Dec. 16   Thai foreign minister claims there has been no payment by the U.S. to induce Thailand to send troops to Vietnam.

1970, Apr. 30   U.S. and South Vietnamese troops invade Cambodia.

June   Symington subcommittee of Senate Foreign Relations Committee reveals true nature of 1967 secret plan for U.S. financing of Thai troops in Vietnam as well as inducements to Thailand to send them there. Premier Thanom announces that Thailand will send volunteers of ethnic Cambodian origin, armed and equipped from aid supplied by U.S., to assist Cambodian forces in Cambodia against the Communists. Secretary of State Rogers, appearing on CBS-TV's "Face the Nation" (June 7), says that the U.S. could be expected to pay for "a substantial part" of any cooperative effort of Asian nations to come to the defense of Cambodia.

July   The Thai government remains undecided about the nature and extent of its commitment to the Lon Nol regime. Despite American urging, it wavers over officially committing its own troops, although the American government announces that Thai troops would be armed by the U.S. Saigon expresses repeated uneasiness over Thai reluctance. Thais finally agree to allow Cambodian officers to recruit Thais of Cambodian descent in Thailand.

Glossary

ARVN   Army of the Republic of Vietnam (South Vietnam)
Cao Dai   Religious–nationalist sect. Virtually an enclave government under the French.
CIDG   Civil Irregular Defense Group
COSVN   Communist operations in South Vietnam (headquarters of); or more popularly known as the Central Office for South Vietnam
DMZ   Demilitarized Zone
DRV   Democratic Republic of Vietnam (North Vietnam)
FUNK   Front Unifié National Khmer (Cambodia)
GVN   Government of Vietnam (South)
Hoa Hao   Nationalistic and xenophobic religious sect founded in the late 1930s. Strongest along the Cambodian border.
ICC   International Control Commission
Khmer Rouge   Red Khmer (Cambodia)
Khmer Serai   Free Khmer (Cambodia)
Lao Issara   Free Lao
NLF   National Liberation Front (South Vietnam)
PL   Pathet Lao
PRU   Provincial Reconnaissance Units
RevDev   revolutionary development
RLG   Royal Laotian Government
ROK   Republic of Korea (South Korea)
Sangkum Reastr Niyum   Popular Socialist Community party (Cambodia)
SEADAG   Southeast Asia Development Advisory Group
SEATO   Southeast Asia Treaty Organization
STANO   surveillance, target acquisition, and night observation
VC   Viet Cong
Viet Cong   Originally a term of opprobrium applied by Diem after 1954 to label his opponents as Communists. However, popularly refers to the various resistance forces that have built on the foundation of the Viet Minh in the South before 1954.
Viet Minh   League for the Independence of Vietnam
VNQDD   Vietnam Quoc Dan Dang. The major Vietnamese underground nationalist party in the 1920s.
WHAM   winning hearts and minds

Selected Bibliography

I. INDOCHINA

*Bastin, J. and H. Benda. *History of Modern Southeast Asia.* Englewood Cliffs, N.J.: Prentice-Hall, 1969. A concise history of Vietnam, Laos, and Cambodia and the other countries in Southeast Asia.

*Chomsky, Noam. *At War with Asia.* New York: Pantheon, 1970. A collection of Chomsky's essays on the war. Includes a report of his journey to Laos and North Vietnam in the spring of 1970.

Hoopes, Townsend. *The Limits of Intervention: An Inside Account of How the Johnson Policy of Escalation in Vietnam Was Reversed.* New York: McKay, 1969. A good account of U.S. policy debates by the former Undersecretary of the Air Force.

Kahin, George McT., ed. *Government and Politics of Southeast Asia,* 2nd ed. Ithaca, N.Y.: Cornell University Press, 1964. The standard work on the countries of Southeast Asia from World War II to the mid-1960s. Specialized bibliographies follow each section.

*Selden, Mark and Edward Friedman, eds. *America's Asia.* New York: Pantheon, 1970. A wide-ranging series of essays covering America's involvement in Asia since 1945, by the new generation of Asia scholars.

*Weisberg, Barry, ed. *Ecocide in Indochina: The Ecology of War.* New York: Harper & Row, 1970. An excellent documentation of America's war against the people and country of Vietnam. It covers such subjects as defoliation, refugees, antipersonnel weapons, craterization.

II. VIETNAM

*Burchett, Wilfred. *Vietnam: Inside Story of the Guerilla War.* New York: International Publishers, 1965. A sympathetic

*Available in paperback.

account of the National Liberation Front based on extensive firsthand observation.

*Chaliand, Gérard. *The Peasants of North Vietnam.* Baltimore: Penguin Books, 1969. One of the few detailed firsthand accounts of rural North Vietnam. Written by a French journalist, the book seeks to explain how and why the peasants continued their struggle despite the massive American bombing.

Devillers, Philippe and Jean Lacouture. *End of a War.* New York: Praeger, 1969. The best account of the Geneva conference of 1954 and the transformation of the French struggle against the Vietnamese into an American one.

Doyon, Jacques. *Les viet cong.* Paris, 1968. A good account by a French journalist who traveled in National Liberation Front territories in 1968.

*Falk, Richard A. *The Vietnam War and International Law.* Princeton, N.J.: Princeton University Press, 1968 (2 vols.). The definitive work on the subject.

*Fall, Bernard, ed. *Ho Chi Minh on Revolution.* New York: New American Library, 1967. Includes the speeches, writings, and letters of Ho from 1920 to 1966.

*Gettleman, Marvin, ed. *Vietnam,* rev. ed. New York: Fawcett, 1970. An excellent selection from the writings of historians, statesmen, and journalists covering the major periods in the history of Indochina. A good collection of basic documents as well.

*Harvey, Frank. *Air War: Vietnam.* New York: Bantam, 1967. A description of the consequences of America's air war on both the Vietnamese and American servicemen.

*Herman, Edward S. and Richard Du Boff. *America's Vietnam Policy: The Strategy of Deception.* Washington, D.C.: Public Affairs Press, 1968. An excellent work on the logic of escalation, the duplicity of America's negotiating position under Lyndon Johnson, and a good summation of such topics as the elections required under the Geneva accords, who is the aggressor against whom, and genocide as an inherent part of American policy.

Herman, Edward S. *"Atrocities" in Vietnam: Myths and Realities.* Pilgrim Press, 1970. A devastating indictment of American actions in Vietnam. Extensive documentation on American war crimes.

*Issacs, Harold. *No Peace for Asia.* Cambridge: MIT Press, 1967. The first comprehensive report on the events in Vietnam in 1945–46 by an American eyewitness. A classic depiction of the evils of French colonialism.

*Kahin, George McT. and John Lewis. *The United States in Vietnam,* rev. ed. New York: Dial Press, 1969. The most complete account of America's role in Vietnam since 1954.

*Lacouture, Jean, *Vietnam: Between Two Truces*. New York: Vintage, 1966. A good, readable account by an eminent French journalist.

*Lacouture, Jean. *Ho Chi Minh: A Political Biography*. New York: Vintage, 1968. The best available biography of Ho in English.

Marr, David. *A History of Vietnamese Anti-Colonialism (1885–1925)*. Berkeley: University of California Press, 1970. A description of the historical background of the Vietnamese struggle against the French.

*Pike, Douglas. *Viet Cong*. Cambridge: MIT Press, 1966. A violently hostile work on the NFL which nonetheless provides good information on their organizational system.

*Raskin, Marcus and Bernard Fall. *The Viet-Nam Reader*. New York: Vintage, 1965. A good collection of articles and documents on American foreign policy in Indochina.

*Schell, Jonathan. *The Village of Ben Suc*. New York: Vintage, 1967. A classic account of a U.S. military operation in a single village in South Vietnam.

*Schurmann, Franz, Peter Dale Scott, and Reginald Zelnick. *The Politics of Escalation in Vietnam*. Boston: Beacon Press, 1966. The story of the process of escalation under Johnson during his highly publicized "peace feelers."

*Zinn, Howard. *The Logic of Withdrawal*. Boston: Beacon Press, 1967. The reasons and the means for U.S. withdrawal from Vietnam.

III. LAOS

Fall, Bernard. *Anatomy of a Crisis: The Laotian Crisis of 1960–61*. New York: Doubleday, 1969. A description of the various minority groups in Laos and a limited analysis of the Pathet Lao.

Halpern, Joel. *Economy and Society of Laos: A Brief Survey*. 1964. Provides useful, basic information.

*McCoy, Al and Nina Adams, eds. *Laos: War and Revolution*. New York: Harper & Row, 1970. The best collection of articles on the American war in Laos.

IV. CAMBODIA

*Armstrong, John. *Sihanouk Speaks*. New York: Walker, 1964. A helpful editing of Sihanouk's writings, speeches, and interviews.

Grant, Jonathan, Jonathan Unger, and Laurence A. G. Moss, eds.

Cambodia: The Widening War in Indochina. New York: Simon & Schuster, 1970. The best collection of articles on Cambodia, its history, the role of Prince Sihanouk, and the implications of the American invasion.

Leifer, Michael. *Cambodia and Neutrality.* Ithaca, N.Y.: Cornell University Press, 1962. A critical account of Sihanouk's attempts to hold Cambodia together through a policy of neutralism.

Lacouture, Jean. *The Demi-Gods.* New York: Vintage, 1970. An interesting section on Sihanouk as a charismatic leader.

Smith, Roger. *Cambodia's Foreign Policy.* Ithaca, N.Y.: Cornell University Press, 1965. A reliable account of Sihanouk's policy of neutrality.